J. C. WRIGHT

SELECTED WRITINGS
AND SPEECHES OF

Abraham Lincoln

EDITED BY

T. HARRY WILLIAMS

HENDRICKS HOUSE, INC.
NEW YORK

ISBN: 0-87532-136-4 (paper)

PRINTED IN THE UNITED STATES OF AMERICA

PREFACE

In compiling this selection of Lincoln's works, I have been guided by one principle or purpose. I have chosen those writings which illustrate Lincoln's political and social philosophy and his views on the great issues of his day. My attempt has been to present Lincoln the philosopher of democracy. I have not tried to present the complete Lincoln.

I have taken these selections from published collections of Lincoln's works. For the most part, I have reproduced the speeches and letters as they are given in these earlier works, including punctuation and spelling. The first editors of Lincoln's works, John G. Nicolay and John Hay, "edited" Lincoln to achieve a formal correctness. The changes they made were of a minor nature and did no violence to Lincoln's meaning. I have taken Nicolay and Hay as the closest possible approach to the original documents. Wherever I have omitted a portion of a speech or a letter, I have indicated that omission by asterisks.

Many people have helped me prepare this book. Two who deserve particular mention are my wife and Miss Vivian Wintz of Louisiana State University. My greatest debt of gratitude is to Paul M. Angle of the Illinois State Historical Society for his invaluable advice and assistance.

T. H. W.

PUBLISHER'S PREFACE TO THE 1980 EDITION

Though the opening of the Robert Todd Lincoln Collection in 1947 increased the amount of material available to Lincoln Scholars, the bulk of this is letters to Lincoln rather than his own work. This increase in material is reflected in the collection of his works prepared by the Abraham Lincoln Association under the editorship of Roy P. Basler. However, interesting and useful as it is, it does not invalidate the earlier collection, edited by John G. Nicolay and John Hay. Therefore we feel that *Selected Writings and Speeches of Abraham Lincoln* by T. Harry Williams merits reprinting as it stands, including the introduction. The only change in this edition is the addition of a short bibliography of more recent books. This appears after the selected bibliography.

H.H.

TABLE OF CONTENTS

AND SOURCES OF THE TEXT

INTRODUCTION

LINCOLN'S POLITICAL AND ECONOMIC PHILOSOPHY

Abraham Lincoln spent the formative years of his life in those four decades before 1860 that historians have named the Middle Period and in that Middle West which a novelist has called the Valley of Democracy. It was a lusty, brawling, growing time, when a young and crude nation was bursting from the frayed historical fetters that bound it to Europe and the past and was announcing loudly to the world that the American republic would henceforth walk its own road, at its own gait, and achieve its own destiny. The road led broad and straight to a glorious destination—that Utopia of which mankind had dreamed for centuries, that perfect state which men had longed for and never attained, but which Americans would create in this God-favored western land. It was a democratic time, the morning star and the cock-crowing of the American democratic faith. The common man was rising and marching to new victories in politics, economics, and culture. All the nation heard the tramp of his eager feet, but they resounded most triumphantly in the middle Valley where the equalitarian, coonskin democracy captured one citadel of power after another in the states. Chills chased up the brass-bound spines of conservatives when the democratic hosts under the leadership of Andrew Jackson seized the national citadel itself and rudely ejected from the places of might the old broadcloth aristocracy that had dominated the government since its inception. It was a time of tremendous economic expansion, a get-rich, speculative, boom time. The Industrial Revolution had just come to the United States, factories were springing into belching existence, railroads were beginning to band the nation. The lush farmlands of the West and the South, waving with corn and cotton, supported in solid comfort a large agrarian population; the agricultural frontier was pushing steadily onward to conquer new regions in the interior. There was a continent to be settled and exploited, a thousand natural resources to be tapped. There were big things to do and big profits to be made. Enthusiastically America rolled up its sleeves to do the job.

The doctrines and dogmas of his times moulded Lincoln's philosophy of government and economics. Americans of the Middle Period believed in a set of principles that has been aptly called the democratic faith. Lincoln subscribed to all of them. One of the articles was a conviction that God had created a moral law, rules of right and wrong, for the government of men. Since men possessed consciences and the power to reason, they were aware of this law and would guide themselves by it. Those Americans who rejected the conventional concept of God accepted the same principle of supreme guidance; they held that laws of nature existed and that men could apprehend them. The moral law, or nature's law, was fundamental and perfect and hence superior to man-made law. The latter must not conflict with the former. Human laws that contravened divine law were illegal and must be changed. And they need not be obeyed. But as a matter of fact few human laws would err in this direction. For as man knew the higher law of God he would make his own laws conform to its pattern. Americans had a high respect for their own man-made fundamental law, the Constitution, which adhered closely to the dictates of the supernatural fundamental law. They might differ vigorously with each other over the correct interpretation of the Constitution, but they all appealed to it as the supreme authority to buttress their clashing contentions.

Another tenet of the faith was a belief in the goodness and intelligence of man. Because he could recognize divine law, man was essentially good. Because he was a reasoning creature, man acted intelligently. It followed that he could govern himself through the medium of democratic government. It also followed that he would increase in goodness and intelligence. This being so, there were no goals of happiness or glory to which man could not aspire. Americans of the Middle Period confidently believed that they could attain the millenium on earth. "Perfectionism" was a word heard often on American lips. Ministers, politicians, intellectuals, and cross-roads grocery philosophers uttered it with easy assurance. Part of this idealistic optimism derived from the extraordinary security which the American nation enjoyed. No threat of foreign danger disturbed the United States. The other countries of the western hemisphere were smaller or weaker; the powers of Europe were too far away to worry an America isolated behind her ocean walls. The American economy was young and expanding, and consequently the country was prosperous and becoming more so. Strains might appear here and there in the general structure, but they were not serious enough to cause any anxiety about the future. Americans could afford to look through rose-colored glasses. But fundamentally the optimism of the times was the result of a conception of the goodness of human nature. And in America man, good and intelligent, would fashion a perfect society.

Stemming from this doctrine of continued human progress was the third article of the democratic faith. In the United States there would be achieved a government and a society that would be the best and the happiest in the world. Here would be the supreme example of democratic, popular government, of, by, and for the people. But this glorious creation would not exist for the good of America alone. American democracy was not an end in itself, but a means to a greater end—world democracy. This country had a mission to perform for humanity, to bring democracy to an oppressed world. It would not be brought on the points of American bayonets nor would it be carried into less fortunate lands by missionary American propagandists. America would insure the triumph of universal democracy by the mere force of its example. Everywhere in the world men desired to govern themselves.

Everywhere they were groping through the darkness of ignorance and superstition toward the goal of democracy. Their way was long and hard. But a bright light beckoned them on, guided their faltering progress, and gave them hope of final victory. That light was the American Union, the greatest and most successful democracy that mankind had ever seen. The liberal parties in the rest of the world would never be discouraged, they would never give up the fight as long as the Union lived, as long as the lamp of democracy burned in the western skies.

The last article in the democratic faith dealt with the economic activities of man and their relationship to the general welfare of society. The economic thought of the men of the Middle Period issued from the economic system in which they lived. That system was capitalism: the private ownership and control of property; prices, wages, all value, determined by the law of supply and demand; the operation of the profit motive in the exchange of goods. The private-owners of property fell into three general groups. There were the small farmers, Jefferson's sturdy yeomanry, who owned and managed their independent holdings. The farmers were in every section of the country, but they were most numerous in the Middle West and the South. In the Valley they constituted the overwhelming majority of the population, and they dominated the politics of the region. In the South they were also the largest class, but here they tended to follow the leadership of the big planters, especially in politics. The planters were the second owning group. These lords of broad acres and many slaves were, of course, restricted to the South. Their numbers were few, but they wielded an influence in their section that made them in effect a ruling caste. They gave to Southern society an aristocratic tone, and they gave to the Southern masses leaders whom the masses usually accepted.[1]

---

[1] This general statement may be qualified by the observation that the influence of the planters was greater in the older Southern state, like Virginia, and lesser in the newer states, such as Mississippi. However, by 1860 Southern society was assuming a common pattern, and planter dominance was general.

The last group of owners consisted of the manufacturers, the men who operated the mills and factories that were mushrooming into existence in the years after 1820. Industrialism was a comparative newcomer on the economic scene. It was centered in the Northeast, although here and there it was reaching out eager fingers into the West and South. The captains of industry were fast becoming the controlling power in the economics and the politics of the East, and at Washington they competed vigorously with the slavocracy for special privileges from Congress. Before 1860, however, the business men never dominated their section as the planters did the South nor were they as influential in the national government as their agrarian rivals.

Certain aspects of this early American capitalism stand out with particular significance. This was a system in which an extraordinarily large number of people owned property and used their property, in the form of plantations, farms, or factories, to make a living. In other words this was a capitalistic system in which most of the people were capitalists. Unlike the contemporary system, relatively few people worked for other people in return for wages or salaries. The only important non-capitalistic group were the Eastern laborers and the Southern slaves. Most of the capitalists were "small" capitalists. "Big Business," in the shape of the giant corporations that developed after 1865 simply did not exist. The industrialists and the planters represented for the men of the Middle Period the spectacle of great wealth concentrated in a few hands. Compared to later periods, the concentration was far from extreme, but it was sufficient to anger the yeoman farmers, who bitingly denounced the plutocracy of the factory and the plantation. Their denunciations, however, were rarely as bitter or as frightened as they became after the Civil War when the farmers came to feel that as a class they were losing out to Big Business and were in danger of slipping to the status of peasants. Before 1860 the American economy was expanding, the vast resources and lands of the young nation awaited exploitation, there was more than enough of everything to go around. All classes faced the future with confidence.

The economic thought of the men of Lincoln's time was essentially democratic and capitalistic. They believed in an economic system in which the great majority of people would be property owners or capitalists. The right to acquire property was a natural right of every man, one of the precious rights guaranteed in the Declaration of Independence. If some men acquired more than others, this was no cause for alarm; as long as all acquired some, society would be happy. Let every man make as much money as he was smart enough to make. But the way to wealth must be open equally to all; no class should enjoy special privileges which gave it an artificial advantage over others. All Americans said this; not all believed it or practiced it. It was here that contradictions appeared in the economic doctrine. The principle of the equality of opportunity logically required that the government follow rigidly at all times a policy of *laissez-faire*. The state should not extend any favors or aids to any economic group. If it did, that group would have an unfair advantage over others, and the great principle of equality would be destroyed. Actually every one of the owning classes worked vigorously to get certain kinds of special privileges from the national government. If they were conscious of the incongruity of their thought and their actions, they rationalized it by saying they needed a privilege to lift them to a position of competing equality with other groups. Another contradiction, more potential than real in this period, was the possibility of conflict between the principles of human rights and property rights. What if the unrestrained right to acquire property resulted in the creation of a powerful plutocracy which would dominate the government, concentrate wealth in its own hands, and in general nullify the American dream of the perfect society? The men of the Middle Period did not face up squarely to this problem, mainly because it was hard for them to envision such a possibility. Many of them, however, did believe that the Southern slavocracy had become so rich and mighty that it threatened, unless it were checked, to weaken the foundations of democracy. They intended to check it.[2]

* * * *

Lincoln's political and economic philosophy embraced all the articles of the democratic faith. He gave eloquent expression to everyone of them during the course of his political life, and he made significant contributions to the development and interpretation of the principles of the faith. These principles did not originate with Lincoln. He found them in books, in political speeches, in government documents, and in the minds of common men. He thought about them, he believed them, he applied the general principles to specific issues. And finally he spoke about them, in unforgettable phrases that stuck in men's minds as did the utterances of no other figure of his day or any other day before or since. But Lincoln did not borrow ideas blindly from his environment and adopt them without analysis. Every belief he ever held was the result of sustained and tough thinking; every viewpoint he ever took was partly determined by the nature of his temperament. His mind had the qualities of deliberation and gradualness and introspection. It took Lincoln a long time to arrive at the formulation of a fundamental idea. Then the idea became a permanent part of his philosophy. His temperament was tolerant, patient, non-censorious, kindly. His mind and nature combined their influence in a common direction. Lincoln's position on most issues was a conservative, middle of the road one; instinctively he inclined toward moderation and avoided the extremes. "Stand with anybody that stands right," he said in 1854. "Stand with him while he is right, and part with him when he goes wrong. Stand with the Abolitionist in restoring the Missouri Compromise, and stand against him when

---

[2] An excellent discussion of the political philosophy of the Middle Period is in Ralph Henry Gabriel, *The Course of American Democratic Thought: An Intellectual History Since 1815* (New York, 1940), 12-25. There is also a good treatment, with the emphasis on economic thought, in Vernon Louis Parrington, *Main Currents in American Thought*, II, *The Romantic Revolution in America* (New York, three volumes in one edition, 1939), iii-x, 138-141.

he attempts to repeal the fugitive-slave law. In the latter case you stand with the Southern disuionist. What of that? You are still right. In both cases you are right. In both cases you expose the dangerous extremes." [3]

The doctrine of the existence of a supernatural fundamental law and the corollary that fundamental human law approximated the higher code was an important part of Lincoln's philosophy. His speeches and state papers are sprinkled with references to the two concepts. In the first inaugural he voiced his belief in their reality when he said: "I hold that in contemplation of universal law and of the Constitution the Union of these States is perpetual." [4] In Lincoln's thought, however, the Constitution or the human law had a greater significance than the divine law. From his understanding of the Constitution stemmed his conception of the nature of the American Union. Two conflicting interpretations of the Constitution faced each other in Lincoln's day, the nationalist interpretation and the state rights interpretation. Lincoln was a nationalist. He believed that the national government was superior to the state governments, that the people were sovereign and not the states, that the Union was a permanent political organism and not a league of states which any member could leave at will. But he was no Hamiltonian who would have centralized supreme power at Washington and made the states mere satrapies. He believed in a federal Union with a guaranteed division of power between the national government and the states. ". . . The right of each state to control its domestic institutions according to its own judgment exclusively, is essential to that balance of powers on which the perfection and endurance of our politics fabric depend," he affirmed.[5] No fears beset Lincoln that a powerful central government would inevitably become an agency of tyranny. "Must a government of necessity be too strong for the liberties of its own people,

---

[3] John G. Nicolay and John Hay (eds.), *Complete Works of Abraham Lincoln* (New York, 1905), II, 243.

[4] Lincoln, *Works*, VI, 173.

[5] *Ibid.*, VI, 88.

or too weak to maintain its own existence?" he asked.[6] He provided an answer to this question in his description of the beneficient working of the principle of majority rule under the Constitution: "A majority held in restraint by constitutional checks and limitations, and always changing easily with deliberate changes of popular opinions and sentiments, is the only true sovereign of a free people. Whoever rejects it does, of necessity, fly to anarchy or to despotism." [7]

Lincoln respected the Constitution, but he was no constitution-worshipper. He revered no documents merely because they were old and fundamental. He loved the Federal Union partly because it was the living embodiment of the work of the Fathers but more because it made common men free. And like most of his contemporaries he recognized the right of revolution. In one remarkable passage he carried the right to change the government by force even farther than the men of his time usually did:

Any people anywhere being inclined and having the power have the right to rise up and shake off the existing government, and form a new one that suits them better. This is a most valuable, a most sacred right—a right which we hope and believe is to liberate the world. Nor is this right confined to cases in which the whole people of an existing government may choose to exercise it. Any portion of such people that can may revolutionize and make their own of so much of the territory as they inhabit. More than this, a majority of any portion of such people may revolutionize, putting down a minority, intermingled with or near about them, who may oppose this movement. Such a minority was precisely the case of the Tories of our own revolution. It is a quality of revolutions not to go by old lines or old laws; but to break up both, and make new ones.[8]

Of all the articles of the democratic faith undoubtedly the

[6] *Ibid.*, VI, 304.
[7] *Ibid.*, VI, 179.
[8] *Ibid.*, I, 338-339.

ones that stirred Lincoln most deeply were those that concerned the goodness of man and his ability to govern himself, and the mission of America to bring democracy to a suffering world. To them he paid the highest tributes of his eloquence. The cardinal test of a democrat is whether he believes the plain people are competent to make decisions in matters of politics and government; many people who profess to be democratic do not meet this test. Lincoln met it squarely. He had no fears of the ignorant masses or of the tyranny of numbers. He had faith in the goodness and intelligence of men. God must have loved the common people, Lincoln was supposed to have said, or He would not have made so many of them. "Why should there not be a patient confidence in the ultimate justice of the people?" he asked in the first inaugural. "Is there any better or equal hope in the world?" [9]

The American Union was a sacred thing to Lincoln. It was sacred not alone because it made men free in America but because it would make them free everywhere. It was what Lincoln liked to call "the last best hope of earth." The Union was the best government ever devised because it was based on a great principle—the principle of equal rights for all men. Here Lincoln went back beyond the Constitution to the Declaration of Independence and its statement that all men were created free and equal and endowed with unalienable rights. He interpreted this to mean that men were born with equal opportunities to make of themselves what they could, to acquire property, to participate in government, to pursue liberty and happiness. "Most governments have been based, practically, on the denial of the equal rights of man . . .; ours began by affirming those rights," he declared. "They said, some men are too ignorant and vicious to share in government. Possibly so, said we; and, by your system, you would keep them ignorant and vicious. We propose to give all a chance; and we expected the weak to grow stronger, the ignorant wiser, and all better and happier together." [10]

[9] *Ibid.*, VI, 183.
[10] *Ibid.*, II, 184.

Lincoln believed that the Union was held together by this idea of equal rights, which permeated both the structure of government and the minds of the people. And this made America uniquely different from all other nations, whose bonds of unity were culture, tradition, or race. America was the great guardian of this idea and she must guard it well, because it would save the world by the force of its example. On his way to Washington in 1861 to become the leader of a divided nation, Lincoln made a brief address at Independence Hall in Philadelphia on February 22. With the Union in process of apparent dissolution as he spoke, he uttered the classic expression of the concept of America's mission to humanity: "I have often inquired of myself what great principle or idea it was that kept this Confederacy so long together. It was not the mere matter of separation of the colonies from the motherland, but that sentiment in the Declaration of Independence which gave liberty not alone to the people of this country, but hope to all the world for all future time. It was that which gave promise that in due time the weights would be lifted from the shoulders of all men, and that all should have an equal chance." [11] And it was this that led Lincoln to fight a war to bring the South back into the Union. If the Union was destroyed the idea it represented was also destroyed. That idea was too precious to be lost.

Lincoln's views about economics were those of the small capitalist—the farmer or the corner groceryman—who was also a laborer. He wanted a system in which all men owned property, and he insisted that all should have equal opportunities to acquire it. He approved of the middle class ideals of acquisitiveness and thrift, but he demanded that competition be open to all. He respected property rights, but he held that there were others more sacred. Labor was necessary to get capital; capital was but the fruit of labor. Therefore labor was more important than capital and must always be so; capital

[11] *Ibid.*, VI, 157. For pertinent comments on this phase of Lincoln's philosophy, see Andrew C. McLaughlin, "Lincoln as a World Figure," *Abraham Lincoln Association Papers, 1924* (Springfield, 1924), 101-104.

must never be put above labor. Lincoln liked the economic order of his time because it gave the laboring man a chance to become a capitalist. "There is no permanent class of hired laborers amongst us . . . ," he said. "The hired laborer of yesterday labors on his own account to-day, and will hire others to labor for him to-morrow. Advancement—improvement in condition—is the order of things in a society of equals." [12] It was possible, he admitted, that some laborers would not rise to be property owners; a few would lack the competence to better themselves and a few would be held back by misfortune. But this was not the fault of the system.[13] Lincoln denied that society was rigidly divided into two classes of employers and workers. The majority of men, he said, neither worked for others nor hired others to work for them. Most men worked for themselves on their own farms or in their own shops. They were both capitalists and laborers.[14] In a speech at New Haven in 1860 Lincoln gave the fullest expression to his small-capitalist philosophy:

> What is the true condition of the laborer? I take it that it is best for all to leave each man free to acquire property as fast as he can. Some will get wealthy. I don't believe in a law to prevent a man from getting rich; it would do more harm than good. So while we do not propose any war upon capital, we do wish to allow the humblest man an equal chance to get rich with everybody else. When one starts poor, as most do in the race of life, free society is such that he knows he can better his condition; he knows that there is no fixed condition of labor for his whole life.[15]

Because labor was necessary to the production of capital, Lincoln placed labor above capital in economic importance. Boldly he proclaimed in his message to Congress in December,

---

[12] Lincoln, *Works*, II, 184-185. It is probable that this passage is misdated and was part of a speech delivered at Cincinnati, September 17, 1859. See Emanuel Hertz, *Abraham Lincoln: A New Portrait* (New York, 1931), II, 757-758.

[13] Lincoln, *Works*, V, 250.

[14] *Ibid.*, V, 247-250.

[15] *Ibid.*, V, 360-361.

1861: "Labor is prior to, and independent of, capital. Capital is only the fruit of labor, and could never have existed if labor had not first existed. Labor is the superior of capital, and deserves much the higher consideration." [16] And to a committee from the Workingmen's Association of New York he said in 1864: "The strongest bond of human sympathy, outside of the family relation, should be one uniting all working people, of all nations, and tongues, and kindreds." Then he read them a little lecture on how the capitalistic system benefited the worker:

> Nor should this lead to a war upon property, or the owners of property. Property is the fruit of labor; property is desirable; is a positive good in the world. That some should be rich shows that others may become rich, and hence is just encouragement to industry and enterprise. Let not him who is houseless pull down the house of another, but let him work diligently and build one for himself, thus by example assuring that his own shall be safe from violence when built.[17]

In the New Haven speech in which Lincoln expounded his views of capitalistic society, he spoke a word to the laboring men in the audience. Referring to a shoe strike in the state, he said: ". . . I am glad to see that a system of labor prevails in New England under which laborers can strike when they want to, where they are not obliged to work under all circumstances, and are not tied down and obliged to labor whether you pay them or not! I like the system which lets a man quit when he wants to, and wish it might prevail everywhere. One of the reasons why I am opposed to slavery is just here." [18] As Lincoln looked at his America in the years just before 1860, he saw rising in the South a threat to democratic capitalism, to the great principle of equal rights, to the Union itself. That threat was slavery. To Lincoln it seemed that the slavocracy

---

[16] *Ibid.*, VII, 57.
[17] *Ibid.*, X, 54.
[18] *Ibid.*, V, 360.

was scheming to spread their institution into all the national territories and finally into the free states. To him this meant catastrophic tragedy. It meant that free labor would be degraded and destroyed by the competition of slave labor. It meant that the idea of equality of opportunity would wither and die and in its place would appear the hateful principle that a small rich class should dominate society and government. It meant the end of America's mission to humanity. Lincoln determined that slavery must be abolished to save the American dream. But it must be abolished gradually so that the nation would not be dstroyed in the process. For if the nation was destroyed, the dream too would be lost.

LINCOLN AND SLAVERY

In 1837, when he was a member of the Illinois legislature, Lincoln made his first public statement about the institution of Negro slavery. He and a colleague introduced a resolution which declared that slavery was founded "on both injustice and bad policy, but that the promulgation of abolition doctrines tends rather to increase than abate its evils," and that Congress had no power to interfere with slavery in the states where it existed.[19] To the end of his life Lincoln held substantially to this position; he never modified or changed the essentials of his early attitude. He believed that slavery was wrong, but he would not compel the owners of slaves to give up their property without their consent. He would not strike at slavery in the Southern states, because the Constitution recognized the right of each state to control its domestic instituions; but he would prevent by national fiat its extension into the national territories. He would pen it up in the South and by choking off its further growth make certain of its eventual and peaceable extinction.

Lincoln heartily disliked the abolitionists, those fierce men and women who demanded the immediate emancipation of the slaves and who if they could not have their way, preferred

---

[19] *Ibid.*, I, 51-52.

to avoid any contaminating contact with slavery by withdrawing the free states from the Union. He detested their fana-
ticism and intolerance and their extreme opinions. "Those
who would shiver into fragments the Union of these States,
tear to tatters its now venerable Constitution, and even burn
the last copy of the Bible, rather than slavery should continue
a single hour, together with all their more halting sympathizers,
have received, and are receiving, their just execration . . . ,"
he declared in 1852.[20] Such as these he never welcomed in
the anti-slavery movement.[21] He disliked the abstract imprac-
ticality of the abolitionists, their failure to realize the complex
problems involved in the sudden emancipation of millions of
slaves, their refusal to recognize that abolition could not be
crammed down Southern throats. As long as the South wanted
slavery, Lincoln thought, it was hopeless to force it to take
freedom. "A universal feeling, whether well or ill-founded,
cannot be safely disregarded," he observed. Even right things
must wait until public opinion accepted them.[22] Finally Lincoln was disturbed by the abolitionists' lack of feeling for the
Union, their willingness to leave it if they could not reform
it right away. To him the preservation of the Union was
infinitely more precious than the striking down of slavery.
"Much as I hate slavery," he said, "I would consent to the
extension of it rather than see the Union dissolved, just as I
would consent to any great evil to avoid a greater one." [23]
Patient in the conviction that the institution would die a natural
death if restricted to the South, he could afford to wait, and
he wanted the abolitionists to keep their mouths shut during
the interim. It was characteristic of Lincoln, with his moderate
nature, to denounce the extremity of the Garrisons and the
Welds. It was also characteristic of him to denounce the aggressive exponents of the sacredness of slavery, "the opposite
extreme— . . . a few but increasing number of men who, for

---

[20] *Ibid.*, II, 172-173.
[21] *Ibid.*, V, 60-61.
[22] *Ibid.*, II, 69-70.
[23] *Ibid.*, II, 236.

the sake of perpetuating slavery, are beginning to assail and to ridicule the white man's charter of freedom, the declaration that 'all men are created free and equal.' " [24]

Lincoln based his opposition to slavery mainly upon democratic and economic grounds. He felt a moral repugnance to the institution, but this was subordinate to his other reasons for disliking it.[25] He believed that slavery and the aristocratic philosophy of its advocates threatened to subvert the democratic idea that all men were created free and equal. Let the principle be established that Negroes were not created with an equal right to earn their bread, he said, and the next step would be to deny the right to certain groups of whites, probably laborers.[26] A vigorous and expanding slavery gave the lie to the American ideal of an equalitarian democratic society and hence it weakened the influence of America as the supreme example of successful democracy upon the rest of the world. It might even destroy America's mission to humanity.[27] Lincoln was deeply moved as he pondered these consequences, and he placed the democratic opposition to slavery on the highest philosophical plane:

> It is the eternal struggle between these two principles—right and wrong—throughout the world. They are the two principles that have stood face to face from the beginning of time; and will ever continue to struggle. The one is the common right of humanity, and the other the divine right of kings. It is the same principle in whatever shape it develops itself. It is the same spirit that says, "You toil and work and earn bread, and I'll eat it." No matter in what shape it comes, whether from the mouth of a king who seeks to bestride the people of his own nation and live by the fruit of their labor, or from one race of men as an

---

[24] *Ibid.*, II, 172-173.
[25] This, of course, is but an opinion and cannot be definitely established. Some Lincoln students would disagree with it.
[26] Lincoln, *Works*, V, 344-345.
[27] *Ibid.*, II, 205.

apology for enslaving another race, it is the same tyrannical principle.[28]

Out of his solicitude for the economic well-being of the laboring masses there arose Lincoln's second reason for seeking the abolition of slavery. He proposed to keep it locked up in the South because that would assure its ultimate extinction. But he had another motive, an economic one, for preventing its expansion. He wanted to keep it out of the as yet unsettled and vast territories of the national government. He demanded that these western lands be consecrated as homes for free laborers. This they could never be if slaveholders could move into them with their Negroes. Free labor could not compete with slave labor. Slavery would drive out most of the white farmers and pauperize those who remained. "The whole nation is interested that the best use shall be made of these territories," he declared. "We want them for homes of free white people. This they cannot be, to any considerable extent, if slavery shall be planted within them. Slave States are places for poor white people to remove from, not to remove to. New free States are the places for poor white people to go to, and better their condition." [29] And again he said, voicing a concept of America as a place of refuge for the oppressed of all nations: "I am in favor of this not merely . . . for our own people who are born amongst us, but as an outlet for free white people everywhere, the world over—in which Hans, and Baptiste, and Patrick, and all other men from all the world, may find new homes and better their condition in life." [30]

It is significant that Lincoln never spoke of the territories as being homes for free black labor. He did not want colored workers there any more than he wanted slaves to compete with whites. In fact, he did not want Negroes in America at all. Lincoln was firmly convinced of the inferiority of the Negroes,

---

[28] *Ibid.,* V, 65.
[29] *Ibid.,* II, 232-233.
[30] *Ibid.,* V, 58-59. See also Paul M. Angle (ed.), *New Letters and Papers of Lincoln* (Boston, 1930), 190, 210.

and he did not believe that two races of different color could live side by side on a basis of equality. For the good of both, he believed that the slaves, when and after they were freed, should be colonized in some other land, preferably Africa.[31] "There is a natural disgust in the minds of nearly all white people at the idea of indiscriminate amalgamation of the white and black races," he exclaimed.[32] He was opposed, he said in 1858, to permitting Negroes to vote, to serve on juries, or to marry with whites.[33] He gave the fullest expression of his views on race relations at Ottawa, Illinois, in a debate with Stephen A. Douglas:

> I have no purpose to introduce political and social equality between the white and the black races. There is a physical difference between the two, which in my judgment, will probably forever forbid their living together upon the footing of perfect equality; and inasmuch as it becomes a necessity that there must be a difference, I, as well as Judge Douglas, am in favor of the race to which I belong having the superior position. I have never said anything to the contrary, but I hold that notwithstanding all this, there is no reason in the world why the negro is not entitled to all the natural rights enumerated in the Declaration of Independence—the right to life, liberty, and the pursuit of happiness. . . . I agree with Judge Douglas he is not my equal in many respects—certainly not in color, perhaps not in moral or intellectual endowment. But in the right to eat bread, without the leave of anybody else, which his own hand earns, he is my equal and the equal of Judge Douglas, and the equal of every living man.[34]

The story of Lincoln's opposition to slavery before the Civil War falls into two periods, divided by the year 1854. Up to that time he manifested a constant but not vehement hostility to the institution. He was for keeping it out of the territories

---

[31] Lincoln, *Works*, II, 337-338.
[32] *Ibid.*, II, 329-330.
[33] *Ibid.*, IV, 90-91.
[34] *Ibid.*, III, 229-230.

and leaving it alone in the states where it existed. During his short term in Congress he supported the Wilmot Proviso, which would have barred slavery from the new territories acquired as a result of the war with Mexico; he introduced a measure to abolish the institution in the District of Columbia with the consent of, and financial compensation for, the owners.[35] He thought that slavery was in a moribund condition, and he was willing to let it die in peace. Then in 1854 an event occurred that galvanized him into action. Congress passed the Kansas-Nebraska Act, providing for the organization of two new territorial governments and their eventual admission as states. These territories were located in a region which by the terms of the Missouri Compromise of 1820 was forbidden ground to slavery. The Kansas-Nebraska Act repealed the earlier prohibition and permitted slaveholders to emigrate into these territories with their property. The legal status of slavery in Kansas and Nebraska was to be determined by the principle of popular sovereignty. This meant that the people in the territories were to decide whether or not they wanted the institution. The advocates of popular sovereignty were always vague as to the exact time when the people would make a decision, but presumably it would come when a territory entered that transitional stage before becoming a state when it chose a territorial legislature to make laws of a purely local nature. The legislature would vote either to establish slavery or to exclude it. If the latter, slaveholders in the territory would have to leave. The Kansas-Nebraska Act stirred men to anger and alarm all over the North. It opened up new areas of expansion to slavery; it repealed an old law which many had come to think sacred and permanent. It seemed that an agressive slavocracy was opening a campaign to extend slavery into all the national territories. It jolted Lincoln out of his assumption that slavery was dying a natural death and brought him onto the field in active opposition to its spread to any place outside of the South.

[35] *Ibid.*, I, 277; II, 66-67, 92, 96-100.

At Peoria, Illinois, in October, 1854, he made the first great speech of his life. It was a long, reasoned, and moderate address, in which he declared his unalterable hostility to the expansion of slavery into any territories where it previously had been excluded. At the outset he made it crystal clear that he had no purpose to interfere in any way with the institution in the states of the South. He voiced no criticism of the Southern people for supporting it: "They are just what we would be in their situation. If slavery did not now exist among them, they would not introduce it. If it did now exist among us, we should not instantly give it up." He confessed that he did not know how to effect a final and satisfactory emancipation of all the slaves. "If all earthly power were given me," he said, "I should not know what to do as to the existing institution." His first impulse would be to free all the blacks and colonize them in Africa. But he realized that colonization was a long and costly process, and in any event he would not force emancipation upon a reluctant South. Turning to the issue of slavery and the territories, he spoke with assured certainty. Congress had no constitutional right to abolish slavery in the states, but it had the unquestioned power to keep it out of the territories. He would exercise the power to the fullest; not a slave must go into the western lands. He was adamant on this point. The territories must be reserved as homes for free whites.[36]

The Kansas-Nebraska Act was but the first in a series of rapidly unfolding events that finally led to bloody civil war. Sectional bitterness and hatred mounted with each incident, and men hardened their minds by the hour against compromise. On the plains of bleeding Kansas the minions of slavery and anti-slavery debated popular sovereignty with Sharp's rifles. The fiery Carolinian, Preston Brooks, caned the abolitionist Charles Sumner on the floor of the Senate, and members of Congress came to their sessions armed with horse pistols. The old Whig party, which had straddled every other issue before,

---

[36] *Ibid.*, II, 205-207.

attempted one last colossal straddle on the slavery question— and split and died without dignity. In its place there appeared the Republican party, young, militant, composed of all the disparate elements which for idealistic and selfish motives wanted to check the expansion of slavery. The Supreme Court, dominated by Democrats, heard the case of Dred Scott, slave, and handed down a decision stating that slaveholders could take their property into any national territory and that Congress could not stop them. John Brown had a vision and received God's command to free the slaves: he made his mad raid on Harper's Ferry and failed, and his body was laid in a martyr's grave. The nation rushed on the feet of angry words to the brink of disunion.

As Lincoln observed these momentous developments, he came increasingly to the conviction that there was on foot a gigantic slaveholders' conspiracy to legalize and establish slavery in the territories and eventually to carry it into the free states themselves. Historians now know that he was mistaken about the conspiracy. The South intended to get what it could in the territories, but there was no organized plot, as Lincoln imagined it, to install slavery everywhere. Most historians also think that he and others who stood with him need not have worried about slavery expanding into the West. They point out that nature had passed a law excluding it, that it never would have been profitable there and hence never would have survived. Perhaps so. This is hindsight which Lincoln did not have. He could only judge the events of his time by the light of his time. And that light told him that the time had come to stop the victorious march of slavery before it conquered the democratic faith. To the convention of Illinois, who in 1858 nominated him as their candidate for the United States Senate, he addressed these fateful words:

'A house divided against itself cannot stand.' I believe this government cannot endure permanently half slave and half free. I do not expect the Union to be dissolved—I do not expect the house to fall—but I do expect it will cease to be divided. It will become all one thing, or all the other. Either the opponents of slavery will arrest the further spread of it, and place it where the public mind shall rest in the belief that it is in the course of ultimate extinction; or its advocates will push it forward till it shall become alike lawful in all the States, old as well as new, North as well as South.[37]

This pronouncement represented no change from Lincoln's previous views. He merely wanted to restore the situation to what it had been before 1854—when slavery existed in a restricted area and was in the course of ultimate extinction. He would do this despite the Dred Scott decision. That decision he considered to be unconstitutional, a piece of legal perversion. It would be changed. When the Republicans came to power, they would see to that.[38] He never dreamed that the South would resist this program, that it would leave the Union before it would give up what it thought its just rights. According to Lincoln's way of thinking, the South would lose no rights that belonged to it. It would merely lose those which it had taken from the North since 1854.

LINCOLN AND THE CIVIL WAR

In 1860 the Republican party chose Lincoln as its presidential candidate, partly because he was more "available" than the other aspirants for the nomination; and he won the election, mainly because the Democratic opposition was divided into a Northern and a Southern wing. He was elected in November but did not take office until March of the following year. The intervening months were among the most terrible in American history. Seven states in the lower South seceded from the Union and assumed an independent status. Then they set about forming a union of their own, the Confederate States. The states which left the old Union did so

---

[37] *Ibid.*, III, 2.
[38] *Ibid.*, II, 320-321; V, 232.

because they believed that the triumph of the Republican party threatened the Southern way of life. In Lincoln's election, they saw the impending destruction of something bigger than slavery: the entire social structure, the culture, the economic order of Dixie. To save the minority South from the alien domination of the majority North, the secession leaders took their states out of the Union. They did so in the conviction that their action was constitutional. They expected no protest from the North. They entertained no hostile designs against the North. They simply wanted to be let alone.

As the secession movement got under way and the first states took their departure, conservative men representing all parties and sections came forward in Congress with proposed compromises to avert further withdrawals and to bring back the states already gone. The sponsors of these measures agreed on certain principles: the adoption of an amendment to the Constitution guaranteeing forever the existence of slavery in the states and the passage of a fugitive slave law satisfactory to the South. On the thorny issue of slavery and the territories, the compromisers differed. Two suggested solutions found a measure of Congressional and popular support. One was to apply the doctrine of popular sovereignty to all the territories. The other, the Crittenden Compromise, proposed to divide the territories on the old Missouri Compromise line of 36° 30'. North of the line slavery would be excluded; South of it the institution would be welcomed.

No compromise could pass Congress unless the Republican party supported it. The Republicans in Congress could not support any of the measures up for consideration until they knew what Lincoln's attitude was. They looked to the president-elect in Springfield for leadership, for instructions to vote for or against compromise. The country looked to Springfield also. Public opinion in all sections was confused. There were many in the South who hoped that secession could be averted. They wanted Lincoln to issue a public statement proclaiming his intention to respect Southern rights. This they could use as an argument against the advocates of immediate secession. Especially in the states of the upper South did the leaders desire Lincoln to speak out. They meant to hold their states in the Union and they intended to arrange a compromise that would satisfy both sections. They wanted Lincoln's help. The Northern people were puzzled and shaken by the crisis that was developing. For years they had heard the South threaten secession in talk that was never followed by action, and they had come to feel that the threats were nothing but bluster. Now the thing was upon them and they knew not what to do. They did not want the Union dissolved, but they did not know how to save it. They would have made a compromise with the South, but they were not sure what and how to compromise. Anxiously they turned their eyes on Springfield.

Out in the little capitol of Illinois, Abraham Lincoln watched the events of the hour and pondered their meaning. He did not understand them. He did not understand the South. He did not appreciate how deeply the Southern leaders felt that his election endangered Southern institutions. That he failed to see the ominous realities of the situation was not surprising. He had not been in Washington since his one term as a Congressman had ended in 1849. Consequently he had not witnessed on the spot the bitterness and the hatred of the sectional controversy as it was reflected in national politics. He was out of touch with Southern politicians. He had observed the struggle from Illinois, and his point of observation was relatively remote from the arena. His horizon was limited, and his opinions were naturally parochial. He could not understand why the South was alarmed because the Republican party was taking over the national government. Again and again he had proclaimed in his speeches that he had no purpose to interfere with slavery in the states. He had publicly recognized the constitutional right of slaveholders to recover their runaway property through the medium of a fugitive slave law. He proposed no attack upon Southern rights as those rights were guaranteed by the Constitution. To exclude slavery from the territories was not denying the South its rights, he believed. It was simply restoring the situation to what it had been from the beginning of the government to 1854; it was restoring the policy laid down by the Founding Fathers of placing slavery where the public could rest in the belief that it was in the course of ultimate extinction. Why should the South object to this? Furthermore Lincoln did not take the threat of secession seriously. He thought that the Southern masses were sincerely devoted to the Union and would prevent their leaders from taking their states out of the Union. He failed to grasp the essential fact that the issue with the South was not slavery but the fear of Northern Domination, now first portended by the Republican triumph. The South wanted more than assurances about slavery in the states. It wanted dominion status. It demanded to know that the Southern way of life was safe. To this all other questions, including the symbolical right to take slaves into the territories, were subordinate.[39]

As the secession crisis expanded, men of all shades of opinion besieged Lincoln for a public statement that would allay Southern fears and avert the withdrawal of other states. He refused. Unconvinced of the seriousness of the situation and not understanding the temper of the South, he saw no reason to speak out. If the Southerners wanted to know where he stood, he exclaimed, let them read his speeches. If he issued a statement, designing men would seize on it and distort its meanings. He remained silent too as to whether as President he would attempt to force the seceded states back into the Union with an exercise of military power. Privately he told several Republican leaders that no state could lawfully leave the Union without the consent of all the others, and that it was the duty of the President to run the machine as it was.[40] These remarks were sufficiently cryptic to indicate that Lincoln was uncertain as to what he would do in the event that a situation developed that he did not believe would develop:

---

[39] Nathaniel Wright Stephenson, *Lincoln: An Account of His Personal Life Especially of Its Springs of Actions as Revealed and Deepened by the Ordeal of War* (Indianapolis, 1924), 101-103, 113-114.

[40] Angle, *New Letters and Papers of Lincoln,* 259-260; Lincoln to Thurlow Weed, December 17, 1860, Lincoln, *Works,* VI, 82.

the secession of a large number of states and the prospect of a permanently divided union.

If Lincoln exercised a negative influence upon public opinion, he exercised a very positive one upon the attitude of his party toward the compromise measures pending in Congress. The Republican chieftains in Washington sought his counsel about these measures. They could not take a position until they knew his position, and because he was the president-elect and the leader of the party they had to follow where he led. Lincoln, therefore, became the decisive factor in determining the fate of the compromises. He was willing to agree to a guarantee for slavery in the states and a fugitive slave act acceptable to the South. But on the vital issue of slavery and the territories he would not budge an inch. He instructed the Republicans to oppose the Crittenden Compromise or popular sovereignty. These schemes settled nothing, he said; both gave to slavery areas in which to expand and hence prolonged its existence. To the argument that the Crittenden proposal did not give slavery a very large or a very suitable area he replied that the South would use its power in the national government to secure the conquest of lands in Latin America where slavery would be profitable, lands that lay well to the south of the line of 36° 30'. So he bade his followers stand firm. The tug had to come sometime, he said, and better now than later.[41] The Republicans obeyed his directions and voted against the compromises. The extreme Southerners also voted against them. The compromises were defeated, and with them the chance that the Union could be preserved by mutual concessions. Why did Lincoln refuse to support any plan that might have stopped the secession movement? Why did this man whose nature was essentially moderate and generous oppose policies of moderation at this fateful hour? Why did he, loving the Union above all things, take a stand that made the dis-

---

[41] Lincoln to William Kellogg, December 11, 1860, *ibid.*, VI, 77-78; *id.* to E. B. Washburne, December 13, *ibid.*, VI, 78-79; *id.* to William H. Seward, February 1, 1861, *ibid.*, VI, 103; *id.* to Lyman Trumbull, December 10, 17, 1860, Gilbert A. Tracy (ed.), *Uncollected Letters of Abraham Lincoln* (Boston, 1917), 171-172.

solution of the Union certain? One possible answer is that he was simply holding to his principles. He believed deeply and sincerely that for the good of America and mankind, slavery must be put on the road to extinction. Now he was hewing to the line, let the results be what they may. Against this explanation rises the fact that Lincoln was always willing to yield some of his principles to save more important ones. And the most important thing in the world to him was the Union. Again and again in the war years just ahead he would give up for the sake of the Union policies in which he believed. It seems probable then that he would have acted in a similar manner in the secession crisis had he understood that the alternative to compromise was the destruction of the Union. But he did not understand the situation. At first he did not think that the South would secede merely because the Republicans had won control of the government. Then when the secession of a number of Southern states became an accomplished fact, he refused to believe that their action would be permanent. He thought that there was a strong union sentiment among the Southern people that would eventually make itself felt. The masses would repudiate their leaders and bring their states back into the nation. All the incoming administration had to do was to convince the South that it had no purpose to interfere with Southern institutions. If the Republicans adopted a conciliatory program, the Union would be restored by peaceable means and by the spontaneous action of the seceded states.[42]

Such a program Lincoln tried to carry through when he became President in March. He placed it before the South and the nation in his inaugural address. Earnestly he assured the people in the seceded states that the government would not attack them unless they first attacked the government. He would waive temporarily the enforcement of national laws in these states. He would not attempt to recover the federal forts

---

[42] For a penetrating analysis of the attitudes of Lincoln and the Republicans during this period, see David M. Potter, *Lincoln and His Party in the Secession Crisis* (New Haven, 1942).

and arsenals which the seceders had captured, although he would "hold, occupy, and possess" those which had not been seized, notably Fort Sumter in Charleston harbor, as symbolic assertions of national authority. He promised that the government would respect every right guaranteed to the South by the Constitution. There would be no interference with slavery in the states or with the rendition to their owners of fugitive slaves.[43] Then he sought to stir the feeling for the Union that he thought existed in the hearts of the Southern masses. He denied the right of secession and asserted the perpetuity of the Union.[44] He pleaded with the Southern people not to destroy it and with it the happiness of all America:

> Physically speaking, we cannot separate. We cannot remove our respective sections from each other, nor build an impassable wall between them. A husband and wife may be divorced, and go out of the presence and beyond the reach of each other; but the different parts of our country cannot do this. They cannot but remain face to face, and intercourse, either amicable or hostile, must continue between them. Is it possible then, to make that intercourse more advantageous or more satisfactory after separation than before? Can aliens make treaties easier than friends can make laws? Can treaties be more faithfully enforced between aliens than laws among friends? [45]

Lincoln's program of peaceable reconstruction was not to be. He attempted to send supplies to the garrison at Fort Sumter, first notifying the government of the Confederacy that he was going to do so. It was not his purpose to provoke hostilities. He was determined to hold on to Sumter as a symbol of national authority. The little garrison was running short of food, and its commander informed Lincoln that unless relief came they would have to give up the fort. Lincoln

---

[43] The inaugural address is in Lincoln, *Works*, VI, 169-185. For comments upon Lincoln's program as announced in the inaugural, see Potter, *Lincoln and His Party*, 320-333.

[44] Lincoln, *Works*, VI, 173-175.

[45] *Ibid.*, VI, 181.

decided to send the relief. But the Confederate government and South Carolina, both of which had writhed for months as they contemplated a federal fort in the middle of Charleston harbor, anticipated him. They demanded the surrender of Sumter, and when the demand was refused they opened fire on the fort and reduced it. The mystic chords of the Union were snapped. War had come at last.

For four bloody years Lincoln guided his country through the toils of civil war. Never once did he waver in his determination that the struggle must be fought through to a victorious conclusion. Never once did he dream of giving up the fight. He had realized, finally, the nature and the deepness of the Southern protest against the majority North. The South had seceded because it would not live under a government controlled by a party that was hostile to Southern institutions. To Lincoln this refusal to accept the results of the election was denying the principles of democracy. If a minority could thus flout the majority, popular government was a failure, the American Union was a farce. Lincoln recognized this when he said in his message to Congress in July, 1861: "And this issue embraces more than the fate of the United States . . . . It forces us to ask: 'Is there, in all republics, this inherent and fatal weakness?' 'Must a government, of necessity, be too strong for the liberties of its own people, or too weak to maintain its own existence?' " [46] This was a war, Lincoln believed, to preserve democratic government in America and to preserve the democratic idea in the world. For if American democracy died, the hope of universal democracy would die with it. "This is essentially a people's contest," he declared. "On the side of the Union it is a struggle for maintaining in the world that form and substance of government whose leading object is to elevate the condition of men—to lift artificial weights from all shoulders; to clear the paths of laudable pursuit for all; to afford all an unfettered start, and a fair chance in the race of life." [47] This was a war to sustain the equality

[46] *Ibid.,* VI, 304.
[47] *Ibid.,* VI, 321.

of economic opportunity and the rights of labor, he said. The triumph of the Confederacy would mean the triumph of the idea that a small wealthy class, the planter aristocracy, was entitled to control the government and use that control for its own material benefit. The slavocracy, he charged, wanted to "place capital on an equal footing with, if not above, labor, in the structure of government." [48] In the Civil War all of Lincoln's mystic faith in democracy came to the fore. But one thought dominated his mind—the vital necessity of maintaining the world's greatest democratic government. This was why he ruthlessly carried on the war until victory was achieved, so ruthlessly that he often trampled on principles that were almost as dear to him as the Union.

To Lincoln the preservation of the Union was the paramount object of the war. That was the purpose for which the war was being fought. The Union dwarfed all other issues. He would save the Union, at any cost and by whatever methods seemed most likely to succeed. In the opening days of the struggle he sought to rally all parties and factions in the North in support of the war. This necessitated a statement of war aims so broad and national that men of every shade of opinion could unite behind them. Lincoln supplied the formula by proclaiming that the restoration of the Union was the sole objective of the war. Presumably this meant that the Union would be restored as it was before 1861, with slavery still in existence. That was the way Lincoln meant it. He was a superb judge of public opinion, and he sensed that the people would sustain almost unanimously a war to preserve the nation. He also knew that the introduction of other issues would divide and confuse them and hinder the war effort. He knew specifically that if the government announced the abolition of slavery as one of the war aims it would lose the support of large numbers of conservative men, particularly in the loyal slave states. Nor did Lincoln desire to make emancipation one of the results of the war. He did not want to see slavery die

---

[48] *Ibid.*, VII, 56-57.

suddenly and violently in the fury of civil conflict. Such an outcome, he thought, would bring more evil than good in its train. "In considering the policy to be adopted for suppressing the insurrection," he said in his message to Congress in December, 1861, "I have been anxious and careful that the inevitable conflict for this purpose shall not degenerate into a violent and remorseless revolutionary struggle. I have therefore, in every case thought it proper to keep the integrity of the Union prominent as the primary object of the contest on our part. . . ." [49] Lincoln's determination to restore the Union by any method even impelled him to throw overboard consideration of party regularity. He appointed Democrats and loyal slaveholders to high civil and military offices. By inviting such men to accept positions in the administration, he hoped to enlarge the Republican organization into an all-inclusive Union party, a "popular front," whose one resolution was to end the war quickly and reestablish the nation.

Lincoln's program of a war for the Union encountered the fierce opposition of a faction of his own party, the radicals. These men hated slavery with a bitter personal emotion. They had welcomed the outbreak of civil conflict as an opportunity come at long last to destroy slavery, and they were determined that the war must not end without its death. The radicals stood for instant emancipation, the confiscation of "rebel" property, the use of colored soldiers and civil and—when it should become expedient—political equality for the Negro. They demanded a war of remorseless and revolutionary violence, the complete subjugation of the South, and a Carthaginian peace. They fought Lincoln bitterly, in Congress, in the newspapers, and on the stump. And they won many a victory over him. Both logic and time aided their cause. For in a sense Lincoln, in trying to restore the Union as it was, proposed the impossible: to conduct the war for the preservation of an institution, slavery, that was one of the important causes of the war. The longer the struggle continued, the more hostile

---

[49] *Ibid.*, VII, 51.

the Northern people became toward slavery, until finally they cried for its destruction. When that time came, Abraham Lincoln, who always considered himself the tribune of the masses, heeded their voice and struck it down.[50]

By the summer of 1862, Lincoln realized that public opinion was swinging to a position where it might demand the abolition of slavery. Now he began to consider whether it would be necessary for him to effect the overthrow of the institution in order to achieve his paramount objective of preserving the Union. He regarded the eventuality with reluctance, but he was willing to sacrifice his opposition to the violent destruction of slavery to the greater policy of the Union. "Still, I must save this government, if possible," he wrote. "What I cannot do, of course I will not do; but it may as well be understood, once for all, that I shall not surrender this game leaving any available card unplayed." [51] He gave the fullest statement of his determination to save the Union, let the means be what they may, in his famous reply to Horace Greeley when that Republican editor begged him in 1862 to issue a military edict freeing the slaves as a military measure:

If there be those who would not save the Union unless they could at the same time save slavery, I do not agree with them. If there be those who would not save the Union unless they could at the same time destroy slavery, I do not agree with them. My paramount object in this struggle is to save the Union, and is not either to save or to destroy slavery. If I could save the Union without freeing any slave, I would do it; and if I could save it by freeing all the slaves, I would do it; and if I could save it by freeing some and leaving others alone, I would also do that. What I do about slavery and the colored race, I do because I believe it helps to save the Union; and what I forbear, I forbear because I do not believe it would help to save the Union.[52]

[50] The struggle between Lincoln and the radical Republicans is treated in T. Harry Williams, *Lincoln and the Radicals* (Madison, Wisconsin, 1941).
[51] Lincoln to Reverdy Johnson, July 26, 1862, Lincoln, *Works*, VII, 293-294.
[52] Lincoln to Horace Greeley, August 22, 1862, *ibid.*, VIII, 15-16.

Lincoln believed that slavery as an institution could be abolished legally only by the states in which it existed or by an amendment to the Constitution. His own conservative inclination favored the first method. As he observed the mounting spirit of radicalism in the country, he decided to move for state emancipation in order to forestall any demand for the violent wartime destruction of slavery. In March, 1862, he sent a message to Congress suggesting a plan for voluntary gradual emancipation to be undertaken by the states, with the federal government providing financial compensation to owners. His idea was to get this scheme started in the loyal slave states. If they adopted it, he thought that the war would be shortened. The seceded states would be discouraged as they saw their sister commonwealths abolishing the institution upon which they had founded their Confederacy; they would realize that even if they won their independence the other slave states would never join them.[53] Presumably Lincoln meant to apply his plan also to the states which had seceded once the war was over.

Congress responded favorably to Lincoln's suggestion, but the slave states were cool to the proposal. They regarded it as an unwarranted federal interference with their institutions. Lincoln appealed to them again and again to act, even calling their Congressmen into personal conferences, but to no avail.[54] He begged them not to be blind to the signs of the times and the swelling strength of the radicals and the ever louder demands for emancipation as a war measure.[55] "The pressure in this direction is still upon me," he said, "and is increasing." [56] With singular blindness, the slave state leaders refused to read the signs. They refused to accept a measure which might have halted the radical campaign for wartime abolition. Lincoln clung tenaciously to the hope that state emancipation could be effected. As late as December, 1862,

[53] *Ibid.*, VII, 112-115.
[54] *Ibid.*, VII, 120-128.
[55] *Ibid.*, VII, 172-173.
[56] *Ibid.*, VII, 276-277.

he was still recommending it to Congress. In a passage of sincere eloquence in his annual message, he said:

> The fiery trial through which we pass will light us down, in honor or dishonor, to the latest generation. We say we are for the Union. The world will not forget that we say this. We know how to save the Union. The world knows we do know how to save it. We—even we here—hold the power and bear the responsibility. In giving freedom to the slave, we assume freedom to the free—honorable alike in what we give and what we preserve. We shall nobly save or meanly lose the last, best hope of earth. Other means may succeed; this could not fail. The way is plain, peaceful, generous, just—a way which, if followed, the world will forever applaud, and God must forever bless.[57]

Even as he was striving for emancipation by state action and failing, Lincoln was considering other ways to head off the radicals and keep the initiative in his own hands. He knew that the radicals, when they were strong enough in Congress, would attempt to pass a drastic confiscation bill providing for the seizure of the property of "rebels," including slaves, thus effecting emancipation in the guise of punishing treason. This prospect alarmed Lincoln; he knew the extreme lengths to which the radicals might go. In July of 1862 his fears were realized. The radical leaders pushed through Congress a confiscation act which he thought highly objectionable. By dint of much pressure and the threat of a veto, he made them tone down some of the provisions. But he recognized that this was a harbinger of worse to come; the radicals would not stop until total victory was theirs. Lincoln decided he must anticipate them. He resolved to issue an executive proclamation freeing the slaves in the rebellious states as a measure of military necessity. His authority to emancipate by edict he found in the war powers of the President. He informed the Cabinet of his purpose on July 22 and read the members a proposed

---

[57] *Ibid.*, VIII, 131.

draft of the proclamation.[58] Then he put the document aside
for two months, waiting for a propitious moment to announce
it to the people. In the meantime he continued to labor for
compensated emancipation and to argue publicly, as he did
with Greeley, for a policy of non-interference with slavery.
This possibly indicates that he hoped it would not be necessary to issue the proclamation, that he was watching the drift
of events for some sign that radicalism was losing strength or
that the end of the war was close at hand. Whatever was in
Lincoln's mind, nothing did occur to change his original resolution that he must forestall the radicals. On September 22,
after the Union victory at Antietam, he issued a "preliminary"
proclamation. In it he asserted that the restoration of the
Union was still the purpose of the war, and he reaffirmed his
support of compensated emancipation. Then he declared that
on January 1 he would free the slaves in any state still in rebellion. Presumably if all the states in the Confederacy laid
down their arms before that date, slavery within their borders
would remain intact.[59]

On January 1 Lincoln issued the final proclamation. It
freed the slaves in the rebellious states, with the exception of
all of Tennessee and designated parts of Louisiana and Virginia—the only areas of the Confederacy controlled by Union
forces and hence the only areas where military emancipation
could be made a reality. In other words Lincoln freed the
slaves where the proclamation was inoperative and held them
in slavery where he could have set them free. The proclamation
was nothing but a paper edict until the Union armies could
occupy the regions designated as in rebellion. Lincoln justified his action as a measure of pure military necessity to weaken
the South's powers to resist. In the whole document there
was not a single declaration of anti-slavery sentiment nor any
statement that emancipation was now one of the aims of the
war.[60] The emancipation proclamation was not the way Lin-

[58] *Ibid.,* VII, 289-290.
[59] *Ibid.,* VIII, 36-41.
[60] *Ibid.,* VIII, 161-164.

coln would have preferred to solve the slavery question. But having issued it he could not go back on it. Eventually as large regions of the South were conquered it operated with some practical effect. The proclamation did not affect the slaves in the loyal slave states nor did it abolish slavery as a legal institution. Not until 1865, with the passage of the Thirteenth amendment, was slavery destroyed as an institution and the slaves freed everywhere. To the amendment Lincoln gave his blessing and support.[61] He had always held that there were only two constitutional methods of abolishing slavery: by state action or by an amendment to the Constitution. He could accept the Thirteenth amendment as effecting the death of slavery in a lawful, decent manner, although he might regret that it did not contain his favorite device of compensation.

In the midst of the war Lincoln turned his thoughts to the problems of reconstruction. He believed that reconstruction was a presidential function, and he decided to start the process even before the war had ended. His purpose was to get the seceded states back in the Union as soon as possible, with all their former privileges and rights restored. Indeed Lincoln contended that they had never been out of the Union, but only out of their proper relation to it. He was opposed to any punitive measures against the Southern people. The plan he worked out was essentially statesmanlike and extremely generous to the defeated South. He first formally announced it on December 3, 1863, in a "proclamation of amnesty and reconstruction." At that time large parts of the South were being occupied by Federal armies, and military governors appointed by Lincoln ruled the conquered regions. It was here that he proposed to inaugurate reconstruction. In his proclamation he offered pardon to all adherents of the Confederacy, except certain high governmental officials, who would take an oath to support the Union and the acts of Congress and his own proclamation concerning slavery. When in any state ten per

[61] *Ibid.*, X, 302-310, message to Congress, December 6, 1864.

cent of the number of voters in 1860 had sworn this oath, they could set up a state government, and he would extend to it executive recognition. If the new government wished to adopt some provision which would recognize and declare the permanent freedom of the former slaves, he would not object.[62] With Lincoln's encouragement and aid, reconstructed governments were established in Louisiana, Tennessee, Arkansas, and Virginia.

Lincoln's plan enraged the radicals. This mild and tender program, they cried, would lose the Republicans the gains of the war. They demanded harsh and retributive justice for the Southern people, the disfranchisment of the leaders of the Confederacy, and enforced abolition of slavery by the seceded states before restoration to the Union. They embodied their ideas in the Wade-Davis bill, which Lincoln disposed of by a pocket veto. They countered by defeating Congressional recognition of his reconstructed governments. The situation was a stalemate as the war ended, but the controversy was just beginning. The coming of peace made reconstruction the dominant issue of the hour. Both Lincoln and the radicals prepared to do battle. The radicals were more confident than ever of victory and more vindictive in their plans for the South. Now they were demanding the grant of the suffrage to the Negroes and military rule for the "conquered provinces" of Dixie. Against them stood Lincoln with his program of a generous peace and an immediately restored Union. On April 11, 1865, Lincoln made the last speech of his life, to a crowd on the White House lawn. He pleaded for the acceptance of the seceded states back into the Union. He would make it easy for them to return. He would not insist that they give the suffrage to the Negroes as a condition of readmission. He hoped that they would grant the vote to the more intelligent Negroes and to those who had been soldiers, but there must be no compulsion from the national government.[63] He de-

---

[62] *Ibid.*, IX, 218-223. See also pp. 247-253, where Lincoln discussed reconstruction in his message to Congress.
[63] *Ibid.*, XI, 84-92.

fended his reconstructed state governments, and painted the results that would follow if these promising beginnings were denied recognition by Congress:

> Now, if we reject and spurn them, we do our utmost to disorganize and disperse them. We, in effect, say to the white man: You are worthless or worse; we will neither help you, nor be helped by you. To the blacks we say: This cup of liberty which these, your old masters, hold to your lips we will dash away from you, and leave you to the chances of gathering the spilled and scattered contents in some vague and undefined when, where, and how.[64]

Lincoln did not live to fight his reconstruction policy through to either victory or defeat. On April 14 at Ford's Theatre, John Wilkes Booth removed with an assassin's bullet the one man who might have beaten the radicals, a man whose common sense, tact, and magnanimity would have served the country well in the difficult years just ahead.

LINCOLN THE WRITER AND ORATOR

When Lord Curzon delivered the Rede lectures at the University of Cambridge in 1913, he chose as his topic "Modern Parliamentary Eloquence." As he finished an exhaustive treatment of the field, he announced that he would name the three masterpieces of modern oratory in the English language. They were the toast of William Pitt after Trafalgar, Lincoln's Gettysburg address, and Lincoln's second inaugural.[65]

So many of Lincoln's speeches and state papers are called great today because they are literature rather than oratory. He influenced men's minds even in his own time more by what he said and how he phrased it than by how he uttered it. His speeches always read much better than they sounded. With the great orators of American history, those men who swayed crowds and conventions by the magnetism of their personalities

---

[64] *Ibid.,* XI, 90.
[65] William E. Barton, *Lincoln at Gettysburg* (Indianapolis, 1930), 127-128.

and the mellow beauty of their voices, Lincoln does not belong. He was not a Henry, a Webster, or a Bryan. This is not to say that Lincoln was an inferior performer on the platform. He could make an effective stump speech, he could present an impressive logical argument that commanded audience attention, and he was a redoubtable opponent in the rough and tumble political debates that were the fashion of the day. But Lincoln the speaker was a second-rate figure. Lincoln the writer stands in the front rank of those few masters of the language who have stirred men's emotions and moved them to action with the magic of words.

There are three well marked periods of development in Lincoln's literary career. The first one ended in 1854. Up to that time his speeches have a certain immaturity about them, both of style and thought. Obviously they are the products of a man who has not yet found himself. They are for the most part the stump speeches of a young politician, slashing attacks on his opponents, broad humor and broader satire, and fervid defences of his own party.[66] In one important respect they departed from the rhetorical fashion of the day, and where they did the results were superior. The orators of that time dealt generously in rounded periods, purple patches, long and overloaded sentences, and pedantic classical and mythological allusions. Frequently their devotion to the forms of rhetoric obscured the meaning of their thought. Lincoln's style was singularly free from these faults. He had his moments of bombast and windy soaring to the stars, but the moments were relatively few. Even in these salad days of his literary development, he was primarily concerned with clarity of expression. He was more interested in communicating a thought to others then in decorating it with pretty phrases. His taste, influenced by his reading of Blackstone, Euclid, Shakespeare, and the Bible, was good and improving. So was his sense of rhythm. He had from the beginning a keen ear for the sound

---

[66] An excellent example of Lincoln's techniques as a stump speaker is in Angle, *New Letters and Papers of Lincoln*, 85-110.

of words. Gradually he was to acquire a mastery of the effective arrangement of them in sentences and paragraphs of cadenced beauty.

The clarity and simplicity of exposition which Lincoln developed in his first period became a permanent characteristic of his literary style. Always he aimed so to phrase his ideas that the common people would understand him. If this necessitated the use of plain, homespun, salty words, words that some people thought undignified, Lincoln did not care. When he was President he once employed "sugar-coated" in an official communication to Congress. The public printer tried to get him to change it, objecting that the word was not one that should appear in a document of this kind. Lincoln replied that if the time ever came when the people did not understand what sugar-coated meant he would stop using it. Homely, down-to-earth folk expressions and vivid, lusty figures of speech were devices he relied upon to drive his meanings home. In one of his debates with Douglas he observed that the Supreme Court's Dred Scott decision had practically nullified Douglas' pet doctrine of popular sovereignty, and referring to the latter asked, "Has it not got down as thin as the homeopathic soup that was made by boiling the shadow of a pigeon that had starved to death?"[67] Writing in 1862 to a man who had protested certain drastic measures adopted by the government to aid the war effort, Lincoln queried sharply, "Would you drop the war where it is? Or would you prosecute it in future with elderstalk squirts charged with rose-water?" [68] He warned General Joseph Hooker in 1863 against the danger of dividing his army on both banks of the Rappahannock: "In one word, I would not take any risk of being entangled upon the river, like an ox jumped half over a fence and liable to be torn by dogs front and rear without a fair chance to gore one way or kick the other." [69] Again writing to Hooker, when Lee was beginning his invasion of the North, Lincoln said,

---

[67] Lincoln, *Works*, IV, 380.
[68] *Ibid.*, VII, 297, Lincoln to Cuthbert Bullit, July 28, 1862.
[69] *Ibid.*, VIII, 291-292, Lincoln to Hooker, June 5, 1863.

"If the head of Lee's army is at Martinsburg and the tail of it on the plank road between Fredericksburg and Chancellorsville, the animal must be very slim somewhere. Could you not break him?" [70]

The second phase of Lincoln's literary career falls between 1854 and 1860. It was a period of growth and improvement. In 1854 he came out of his legal retirement to fight the Kansas-Nebraska bill, and for the next six years he was on the hustings constantly denouncing the expansion of slavery. These are the years of the Peoria speech, the great debates with Douglas, the Cooper Union address, when Lincoln spoke all over Illinois, in other Middle Western states, and in the East, when he first acquired a national reputation. The speeches that Lincoln made in this second phase were in marked contrast to his earlier efforts. Gone was the broad humor, its place taken by an all-pervading seriousness. Gone too was the occasional floridity; now Lincoln used only short, plain words as he strove to impale his message in the Northern mind. No longer did he slash into his opponents with all the varied verbal weapons of the hard-hitting stump speaker; moderation, fairness, and humility characterized his utterances now. Lincoln had found himself by finding a cause, a cause that was bigger than he, and the realization made him humble and great.

The speeches of the Lincoln of the second phase are superb examples of political argumentation. They represent significant contributions to the literature of political theory and to the democratic faith. But they are not the speeches that men remembered and quoted, they are not the writings of Lincoln that have become a part of the American heritage. This is because up to 1860 his literary style lacked one quality to make it great. It had the virtues of simplicity, clarity, cadence, logic, the ordered march of ideas. It did not have beauty or poetry. Lincoln's writings before 1860 were almost bare of imagery.[71]

---

[70] *Ibid.*, VIII, 315, Lincoln to Hooker, June 14, 1863.
[71] See *ibid.*, II, 327-328, for a rare example of imagery before 1860.

Then, starting with the first inaugural in 1861, an exquisite poetic imagery suddenly appears in his language. The last paragraph of that address, composed with the aid of William H. Seward, is Lincoln's first great and beautiful production:[72]

> I am loath to close. We are not enemies, but friends. We must not be enemies. Though passion may have strained, it must not break our bonds of affection. The mystic chords of memory, stretching from every battle-field and patriot grave to every living heart and hearthstone all over this broad land, will yet swell the chorus of the Union when again touched, as surely, they will be, by the better angels of our nature.[73]

It was as if the ordeal of seccession and war had touched some hidden spring in his being and brought out all the mystic poetry of his nature that he had restrained in the years before. His addresses and state papers of the war years have an "eloquence which rises from the heart when life has been felt in its tragic reality. . . . Such words come only to those who have been purified by fire; they are the distillation of bitter experience."[74] This is the Lincoln who wrote the moving plea for compensated emancipation in his message to Congress in December, 1862;[75] who at Gettysburg stated the democratic faith better than anyone else has before or since;[76] who composed the letter to Mrs. Bixby, one of the few fine letters of consolation ever written.[77] And this is the Lincoln who in the second inaugural, near the close of the war, spoke in words of solemn beauty as he looked into the future just ahead:

> Fondly do we hope—fervently do we pray—that this mighty scourge of war may speedily pass away. Yet, if

---

[72] Lincoln's original draft of the inaugural, the changes suggested by Seward, and Lincoln's revisions of Seward's suggestions are in John G. Nicolay and John Hay, *Abraham Lincoln: A History* (New York, 1890), III, 327-344.
[73] Lincoln, *Works*, VI, 185.
[74] Parrington, *Main Currents in American Thought*, II; *The Romantic Revolution in America*, 159.
[75] Lincoln, *Works*, VIII, 131.
[76] *Ibid.*, IX, 209-210.
[77] *Ibid.*, X, 274-275.

God wills that it continue until all the wealth piled by the bondsman's two hundred and fifty years of unrequited toil shall be sunk, and until every drop of blood drawn with the lash shall be paid by another drawn with the sword, as was said three thousand years ago, so still it must be said, "The judgments of the Lord are true and righteous altogether."

With malice toward none; with charity for all; with firmness in the right, as God gives us to see the right, let us strive on to finish the work we are in; to bind up the nation's wounds; to care for him who shall have borne the battle, and for his widow and his orphan—to do all which may achieve and cherish a just and lasting peace between ourselves, and with all nations.[78]

COLLECTIONS OF LINCOLN'S WORKS

When John G. Nicolay and John Hay, Lincoln's secretaries, were working on their ten volume biography of the departed President, they collected hundreds of Lincoln letters and papers. Some of these were published in the life, which appeared in 1890. Then Robert Todd Lincoln, son of the President, suggested to the secretaries that they edit Lincoln's works. They complied, and in 1894 brought out the *Complete Works of Abraham Lincoln* in two volumes. New Lincoln papers continued to come to light every year, and in 1905 there was published a "supplement and reissue" of the 1894 edition in twelve volumes by the Tandy-Thomas Company. The 1905 collection contains 2,243 items, 486 of which were not in the 1894 edition. It is still the best and most complete edition of Lincoln's works. In 1905-1906, Arthur Brooks Lapsley edited the *Writings of Abraham Lincoln* in eight volumes. The Lapsley set is smaller by one-third than the

[78] *Ibid.,* XI, 46-47. For material on Lincoln the writer, see Paul M. Angle, "Lincoln's Power with Words," *Abraham Lincoln Association Papers, 1934* (Springfield, 1935), 59-87; Stephenson, *Lincoln,* 135-138; Daniel Kilham Dodge, *Abraham Lincoln, Master of Words* (New York, 1924); Luther Emerson Robinson, *Abraham Lincoln as a Man of Letters* (Chicago, 1918).

Nicolay and Hay collection, and on the whole is not as good.[79]

Nicolay and Hay were tireless collectors and competent editors. Only one item in their edition is open to the accusation of being spurious.[80] Only fourteen items are known to be misdated.[81] Nevertheless the secretaries had their editorial faults, particularly when judged by modern historical standards. They "edited" Lincoln to give his language a formal correctness. They corrected his misspellings, supplied right capital letters for wrong ones, altered his punctuation marks, and changed his line and paragraph arrangements.[82] They did not, however, indulge in any real censorship of Lincoln's writings as Jared Sparks did with those of Washington.

In addition to the Nicolay and Hay edition, there are several shorter works containing valuable and vital material to a study of Lincoln. In 1900 Miss Ida Tarbell published some new Lincoln documents in the second volume of her life of the President. Shortly her most important items were included in other books of a more comprehensive nature. Gilbert A. Tracy brought out in 1917 his *Uncollected Letters* of Lincoln, containing 359 items not in the *Complete Works*, a significant and well-edited book.[83] In 1927 Brown University issued a volume of Lincoln letters from manuscripts in its possession and hitherto unpublished. In 1930 appeared Paul M. Angle's expertly edited *New Letters and Papers*, supplementing Nicolay and Hay and Tracy with 430 new items. The industrious collector, Emanuel Hertz, published in 1931 a two-volume

[79] A convenient summary of the history of the publication of Lincoln's works is in Angle, *New Letters and Papers of Lincoln*, vii-x.

[80] This is the letter to George Pickett in volume I, 191-192, which is probably spurious.

[81] There is a list of the misdated items in an article, "Misdated Lincoln letters and Speeches," in *Bulletin of the Abraham Lincoln Association*, number 24, September, 1931, 7-9. A probable misdating of another item is discussed in Hertz, *Lincoln*, II, 757-758.

[82] James G. Randall, "Has the Lincoln Theme Been Exhausted?", *American Historical Review*, XLI, number 2 (1936), 274-275.

[83] There are four spurious letters in the Tracy book. They are the ones to Peter Hitchcock, December 24, 1849; to James Lemen, March 2, 1857; to John J. Crittenden, December 22, 1859; to Alexander H. Stephens, January 19, 1860. See Paul M. Angle, "Four Spurious Lincoln Letters," *Bulletin of the Abraham Lincoln Association*, number 21, December, 1930, 5-9.

biography, the second volume consisting entirely of documents. His items were new discoveries and previously printed papers that had not appeared in complete or exact form. Hertz's book is marred by careless editing.[84]

Not all of Lincoln's papers are available in published form. The Lincoln collection in the Library of Congress, deposited by Robert Todd Lincoln, is closed to investigators until 1947. There are 108 Lincoln autographs in this collection that have not been published.[85] In addition there are Lincoln items in the possession of private collectors as well as in collections of the papers of other men in the Library of Congress and in libraries throughout the country.

The important published collections of Lincoln's works, arranged alphabetically by the names of the editors, are:

Angle, Paul M. *New Letters and Papers of Lincoln.* Boston, 1940.

Brown University. *Lincoln Letters Hitherto Unpublished in the Library of Brown University and Other Providence Libraries.* Providence, 1927.

Hertz, Emanuel. *Abraham Lincoln: A New Portrait.* Volume II. New York, 1931.

Lapsley, Arthur Brooks. *The Writings of Abraham Lincoln.* Eight volumes. New York, 1905-1906.

Nicolay, John G. and Hay, John. *Complete Works of Abraham Lincoln.* Two volumes. New York, 1894.

————. *Complete Works of Abraham Lincoln.* Twelve volumes. New York, 1905.

Tarbell, Ida M. *The Life of Abraham Lincoln.* Volume II. New York, 1900.

Tracy, Gilbert A. *Uncollected Letters of Abraham Lincoln.* Boston, 1917.

---

[84] The following items in Hertz are spurious: the letter to Melloni, p. 623; the letter to the secretary of the St. Marie Brass Band and St. Cecilia Society, p. 791; the promissory note to L. S. Benedict, p. 791; the memorandum on corporations, p. 954; the letter to Taylor, p. 957.

[85] A list of these letters is in Hertz, *Lincoln*, II, 970-977.

CHRONOLOGICAL OUTLINE

1809 Birth of Lincoln, February 12, near Hodgenville, Kentucky.

1816 The Lincoln family moves to southern Indiana.

1820 Congress adopts the Missouri Compromise forbidding slavery in the national territories north of the line 36° 30'.

1830 The Lincoln family moves from Indiana to Illinois.

1831 Lincoln becomes a storekeeper in New Salem, Illinois.

1832 Eastern abolitionists found the New England Anti-Slavery society, the first of its kind in the United States.

Lincoln runs for the state legislature as a Whig and is defeated.

Lincoln participates in the Black Hawk war, an Indian uprising, as a member of the Illinois militia.

1833 Lincoln becomes postmaster of New Salem.

1834 Lincoln again runs for the legislature and is elected.

1836 Texas revolts against Mexico and declares her independence.

Lincoln is reelected to the legislature.

1837 Lincoln is admitted to the bar. He becomes the law partner of John T. Stuart in Springfield.

1838 Lincoln retains his seat in the legislature.

1840 Lincoln is again elected to the legislature. He campaigns for William Henry Harrison, the Whig presidential candidate.

1841 Lincoln becomes the law partner of Stephen T. Logan.

1844 Lincoln campaigns for the election of the Whig candidate, Henry Clay, for President.

Lincoln forms a law partnership with William Herndon.

1845   The United States annexes Texas.

1846   The Whigs of Lincoln's district nominate him as their candidate for the House of Representatives. He is elected.

The United States declares war on Mexico.

The Wilmot Proviso, forbidding slavery in any territory acquired from Mexico, is introduced in Congress but does not pass.

1847   Lincoln takes his seat in Congress. He offers a set of resolutions designed to convict President James K. Polk and the Democrats of having started the war against Mexico.

1848   In a House speech Lincoln attacks Polk for having launched an aggressive war against Mexico.

The treaty of Guadalupe Hidalgo ends the Mexican War.

Lincoln campaigns for Zachary Taylor, the Whig nominee for President.

1849   Lincoln tries to introduce a bill in the House providing for compensated emancipation.

Lincoln's term as Congressman expires, and under an arrangement with Whig leaders in his district to pass around the office, he does not become a candidate for reelection.

He returns to Springfield to practice law.

1850   The Compromise of 1850, designed to settle the controversies arising out of the issue of slavery in the territories acquired from Mexico, is passed by Congress.

1854   Congress passes the Kansas-Nebraska Act, repealing the Missouri Compromise and opening new territory to slavery.

Lincoln actively opposes the Kansas-Nebraska Act, delivering speeches denouncing it.

Anti-Nebraska men in the Illinois legislature talk about

choosing Lincoln as United States Senator, but Lyman Trumbull is elected with Lincoln's help.

1856　Lincoln joins the new Republican party.

He campaigns for John C. Frémont, the Republican presidential candidate, who is defeated by the Democrat, James Buchanan.

1857　The Supreme Court, in the Dred Scott decision, holds that neither Congress nor a territorial legislature can exclude slavery from a territory.

In Kansas the pro-slavery and anti-slavery forces engage in acts of violence against each other.

1858　The Illinois Republicans nominate Lincoln as their candidate for the United States Senate seat held by Stephen. A. Douglas. Lincoln challenges Douglas to a series of debates, and the Lincoln-Douglas debates take place.

1859　The legislature elects Douglas as Senator.

The abolitionist, John Brown, makes his raid on Harper's Ferry, Virginia.

Lincoln continues to make speeches denouncing the expansion of slavery.

1860　Lincoln speaks at Cooper Institute, New York, his first appearance before a New York audience.

The Republican national convention nominates Lincoln for President. He is elected.

South Carolina secedes from the Union because the Republicans have won the election, December.

1861　Six more Southern states secede. They and South Carolina form the Confederate States of America, January-February.

Lincoln becomes President, March 4.

The Confederate government orders the reduction of Fort Sumter, and the Civil War begins, April.

Four more southern states secede and join the Confederacy, April-June.

Congress meets in special session, July 4.

The Union army is defeated at Bull Run or Manassas, July.

Lincoln appoints George B. McClellan to command all the Union armies, July.

Congress passes the first Confiscation Act, August.

Lincoln overrules John C. Frémont when that officer issues an emancipation proclamation and later removes Frémont from the Western command, August-November.

Congress meets in regular session, and Lincoln delivers his first annual message, December.

1862   Lincoln appoints Edwin M. Stanton as Secretary of War, January.

General Ulysses S. Grant captures Forts Henry and Donelson in the West, February.

Lincoln and McClellan disagree about the best way to attack Richmond. The general gets his way, January-March.

Lincoln submits to Congress, March 6, a plan for compensated emancipation by state action.

Lincoln removes McClellan as general-in-chief, but continues him as commander of the Army of the Potomac, March.

The drawn battle of Shiloh is fought in Tennessee, April.

McClellan starts his campaign, April.

The Federal navy captures New Orleans, April.

General David Hunter issues an emancipation proclamation, and Lincoln revokes it, May.

McClellan advances toward Richmond but is forced to retreat. Lincoln orders his army withdrawn from the Peninsula, May-August.

Lincoln determines to issue an emancipation proclamation but waits for a victory to make it public. Congress passes the second Confiscation Act, July.

Lincoln appoints John Pope to command the eastern

army, and Pope is defeated at the battle of Second Manassas, August.

McClellan, reappointed to the command, halts Robert E. Lee's Confederate army at Antietam. Lincoln issues the preliminary emancipation proclamation, September.

Lincoln removes McClellan and puts Burnside in command of the Army of the Potomac, November.

Lincoln delivers his annual message to Congress, December.

Burnside suffers a crushing defeat at Fredericksburg, December.

1863 Lincoln issues the final emancipation proclamation, January.

General Joseph Hooker succeeds Burnside, January.

Hooker is defeated at Chancellorsville, May.

George G. Meade succeeds Hooker, June.

Meade defeats Lee at Gettysburg, and Grant takes Vicksburg, July.

Lincoln speaks at the Gettysburg National Cemetery, November 19.

Grant defeats the Confederates at Chattanooga, November.

Lincoln issues a proclamation of amnesty and reconstruction and delivers his annual message to Congress, December.

1864 Lincoln makes Grant commander of all the Union armies, March.

Grant starts his campaign to capture Richmond and sends William T. Sherman against Atlanta, May.

The Union party nominates Lincoln for President, June.

Grant loses 55,000 men at Cold Harbor and other battles and does not take Richmond, May-June.

Congress passes the Wade-Davis bill, the radical reconstruction plan, and Lincoln kills it with a pocket veto, July.

The radical Republicans hatch schemes to force withdrawal of Lincoln as a candidate, July-August.

The Democrats nominate McClellan for President, August.

Sherman captures Atlanta, September.

Lincoln is reelected, November.

He delivers his annual message to Congress, December.

1865 The radicals defeat Congressional recognition of Lincoln's reconstructed state governments, February.

Lincoln is inaugurated for a second term, March.

Richmond is captured, and Lincoln visits the fallen city. Lee surrenders, April.

Lincoln delivers his last public address, a plea for his plan of reconstruction, April 11.

John Wilkes Booth shoots Lincoln at Ford's Theatre, April 14.

Lincoln dies, April 15.

SELECTED BIBLIOGRAPHY

The works listed here are but a minute part of the voluminous literature dealing with Lincoln. They include, however, most of the best things that have been done. For fuller information the reader is referred to Daniel Fish, *Lincoln Literature* (Minneapolis, 1900), and the same author's "Lincoln Bibliography," in volume XI of the *Complete Works*. The latter title has also been published separately (New York, 1906, and Rock Island, 1926). Paul M. Angle has compiled a brief but excellent bibliography in his two articles, "Basic Lincolniana," in *Bulletin of the Abraham Lincoln Association*, number 43, June 1936, 5-9, and *ibid.*, number 44, September, 1936, 3-9.

Angle, Paul M. *Lincoln: 1854-1861*. Springfield, 1933.

——— *"Here I Have Lived": A History of Lincoln's Springfield, 1821-1865*. Springfield, 1935.

——— "Lincoln's Power with Words," *Abraham Lincoln Association Papers, 1934*, pp. 59-87. Springfield, 1935.

Barton, William E. *The Life of Abraham Lincoln*. Two volumes. Indianapolis, 1925.

——— *A Beautiful Blunder: The True Story of Lincoln's Letter to Mrs. Lydia A. Bixby*. Indianapolis, 1926.

——— *Lincoln at Gettysburg*. Indianapolis, 1930.

Beveridge, Albert J. *Abraham Lincoln, 1809-1858*. Two volumes. Boston, 1928.

Cole, Arthur C. "Abraham Lincoln and the South," *Abraham Lincoln Association Papers, 1928*, pp. 47-78. Springfield, 1928.

Dodge, Daniel Kilham. *Abraham Lincoln, Master of Words*. New York, 1924.

Herndon, William Henry and Weik, Jesse W. *Herndon's Lincoln: The True Story of a Great Life.* Three volumes. Chicago, 1889. A critical edition in one volume, edited by Paul M. Angle, New York, 1930, is superior to the 1889 edition.

Hill, Frederick T. *Lincoln the Lawyer.* New York, 1906.

McCarthy, Charles H. *Lincoln's Plan of Reconstruction.* New York, 1901.

McLaughlin, Andrew C. "Lincoln as a World Figure," *Abraham Lincoln Association Papers, 1924,* pp. 95-126. Springfield, 1924.

———— "Lincoln, the Constitution, and Democracy," *Abraham Lincoln Association Papers, 1936,* pp. 25-59. Springfield, 1937.

Nevins, Allan. "Lincoln's Plans for Reunion," *Abraham Lincoln Association Papers, 1930,* pp. 51-92. Springfield, 1931.

Newton, Joseph Fort. *Lincoln and Herndon.* Cedar Rapids, Iowa, 1910.

Nicolay, John G. *A Short Life of Abraham Lincoln.* New York, 1902.

Nicolay, John G. and Hay, John. *Abraham Lincoln: A History.* Ten volumes. New York, 1890.

Potter, David M. *Lincoln and His Party in the Secession Crisis.* New Haven, 1942.

Pratt, Harry E. *Lincoln: 1809-1839.* Springfield, 1941.

———— *Lincoln: 1840-1846.* Springfield, 1939.

Randall, James G. *Constitutional Problems Under Lincoln.* New York, 1926.

———— "Has the Lincoln Theme Been Exhausted?", *American Historical Review,* XLI, number 2, 1936, pp. 270-294.

Robinson, Luther E. *Abraham Lincoln as a Man of Letters.* Chicago, 1918.

Sandburg, Carl. *Abraham Lincoln: The Prairie Years.* Two volumes. New York, 1926.

————— *Abraham Lincoln: The War Years.* Four volumes. New York, 1939.

Stephenson, Nathaniel W. *Lincoln: An Account of His Personal Life Especially of Its Springs of Action as Revealed and Deepened by the Ordeal of War.* Indianapolis, 1924.

Tarbell, Ida M. *The Life of Abraham Lincoln.* Two volumes. New York, 1900.

Thomas, Benjamin P. *Lincoln: 1847-1858.* Springfield, 1936.

Williams, T. Harry. *Lincoln and the Radicals.* Madison, Wisconsin, 1941.

A SHORT ADDITIONAL BIBLIOGRAPHY

Basler, Roy P., ed., *The Collected Works of Abraham Lincoln,* New Brunswick, N.J., Rutgers University Press, 9 volumes, 1953–1956. This contains practically all of Lincoln's known writings.

BIOGRAPHIES:

Randall, James G., *Lincoln the President,* New York, Dodd Mead, 4 volumes, 1945–1955. A critical and sympathetic work by a very competent historian.

Sandburg, Carl, *Abraham Lincoln: The Prairie Years and the War Years,* New York, Harcourt Brace, 6 volumes 1926–1939. The vividness of Sandburg's writing recaptures the past in an authentic way.

Thomas, Benjamin P., *Abraham Lincoln, a Biography,* New York, Knopf, 1952. The best of the one volume biographies.

OTHER WORKS OF INTEREST:

Donald, David, *Lincoln Reconsidered,* New York, Knopf, 1956. Essays on Lincoln.

Meserve, Frederick Hill, and Carl Sandburg, *The Photographs of Abraham Lincoln,* New York, Harcourt Brace, 1944. A collection of most of the known photographs of Lincoln.

Mitgang, Herbert, *Lincoln as They Saw Him,* New York, Rinehart, 1956. A collection of contemporary newspaper accounts.

SELECTED WRITINGS
AND SPEECHES OF
ABRAHAM LINCOLN

REPUTED FIRST POLITICAL SPEECH, MARCH, 1832 [1]

This droll document was one of Lincoln's first political productions. He was a candidate for the Illinois legislature, and in this speech he summarized his already announced political views. He was a Whig, and he endorsed the national platform of the party, which advocated the chartering of a national bank by Congress, appropriations of money by the national government to build such internal improvements as canals and roads, and a tariff to protect American producers against European competition.

FELLOW-CITIZENS: I presume you all know who I am. I am humble Abraham Lincoln. I have been solicited by many friends to become a candidate for the Legislature. My politics are short and sweet, like the old woman's dance. I am in favor of a national bank. I am in favor of the internal improvement system, and a high protective tariff. These are my sentiments and political principles. If elected, I shall be thankful; if not it will be all the same.

PROTEST IN THE ILLINOIS LEGISLATURE ON THE SUBJECT OF SLAVERY, MARCH 3, 1837 [2]

By 1837 the abolitionist movement was in full-swing. Abolitionist societies and newspapers appeared in Illinois. The Illinois legislature adopted resolutions condemning abolitionist doctrines and denying the power of the national government to abolish slavery in the states or the District of Columbia. Lincoln, while holding no brief for the abolitionists, thought that the legislature's resolutions went too far in the other direction. To make his own position clear, he offered this protest.

[1] John G. Nicolay and John Hay (eds.), *Complete Works of Abraham Lincoln* (New York, 1905), XI, 97-98.
[2] Lincoln, *Complete Works*, I, 51-52.

RESOLUTIONS upon the subject of domestic slavery having passed both branches of the General Assembly at its present session, the undersigned hereby protest against the passage of the same.

They believe that the institution of slavery is founded on both injustice and bad policy, but that the promulgation of abolition doctrines tends rather to increase than abate its evils.

They believe that the Congress of the United States has no power under the Constitution to interfere with the institution of slavery in the different States.

They believe that the Congress of the United States has the power, under the Constitution, to abolish slavery in the District of Columbia, but that the power ought not to be exercised, unless at the request of the people of the District.

The difference between these opinions and those contained in the said resolutions is their reason for entering this protest.

DAN STONE,

A. LINCOLN,

Representatives from the County of Sangamon.

ADDRESS BEFORE THE YOUNG MEN'S LYCEUM OF SPRINGFIELD, ILLINOIS, JANUARY 27, 1838 [1]

> This is one of Lincoln's earliest speeches of which there is a record. It shows the young Lincoln's idealistic concept of American democracy and illustrates his literary style as developed at that time. The description of how a dictator might rise to power in the United States is realistic.

AS a subject for the remarks of the evening, "The perpetuation of our political institutions" is selected.

In the great journal of things happening under the sun, we, the American people, find our account running under date of the nineteenth century of the Christian era. We find ourselves

---

[1] Lincoln, *Complete Works*, I, 35-50. In the *Works* the speech is misdated January 27, 1837. The correct date is 1838.

in the peaceful possession of the fairest portion of the earth as regards extent of territory, fertility of soil, and salubrity of climate. We find ourselves under the government of a system of political institutions conducing more essentially to the ends of civil and religious liberty than any of which the history of former times tells us. We, when mounting the stage of existence, found ourselves the legal inheritors of these fundamental blessings. We toiled not in the acquirement or establishment of them; they are a legacy bequeathed us by a once hardy, brave, and patriotic, but now lamented and departed, race of ancestors. Theirs was the task (and nobly they performed it) to possess themselves and through themselves us, of this goodly land, and to uprear upon its hills and its valleys a political edifice of liberty and equal rights; 'tis ours only to transmit these—the former unprofaned by the foot of an invader, the latter undecayed by the lapse of time and untorn by usurpation —to the latest generation that fate shall permit the world to know. This task of gratitude to our fathers, justice to ourselves, duty to posterity, and love for our species in general, all imperatively require us faithfully to perform.

How then shall we perform it? At what point shall we expect the approach of danger? By what means shall we fortify against it? Shall we expect some transatlantic military giant to step the ocean and crush us at a blow? Never! All the armies of Europe, Asia, and Africa combined, with all the treasure of the earth (our own excepted) in their military chest, with a Bonaparte for a commander, could not by force take a drink from the Ohio or make a track on the Blue Ridge in a trial of a thousand years.

At what point, then, is the approach of danger to be expected? I answer, If it ever reach us it must spring up amongst us; it cannot come from abroad. If destruction be our lot we must ourselves be its author and finisher. As a nation of freemen we must live through all time, or die by suicide.

I hope I am over wary; but if I am not, there is even now something of ill omen amongst us. I mean the increasing disregard for law which pervades the country—the growing disposition to substitute the wild and furious passions in lieu of the sober judgment of courts, and the worse than savage mobs for the executive ministers of justice. This disposition is awfully fearful in any community; and that it now exists in ours, though grating to our feelings to admit, it would be a violation of truth and an insult to our intelligence to deny. Accounts of outrages committed by mobs form the every-day news of the times. They have pervaded the country from New England to Louisiana; they are neither peculiar to the eternal snows of the former nor the burning suns of the latter; they are not the creature of climate, neither are they confined to the slaveholding or the non-slaveholding States. Alike they spring up among the pleasure-hunting masters of Southern slaves, and the order-loving citizens of the land of steady habits. Whatever then their cause may be, it is common to the whole country.

*   *   *   *

But you are perhaps ready to ask, "What has this to do with the perpetuation of our political institutions?" I answer, "It has much to do with it." Its direct consequences are, comparatively speaking, but a small evil, and much of its danger consists in the proneness of our minds to regard its direct as its only consequences. * * * * When man take it in their heads today to hang gamblers or burn murderers, they should recollect that in the confusion usually attending such transactions they will be as likely to hang or burn some one who is neither a gambler nor a murderer as one who is, and that, acting upon the example they set, the mob of to-morrow may, and probably will, hang or burn some of them by the very same mistake. And not only so; the innocent, those who have ever set their faces against violations of law in every shape, alike with the guilty fall victims to the ravages of mob law; and thus it goes up, step by step, till all the walls erected for the defense of the persons and property of individuals are trodden down and disregarded. But all this, even, is not the full extent of the evil.

By such examples, by instances of the perpetrators of such acts going unpunished, the lawless in spirit are encouraged to become lawless in practice; and having been used to no restraint but dread of punishment, they thus become absolutely unrestrained. Having ever regarded government as their deadliest bane, they make a jubilee of the suspension of its operations, and pray for nothing so much as its total annihilation. While, on the other hand, good men, men who love tranquillity, who desire to abide by the laws and enjoy their benefits, who would gladly spill their blood in the defense of their country, seeing their property destroyed, their families insulted, and their lives endangered, their persons injured, and seeing nothing in prospect that forebodes a change for the better, become tired of and disgusted with a government that offers them no protection, and are not much averse to a change in which they imagine they have nothing to lose. Thus, then, by the operation of this mobocratic spirit which all must admit is now abroad in the land, the strongest bulwark of any government, and particularly of those constituted like ours, may effectually be broken down and destroyed—I mean the attachment of the people. Whenever this effect shall be produced among us; whenever the vicious portion of population shall be permitted to gather in bands of hundreds and thousands, and burn churches, ravage and rob provision-stores, throw printing-presses into rivers, shoot editors, and hang and burn obnoxious persons at pleasure and with impunity, depend on it, this government cannot last. By such things the feelings of the best citizens will become more or less alienated from it, and thus it will be left without friends, or with too few, and those few too weak to make their friendship effectual. At such a time, and under such circumstances, men of sufficient talent and ambition will not be wanting to seize the opportunity, strike the blow, and overturn that fair fabric which for the last half century has been the fondest hope of the lovers of freedom throughout the world.

I know the American people are much attached to their government; I know they would endure evils long and patiently before they would ever think of exchanging it for another—yet, notwithstanding all this, if the laws be continually despised and disregarded, if their rights to be secure in their persons and property are held by no better tenure than the caprice of a mob, the alienation of their affections from the government is the natural consequence; and to that, sooner or later, it must come.

Here, then, is one point at which danger may be expected. The question recurs, "How shall we fortify against it?" The answer is simple. Let every American, every lover of liberty, every well-wisher to his posterity swear by the blood of the Revolution never to violate in the least particular the laws of the country, and never to tolerate their violation by others. As the patriots of seventy-six did to the support of the Declaration of Independence, so to the support of the Constitution and laws let every American pledge his life, his property, and his sacred honor—let every man remember that to violate the law is to trample on the blood of his father, and to tear the charter of his own and his children's liberty. Let reverence for the laws be breathed by every American mother to the lisping babe that prattles on her lap; let it be taught in schools, in seminaries, and in colleges; let it be written in primers, spelling-books, and in almanacs; let it be preached from the pulpit, proclaimed in legislative halls, and enforced in courts of justice. And, in short, let it become the political religion of the nation; and let the old and the young, the rich and the poor, the grave and the gay of all sexes and tongues and colors and conditions, sacrifice unceasingly upon its altars.

While ever a state of feeling such as this shall universally or even very generally prevail throughout the nation, vain will be every effort, and fruitless every attempt, to subvert our national freedom.

* * * *

There is no grievance that is a fit object of redress by mob law. In any case that may arise, as for instance, the promulgation of abolitionism, one of two positions is necessarily true—that is, the thing is right within itself, and therefore deserves the protection of all law and all good citizens, or it is wrong, and therefore proper to be prohibited by legal enactments; and in neither case is the interposition of mob law either necessary, justifiable, or excusable.

But it may be asked, "Why suppose danger to our political institutions? Have we not preserved them for more than fifty years? And why may we not for fifty times as long?"

We hope there is no sufficient reason. We hope all danger may be overcome; but to conclude that no danger may ever arise would itself be extremely dangerous. There are now, and will hereafter be, many causes, dangerous in their tendency, which have not existed heretofore, and which are not too insignificant to merit attention. That our government should have been maintained in its original form, from its establishment until now, is not much to be wondered at. It had many props to support it through that period, which now are decayed and crumbled away. Through that period it was felt by all to be an undecided experiment; now it is understood to be a successful one. Then, all that sought celebrity and fame and distinction expected to find them in the success of that experiment. Their all was staked upon it; their destiny was inseparably linked with it. Their ambition aspired to display before an admiring world a practical demonstration of the truth of a proposition which had hitherto been considered at best no better than problematical—namely, the capability of a people to govern themselves. If they succeeded they were to be immortalized; their names were to be transferred to counties, and cities, and rivers, and mountains; and to be revered and sung, toasted through all time. If they failed, they were to be called knaves, and fools, and fanatics for a fleeting hour; then to sink and be forgotten. They succeeded. The experiment is successful, and thousands have won their deathless names in making it so. But the game is caught; and I believe it is true that with the catching end the pleasures of the chase. This field of glory is harvested, and the crop is already appropriated. But new reapers will arise, and they too will seek a field. It is to deny what the history of the world tells us is true, to suppose that men of ambition and talents will not continue to spring up amongst us. And when they do, they will as naturally seek the gratification of their ruling passion as others have done before them. The question then is, Can that gratification be found in supporting and maintaining an edifice that has been erected by others? Most certainly it cannot. Many great and good men, sufficiently qualified for any task they should undertake, may ever be found whose ambition would aspire to nothing beyond a seat in Congress, a gubernatorial or a presidential chair; but such belong not to the family of the lion, or the tribe of the eagle. What! think you these places would satisfy an Alexander, a Caesar, or a Napoleon? Never! Towering genius disdains a beaten path. It seeks regions hitherto unexplored. It sees no distinction in adding story to story upon the monuments of fame erected to the memory of others. It denies that it is glory enough to serve under any chief. It scorns to tread in the footsteps of any predecessor, however illustrious. It thirsts and burns for distinction; and if possible, it will have it, whether at the expense of emancipating slaves or enslaving freemen. Is it unreasonable, then, to expect that some man possessed of the loftiest genius, coupled with ambition sufficient to push it to its utmost stretch, will at some time spring up among us? And when such an one does, it will require the people to be united with each other, attached to the government and laws, and generally intelligent, to successfully frustrate his designs.

Distinction will be his paramount object, and although he would as willingly, perhaps more so, acquire it by doing good as harm, yet, that opportunity being past, and nothing left to be done in the way of building up, he would set boldly to the task of pulling down.

Here then is a probable case, highly dangerous, and such an one as could not have well existed heretofore.

———

ADDRESS BEFORE THE SPRINGFIELD WASHING-
TONIAN TEMPERANCE SOCIETY,
FEBRUARY 22, 1842 [1]

The temperance movement was one of the many reforms advocated in this period to better the lot of humanity. Lincoln supported it. This address was disliked by some temperance people because of Lincoln's tolerant words about hard drinkers. The Washingtonian Society was an organization of reformed drunkards.

ALTHOUGH the temperance cause has been in progress for near twenty years, it is apparent to all that it is just now being crowned with a degree of success hitherto unparalleled.

The list of its friends is daily swelled by the additions of fifties, of hundreds, and of thousands. The cause itself seems suddenly transformed from a cold abstract theory to a living, breathing, active, and powerful chieftain, going forth "conquering and to conquer." The citadels of his great adversary are daily being stormed and dismantled; his temple and his altars, where the rites of his idolatrous worship have long been performed, and where human sacrifices have long been wont to be made, are daily desecrated and deserted. The triumph of the conqueror's fame is sounding from hill to hill, from sea, and from land to land, and calling millions to his standard at a blast.

For this new and splendid success we heartily rejoice. That that success is so much greater now than heretofore is doubtless owing to rational causes; and if we would have it continue, we shall do well to inquire what those causes are.

The warfare heretofore waged against the demon intemperance has somehow or other been erroneous. Either the champions engaged or the tactics they adopted have not been the most proper. These champions for the most part have been preachers, lawyers, and hired agents. Between these and the mass of mankind there is a want of approachability, if the term

[1] Lincoln, *Complete Works*, I, 193-209.

be admissible, partially, at least, fatal to their success. They are supposed to have no sympathy of feeling or interest with those very persons whom it is their object to convince and persuade.

And again, it is so common and so easy to ascribe motives to men of these classes other than those they profess to act upon. The preacher, it is said, advocates temperance because he is a fanatic, and desires a union of the church and state; the lawyer from his pride and vanity of hearing himself speak; and the hired agent for his salary. But when one who has long been known as a victim of intemperance bursts the fetters that have bound him, and appears before his neighbors "clothed and in his right mind," a redeemed specimen of long-lost humanity, and stands up, with tears of joy trembling in his eyes, to tell of the miseries once endured, now to be endured no more forever; of his once naked and starving children, now clad and fed comfortably; of a wife long weighed down with woe, weeping, and a broken heart, now restored to health, happiness, and a renewed affection; and how easily it is all done, once it is resolved to be done; how simple his language!—there is a logic and an eloquence in it that few with human feelings can resist. They cannot say that he desires a union of church and state, for he is not a church member; they cannot say he is vain of hearing himself speak, for his whole demeanor shows he would gladly avoid speaking at all; they cannot say he speaks for pay, for he receives none, and asks for none. Nor can his sincerity in any way be doubted, or his sympathy for those he would persuade to imitate his example be denied.

In my judgment, it is to the battles of this new class of champions that our late success is greatly, perhaps chiefly, owing. But, had the old-school champions themselves been of the most wise selecting, was their system of tactics the most judicious? It seems to me it was not. Too much denunciation against dram-sellers and dram-drinkers was indulged in. This I think was both impolitic and unjust. It was impolitic, because it is not much in the nature of man to be driven to anything; still less to be driven about that which is exclusively his own business; and least of all where such driving is to be submitted to at the expense of pecuniary interest or burning appetite. When the dram-seller and drinker were incessantly told—not in accents of entreaty and persuasion, diffidently addressed by erring man to an erring brother, but in the thundering tones of anathema and denunciation with which the lordly judge often groups together all the crimes of the felon's life, and thrusts them in his face just ere he passes sentence of death upon him—that they were the authors of all the vice and misery and crime in the land; that they were the manufacturers and material of all the thieves and robbers and murderers that infest the earth; that their houses were the workshops of the devil; and that their persons should be shunned by all the good and virtuous, as moral pestilences—I say, when they were told all this, and in this way, it is not wonderful that they were slow, very slow, to acknowledge the truth of such denunciations, and to join the ranks of their denouncers in a hue and cry against themselves.

To have expected them to do otherwise than they did—to have expected them not to meet denunciation with denunciation, crimination with crimination, and anathema with anathema—was to expect a reversal of human nature, which is God's decree and can never be reversed.

When the conduct of men is designed to be influenced, persuasion, kind, unassuming persuasion, should ever be adopted. It is an old and a true maxim "that a drop of honey catches more flies than a gallon of gall." So with men. If you would win a man to your cause, first convince him that you are his sincere friend. Therein is a drop of honey that catches his heart, which, say, what he will, is the great highroad to his reason, and which, when once gained, you will find but little trouble in convincing his judgment of the justice of your cause, if indeed that cause really be a just one. On the contrary, assume to dictate to his judgment, or to command his action, or to mark him as one to be shunned and despised, and he will retreat within himself, close all the avenues to his head and his heart; and though your cause be naked truth itself, transformed to the heaviest lance, harder than steel, and sharper than steel can be made, and though you throw it with more than herculean force and precision, you shall be no more able to pierce him than to penetrate the hard shell of a tortoise with a rye straw. Such is man, and so must he be understood by those who would lead him, even to his own best interests.

———

SPEECH IN THE UNITED STATES HOUSE OF REPRESENTATIVES, JANUARY 12, 1848 [1]

In 1846 the United States declared war upon Mexico. At that time the Democrat, James K. Polk, was President, and the Democrats controlled Congress. Many members of Lincoln's Whig party felt that the war was an unjust one, that the United States had been the aggressor, and that the purpose of the war was to secure territory for the expansion of slavery or to make political capital for the Democrats. The Whigs opposed the declaration of war and denounced it afterwards, although they supported appropriations to carry it on. Lincoln did not become a member of Congress until December, 1847. This speech expressed his views and those of his party toward the war, then nearly over. It damaged him politically in Illinois at the time, and was used against him in later campaigns.

MR. Chairman: Some if not all the gentlemen on the other side of the House who have addressed the committee within the last two days have spoken rather complainingly, if I have rightly understood them, of the vote given a week or ten days ago declaring that the war with Mexico was unnecessarily and unconstitutionally commenced by the President. I admit that such a vote should not be given in mere party wantonness, and that the one given is justly censurable, if it have no other or better foundation. I am one of those who joined in that vote; and I did so under my best impression of the truth of the case. How I got this impression, and how it

———

[1] Lincoln, *Complete Works*, I, 327-345.

may possibly be remedied, I will now try to show. When the war began, it was my opinion that all those who because of knowing too little, or because of knowing too much, could not conscientiously oppose the conduct of the President in the beginning of it should nevertheless, as good citizens and patriots, remain silent on that point, at least till the war should be ended. Some leading Democrats, including ex-President Van Buren, have taken this same view, as I understand them; and I adhered to it and acted upon it, until since I took my seat here; and I think I should still adhere to it were it not that the President and his friends will not allow it to be so. Besides the continual effort of the President to argue every silent vote given for supplies into an indorsement of the justice and wisdom of his conduct; besides that singularly candid paragraph in his late message in which he tells us that Congress with great unanimity had declared that "by the act of the Republic of Mexico, a state of war exists between that Government and the United States," when the same journals that informed him of this also informed him that when that declaration stood disconnected from the question of supplies sixty-seven in the House, and not fourteen merely, voted against it; besides this open attempt to prove by telling the truth what he could not prove by telling the whole truth—demanding of all who will no[t] submit to be misrepresented, in justice to themselves, to speak out,—besides all this, one of my colleagues [Mr. Richardson] at a very early day in the session brought in a set of resolutions expressly indorsing the original justice of the war on the part of the President. Upon these resolutions when they shall be put on their passage I shall be compelled to vote; so that I cannot be silent if I would. Seeing this, I went about preparing myself to give the vote understandingly when it should come. I carefully examined the President's message, to ascertain what he himself had said and proved upon the point. The result of this examination was to make the impression that, taking for true all the President states as facts, he falls far short of proving his justification; and that the President would have gone farther with his

proof if it had not been for the small matter that the truth
would not permit him. Under the impression thus made I gave
the vote before mentioned. I propose now to give concisely the
process of the examination I made, and how I reached the conclusion I did. The President, in his first war message of May,
1846, declares that the soil was ours on which hostilities were
commenced by Mexico, and he repeats that declaration almost
in the same language in each successive annual message, thus
showing that he deems that point a highly essential one. In
the importance of that point I entirely agree with the President.
To my judgment it is the very point upon which he should be
justified, or condemned. In his message of December, 1846,
it seems to have occurred to him, as is certainly true, that title
—ownership—to soil or anything else is not a simple fact, but
is a conclusion following on one or more simple facts; and that
it was incumbent upon him to present the facts from which he
concluded the soil was ours on which the first blood of the war
was shed.

Accordingly, a little below the middle of page twelve in the
message last referred to he enters upon that task; forming an
issue and introducing testimony, extending the whole to a little
below the middle of page fourteen. Now, I propose to try to
show that the whole of this—issue and evidence—is from beginning to end the sheerest deception. The issue, as he presents it, is
in these words: "But there are those who, conceding all this to
be true, assume the ground that the true western boundary of
Texas is the Nueces, instead of the Rio Grande; and that, therefore, in marching our army to the east bank of the latter river,
we passed the Texas line and invaded the territory of Mexico."
Now this issue is made up of two affirmatives and no negative.
The main deception of it is that it assumes as true that one river
or the other is necessarily the boundary; and cheats the super-
ficial thinker entirely out of the idea that possibly the boundary
is somewhere between the two, and not actually at either. A
further deception is that it will let in evidence which a true
issue would exclude. A true issue made by the President would

be about as follows: "I say the soil was ours, on which the first blood was shed; there are those who say it was not."

I now proceed to examine the President's evidence as applicable to such an issue. When that evidence is analyzed, it is all included in the following propositions:

(1) That the Rio Grande was the western boundary of Louisiana as we purchased it of France in 1803.

(2) That the Republic of Texas always claimed the Rio Grande as her western boundary.

(3) That by various acts she had claimed it on paper.

(4) That Santa Anna in his treaty with Texas recognized the Rio Grande as her boundary.

(5) That Texas before, and the United States after, annexation had exercised jurisdiction beyond the Nueces—between the two rivers.

(6) That our Congress understood the boundary of Texas to extend beyond the Nueces.

Now for each of these in its turn. His first item is that the Rio Grande was the western boundary of Louisiana, as we purchased it of France in 1803; and seeming to expect this to be disputed, he argues over the amount of nearly a page to prove it true; at the end of which he lets us know that by the treaty of 1819 we sold to Spain the whole country from the Rio Grande eastward to the Sabine. Now, admitting for the present that the Rio Grande was the boundary of Louisiana, what, under heaven, had that to do with the present boundary between us and Mexico? How, Mr. Chairman, the line that once divided your land from mine can still be the boundary between us after I have sold my land to you is to me beyond all comprehension. And how any man, with an honest purpose only of proving the truth, could ever have thought of introducing such a fact to prove such an issue is equally incomprehensible. His next piece of evidence is that "the Republic of Texas always claimed this river (Rio Grande) as her western boundary." That is not true, in fact. Texas has claimed it, but she has not

always claimed it. There is at least one distinguished exception.
Her State constitution—the republic's most solemn and well-
considered act; that which may, without impropriety, be called
her last will and testament, revoking all others—makes no such
claim. But suppose she had always claimed it. Has not Mexico
always claimed the contrary? So that there is but claim against
claim, leaving nothing proved until we get back of the claims
and find which has the better foundation. Though not in the
order in which the President presents his evidence, I now consider that class of his statements which are in substance nothing
more than that Texas has, by various acts of her Convention
and Congress, claimed the Rio Grande as her boundary, on
paper. I mean here what he says about the fixing of the Rio
Grande as her boundary in her old constitution (not her State
constitution), about forming congressional districts, counties,
etc. Now all of this is but naked claim; and what I have already
said about claims is strictly applicable to this. If I should claim
your land by word of mouth, that certainly would not make it
mine; and if I were to claim it by a deed which I had made
myself, and with which you had had nothing to do, the claim
would be quite the same in substance—or rather, in utter noth-
ingness. I next consider the President's statement that Santa
Anna[1] in his treaty with Texas recognized the Rio Grande as
the western boundary of Texas. Besides the position so often
taken, that Santa Anna while a prisoner of war, a captive, could
not bind Mexico by a treaty, which I deem conclusive—besides
this, I wish to say something in relation to this treaty, so called
by the President, with Santa Anna. If any man would like to
be amused by a sight of that little thing which the President
calls by that big name, he can have it by turning to "Nile's
Register," Vol. L, p. 336. And if any one should suppose that
"Nile's Register" is a curious repository of so mighty a document as a solemn treaty between nations, I can only say that I
learned to a tolerable degree of certainty, by inquiry at the

---

[1] Santa Anna, dictator of Mexico and general of the Mexican army defeated
by the Texans.

State Department, that the President himself never saw it anywhere else. By the way, I believe I should not err if I were to declare that during the first ten years of the existence of that document it was never by anybody called a treaty—that it was never so called till the President, in his extremity, attempted by so calling it to wring something from it in justification of himself in connection with the Mexican war. It has none of the distinguishing features of a treaty. It does not call itself a treaty. Santa Anna does not therein assume to bind Mexico; he assumes only to act as the President-Commander-in-Chief of the Mexican army and navy; stipulates that the then present hostilities should cease, and that he would not himself take up arms, nor influence the Mexican people to take up arms, against Texas during the existence of the war of independence. He did not recognize the independence of Texas; he did not assume to put an end to the war, but clearly indicated his expectation of its continuance; he did not say one word about boundary, and, most probably, never thought of it. It is stipulated therein that the Mexican forces should evacuate the territory of Texas, passing to the other side of the Rio Grande; and in another article it is stipulated that, to prevent collisions between the armies, the Texas army should not approach nearer than within five leagues—of what is not said, but clearly, from the object stated, it is of the Rio Grande. Now, if this is a treaty recognizing the Rio Grande as the boundary of Texas, it contains the singular features of stipulating that Texas shall not go within five leagues of her own boundary.

Next comes the evidence of Texas before annexation, and the United States afterward, exercising jurisdiction beyond the Nueces and between the two rivers. This actual exercise of jurisdiction is the very class or quality of evidence we want. It is excellent so far as it goes; but does it go far enough? He tells us it went beyond the Nueces, but he does not tell us it went to the Rio Grande. He tells us jurisdiction was exercised between the two rivers, but he does not tell us it was exercised over all the territory between them. Some simple-minded people think it is possible to cross one river and go beyond it without going all the way to the next, that jurisdiction may be exercised between two rivers without covering all the country between them. I know a man, not very unlike myself, who exercised jurisdiction over a piece of land between the Wabash and the Mississippi; and yet so far is this from being all there is between those rivers that it is just one hundred and fifty-two feet long by fifty feet wide, and no part of it much within a hundred miles either. He has a neighbor between him and the Mississippi,—that is, just across the street, in that direction—whom I am sure he could neither persuade nor force to give up his habitation; but which nevertheless he could certainly annex, if it were to be done by merely standing on his own side of the street and claiming it, or even sitting down and writing a deed for it.

But next the President tells us the Congress of the United States understood the State of Texas they admitted into the Union to extend beyond the Nueces. Well, I suppose they did. I certainly so understood it. But how far beyond? That Congress did not understand it to extend clear to the Rio Grande is quite certain, by the fact that their joint resolutions for admission expressly leaving all questions of boundary to future adjustment. And it may be added that Texas herself is proved to have had the same understanding of it that our Congress had, by the fact of the exact conformity of her new constitution to those resolutions.

I am now through the whole of the President's evidence; and it is a singular fact that if any one should declare the President sent the army into the midst of a settlement of Mexican people who had never submitted, by consent or by force, to the authority of Texas or of the United States, and that there and thereby the first blood of the war was shed, there is not one word in all the President has said which would either admit or deny the declaration. This strange omission it does seem to me could not have occurred but by design. My way of living leads me to be about the courts of justice; and there I have sometimes seen a good lawyer, struggling for his client's neck in a desperate case, employing every artifice to work round, befog, and cover up with many words some point arising in the case which he dared not admit and yet could not deny. Party bias may help to make it appear so, but with all the allowance I can make for such bias, it still does appear to me that just such, and from just such necessity, is the President's struggle in this case.

Some time after my colleague [Mr. Richardson] introduced the resolutions I have mentioned, I introduced a preamble, resolution, and interrogations, intended to draw the President out, if possible, on this hitherto untrodden ground. To show their relevancy, I propose to state my understanding of the true rule for ascertaining the boundary between Texas and Mexico. It is that wherever Texas was exercising jurisdiction was hers; and wherever Mexico was exercising jurisdiction was hers; and that whatever separated the actual exercise of jurisdiction of the one from that of the other was the true boundary between them. If, as is probably true, Texas was exercising jurisdiction along the western bank of the Nueces, and Mexico was exercising it along the eastern bank of the Rio Grande, then neither river was the boundary; but the uninhabited country between the two was. The extent of our territory in that region depended not on any treaty-fixed boundary (for no treaty had attempted it), but on revolution. Any people anywhere being inclined and having the power have the right to rise up and shake off the existing government, and form a new one that suits them better. This is a most valuable, a most sacred right —a right which we hope and believe is to liberate the world. Nor is this right confined to cases in which the whole people of an existing government may choose to exercise it. Any portion of such people that can may revolutionize and make their own of so much of the territory as they inhabit. More than this, a majority of any portion of such people may revolutionize, putting down a minority, intermingled with or near about them, who may oppose this movement. Such minority was precisely the case of the Tories of our own revolution. It is a quality of revolutions not to go by old lines or old laws; but to break up both, and make new ones.

As to the country now in question, we bought it of France in 1803, and sold it to Spain in 1819, according to the President's statements. After this, all Mexico, including Texas, revolutionized against Spain; still later Texas revolutionized against Mexico. In my view, just so far as she carried her revolution by obtaining the actual, willing or unwilling, submission of the people, so far the country was hers, and no farther. Now, sir, for the purpose of obtaining the very best evidence as to whether Texas had actually carried her revolution to the place where the hostilities of the present war commenced, let the President answer the interrogatories I proposed, as before mentioned, or some other similar ones. Let him answer fully, fairly, and candidly. Let him answer with facts and not with arguments. Let him remember he sits where Washington sat, and so remembering, let him answer as Washington would answer. As a nation should not, and the Almighty will not, be evaded, so let him attempt no evasion—no equivocation. And if, so answering, he can show that the soil was ours where the first blood of the war was shed,—that it was not within an inhabited country, or, if within such, that the inhabitants had submitted themselves to the civil authority of Texas or of the United States, and that the same is true of the site of Fort Brown,—then I am with him for his justification. In that case I shall be most happy to reverse the vote I gave the other day. I have a selfish motive for desiring that the President may do this—I expect to gain some votes, in connection with the war, which, without his so doing, will be of doubtful propriety in my own judgment, but which will be free from the doubt if he does so. But if he can not or will not do this,—if on any pretense or no pretense he shall refuse or omit it—then I shall be fully convinced of what I more than suspect already—that he is deeply conscious of being in the wrong; that he feels the blood of this war, like the blood of Abel, is crying to Heaven against him; that originally having some strong motive—what,

I will not stop now to give my opinion concerning—to involve
the two countries in a war, and trusting to escape scrutiny by
fixing the public gaze upon the exceeding brightness of military
glory,—that attractive rainbow that arises in showers of blood
—that serpent's eye that charms to destroy,—he plunged into it,
and has swept on and on till, disappointed in his calculation of
the ease with which Mexico might be subdued, he now finds
himself he knows not where. How like the half-insane
mumbling of a fever dream is the whole part of his late message! At one time telling us that Mexico has nothing whatever
that we can get but territory; at another showing us how we
can support the war by levying contributions on Mexico. At
one time urging the national honor, the security of the future,
the prevention of foreign interference, and even the good of
Mexico herself as among the objects of the war; at another
telling us that "to reject indemnity, by refusing to accept a
cession of territory, would be to abandon all our just demands,
and to wage the war bearing all its expenses, without a purpose
or definite object." So then this national honor, security of
the future, and everything but territorial indemnity may be
considered the no-purpose and indefinite objects of the war!
But, having it now settled that territorial indemnity is the only
object, we are urged to seize, by legislation here, all that he
was content to take a few months ago, and the whole province
of Lower California to boot, and to still carry on the war—to
take all we are fighting for, and still fight on. Again, the
President is resolved under all circumstances to have full territorial indemnity for the expenses of the war; but he forgets to
tell us how we are to get the excess after those expenses shall
have surpassed the value of the whole of the Mexican territory.
So again, he insists that the separate national existence of
Mexico shall be maintained; but he does not tell us how this
can be done, after we shall have taken all her territory. Lest
the questions I have suggested be considered speculative merely,
let me be indulged a moment in trying to show they are not.
The war has gone on some twenty months; for the expenses of

which, together with an inconsiderable old score, the President now claims about one half of the Mexican territory, and that by far the better half, so far as concerns our ability to make anything out of it. It is comparatively uninhabited; so that we could establish land offices in it, and raise some money in that way. But the other half is already inhabited, as I understand it, tolerably densely for the nature of the country, and all its lands, or all that are valuable, already appropriated as private property. How then are we to make anything out of these lands with this encumbrance upon them? or how remove the encumbrance? I suppose no one would say we should kill the people, or drive them out, or make slaves of them; or confiscate their property. How, then, can we make much out of this part of the territory? If the prosecution of the war has in expenses already equaled the better half of the country, how long its future prosecution will be in equaling the less valuable half is not speculative, but a practical question, pressing closely upon us. And yet it is a question which the President seems never to have thought of. As to the mode of terminating the war and securing peace, the President is equally wandering and indefinite. First, it is to be done by a more vigorous prosecution of the war in the vital parts of the enemy's country; and after apparently talking himself tired on this point, the President drops down into a half-despairing tone, and tells us that "with a people distracted and divided by contending factions, and a government subject to constant changes by successive revolutions, the continued success of our arms may fail to secure a satisfactory peace." Then he suggests the propriety of wheedling the Mexican people to desert the counsels of their own leaders, and, trusting in our protestations, to set up a government from which we can secure a satisfactory peace; telling us that "this may become the only mode of obtaining such a peace." But soon he falls into a doubt of this too; and then drops back onto the already half-abandoned ground of "more vigorous prosecution." All this shows that the President is in nowise satisfied with his own positions.

First he takes up one, and in attempting to argue us into it he argues himself out of it, then seizes another and goes through the same process, and then, confused at being able to think of nothing new, he snatches up the old one again, which he has some time before cast off. His mind, taxed beyond its power, is running hither and thither, like some tortured creature on a burning surface, finding no position on which it can settle down and be at ease.

Again, it is a singular omission in this message that it nowhere intimates when the President expects the war to terminate. At its beginning, General Scott[1] was by this same President driven into disfavor, if not disgrace, for intimating that peace could not be conquered in less than three or four months. But now, at the end of about twenty months, during which time our arms have given us the most splendid successes, every department and every part, land and water, officers and privates, regulars and volunteers, doing all that men could do, and hundreds of things which it had ever before been thought men could not do—after all this, this same President gives us a long message, without showing us that as to the end he himself has even an imaginary conception. As I have before said, he knows not where he is. He is a bewildered, confounded, and miserably perplexed man. God grant he may be able to show there is not something about his conscience more painful than all his mental perplexity.

SPEECH IN THE UNITED STATES HOUSE OF REPRESENTATIVES, JULY 27, 1848 [2]

This is part of a "stump speech" delivered by Lincoln in Congress. The presidential campaign of 1848 was about to begin, and Lincoln started his participation in it with this speech in the House. The Whigs had nominated General Zachary Taylor, the hero of the Mexican War; the Demo-

---

[1] General Winfield Scott.
[2] Lincoln, *Complete Works*, II, 59-88.

crats had put up General Lewis Cass, whose title was more
honorary than anything else. The Democrats had criticized
Taylor as a soldier who knew nothing about statecraft, a
man without principles. At the same time they tried to
capitalize on Cass' military reputation. Lincoln opened his
speech by saying Taylor possessed very good principles.
Then he attacked the Democrats for riding two horses, and
paid his respects to Cass' military exploits. The speech is an
excellent illustration of Lincoln's stump style.

*   *   *   *

BUT I suppose I cannot reasonably hope to convince you
that we have any principles. The most I can expect is to
assure you that we think we have, and are quite contented
with them. The other day one of the gentlemen from Georgia
[Mr. Iverson], an eloquent man, and a man of learning, so
far as I can judge, not being learned myself, came down upon
us astonishingly. He spoke in what the "Baltimore American"
calls the "scathing and withering style." At the end of his
second severe flash I was struck blind, and found myself feeling with my fingers for an assurance of my continued existence. A little of the bone was left, and I gradually revived.
He eulogized Mr. Clay in high and beautiful terms, and then
declared that we had deserted all our principles, and had
turned Henry Clay out, like an old horse, to root. This is
terribly severe. It cannot be answered by argument—at least I
cannot so answer it. I merely wish to ask the gentleman if the
Whigs are the only party he can think of who sometimes turn
old horses out to root. Is not a certain Martin Van Buren an
old horse which your own party have turned out to root?
and is he not rooting a little to your discomfort about now?
But in not nominating Mr. Clay we deserted our principles,
you say. Ah! In what? Tell us, ye men of principle, what
principle we violated. We say you did violate principle in discarding Van Buren, and we can tell you know. You violated
the primary, the cardinal, the one great living principle of all
democratic representative government—the principle that the
representative is bound to carry out the known will of his

constituents. A large majority of the Baltimore convention of 1844 were, by their constituents, instructed to procure Van Buren's nomination if they could. In violation—in utter glaring contempt—of this, you rejected him—rejected him, as the gentleman from New York [Mr. Birdsall] the other day expressly admitted, for availability—that same "general availability" which you charge upon us, and daily chew over here, as something exceedingly odious and unprincipled. But the gentleman from Georgia [Mr. Iverson] gave us a second speech yesterday, all well considered and put down in writing, in which Van Buren was scathed and withered a "few" for his present position and movements. I cannot remember the gentleman's precise language; but I do remember he put Van Buren down, down, till he got him where he was finally to "stink" and "rot."

Mr. Speaker, it is no business or inclination of mine to defend Martin Van Buren in the war of extermination now waging between him and his old admirers. I say, "Devil take the hind-most"—and foremost. But there is no mistaking the origin of the breach; and if the curse of "stinking" and "rotting" is to fall on the first and greatest violators of principle in the matter, I disinterestedly suggest that the gentleman from Georgia and his present co-workers are bound to take it upon themselves. But the gentleman from Georgia further says we have deserted all our principles, and taken shelter under General Taylor's military coat-tail, and he seems to think this is exceedingly digrading. Well, as his faith is, so be it unto him. But can he remember no other military coat-tail under which a certain other party have been sheltering for near a quarter of a century? Has he no acquaintance with the ample military coat-tail of General Jackson? Does he not know that his own party have run the five last presidential races under that coat-tail? And that they are now running the sixth under the same cover. Yes, sir, that coat-tail was used not only for General Jackson himself, but has been clung to, with the grip of death, by every Democratic candidate since.

You have never ventured, and dare not now venture, from under it. Your campaign papers have constantly been "Old Hickories," with rude likenesses of the old general upon them; hickory poles and hickory brooms your never-ending emblems; Mr. Polk himself was "Young Hickory," "Little Hickory," or something so; and even now your campaign paper here is proclaiming that Cass and Butler are of the true "Hickory stripe." Now, sir, you dare not give it up. Like a horde of hungry ticks you have stuck to the tail of the Hermitage lion to the end of his life; and you are still sticking to it, and drawing a loathsome sustenance from it, after he is dead. A fellow once advertised that he had made a discovery by which he could make a new man out of an old one, and have enough of the stuff left to make a little yellow dog. Just such a discovery has General Jackson's popularity been to you. You not only twice made President of him out of it, but you had enough of the stuff left to make Presidents of several comparatively small men since; it is your chief reliance now to make still another.

Mr. Speaker, old horses and military coat-tails, or tails of any sort, are not figures of speech such as I would be the first to introduce into discussions here; but as the gentleman from Georgia has thought fit to introduce them, he and you are welcome to all you have made, or can make by them. If you have any more old horses, trot them out; any more tails, just cock them and come at us. I repeat, I would not introduce this mode of discussion here; but I wish gentlemen on the other side to understand that the use of degrading figures is a game at which they may not find themselves able to take all the winnings. ["We give it up!"] Aye, you give it up, and well you may; but for a very different reason from that which you would have us understand. The point—the power to hurt— of all figures consists in the truthfulness of their application; and, understanding this, you may well give it up. They are weapons which hit you, but miss us.

But in my hurry I was very near closing this subject of military tails before I was done with it. There is one entire article of the sort I have not discussed yet,—I mean the military tail you Democrats are now engaged in dovetailing into the great Michigander. Yes, sir; all his biographies (and they are legion) have him in hand, tying him into a military tail, like so many mischievous boys tying a dog to a bladder of beans. True the material they have is very limited, but they drive at it might and main. He *in*vaded Canada without resistance, and he *out*vaded it without pursuit. As he did both under orders, I suppose there was to him neither credit not discredit in them; but they constitute a large part of the tail. He was not at Hull's surrender, but he was close by; he was volunteer aid to General Harrison on the day of the battle of the Thames; and as you said in 1840 Harrison was picking huckleberries two miles off while the battle was fought, I suppose it is a just conclusion with you to say Cass was aiding Harrison to pick huckleberries. This is about all, except the mooted question of the broken sword. Some authors say he broke it, some say he threw it away, and some others, who ought to know, say nothing about it. Perhaps it would be a fair historical compromise to say, if he did not break it, he did not do anything else with it.[1]

By the way, Mr. Speaker, did you know I am a military hero? Yes, sir; in the days of the Black Hawk war[2] I fought, bled, and came away. Speaking of General Cass's career reminds me of my own. I was not at Stillman's defeat, but I was about as near it as Cass was to Hull's surrender; and, like him, I saw the place very soon afterward. It is quite certain I did not break my sword, for I had none to break; but I bent a musket pretty badly on one occasion. If Cass broke his sword, the idea is he broke it in desperation; I bent the musket by accident. If General Cass went in advance of me in picking huckleberries, I guess I surpassed him in charges upon the wild onions. If he saw any live, fighting Indians, it was more

---

[1] These references are to Cass' military career in the War of 1812.
[2] The Black Hawk war was an Indian uprising in Illinois in 1832.

than I did; but I had a good many bloody struggles with the mosquitoes, and although I never fainted from the loss of blood, I can truly say I was often very hungry. Mr. Speaker, if I should ever conclude to doff whatever our Democratic friends may suppose there is of black-cockade federalism about me, and therefore they shall take me up as their candidate for the presidency, I protest they shall not make fun of me, as they have of General Cass, by attempting to write me into a military hero.

FRAGMENT ON SLAVERY [JULY 1, 1854?] [1]

This fragment was found among Lincoln's papers undated. Nicolay and Hay tentatively fixed it as having been written in 1854. It may have been composed at a somewhat later date.

IF A can prove, however conclusively, that he may of right enslave B, why may not B snatch the same argument and prove equally that he may enslave A? You say A is white and B is black. It is color, then; the lighter having the right to enslave the darker? Take care. By this rule you are to be slave to the first man you meet with a fairer skin than your own. You do not mean color exactly? You mean the whites are intellectually the superiors of the blacks, and therefore have the right to enslave them? Take care again. By this rule you are to be slave to the first man you meet with an intellect superior to your own. But, say you, it is a question of interest, and if you make it your interest you have the right to enslave another. Very well. And if he can make it his interest he has the right to enslave you.

---

[1] Lincoln, *Complete Works*, II, 186.

SPEECH AT PEORIA, ILLINOIS, IN REPLY TO
SENATOR DOUGLAS, OCTOBER 16, 1854 [1]

> The passage of the Kansas-Nebraska Act in 1854, repealing
> the Missouri Compromise of 1820 and opening new territory
> to slavery, stirred Lincoln to action. The Kansas-Nebraska
> Act had been sponsored in Congress by Senator Stephen A.
> Douglas, leader of the Illinois Democrats. Douglas de-
> fended his bill in a speech at Springfield on October 4, and
> Lincoln replied to him. On October 16 Douglas spoke at
> Peoria, and again Lincoln was on hand to answer. Lincoln's
> speech at Peoria was an amplification of the one he had
> given at Springfield. It is his first great address. He opened
> it with an historical account of the slavery issue up to 1854.
> This section is omitted.

* * * *

THIS is the repeal of the Missouri Compromise. The foregoing history may not be precisely accurate in every particular, but I am sure it is sufficiently so for all the use I shall
attempt to make of it, and in it we have before us the chief
material enabling us to judge correctly whether the repeal of
the Missouri Compromise is right or wrong. I think, and shall
try to show, that it is wrong—wrong in its direct effect, letting
slavery into Kansas and Nebraska, and wrong in its prospective
principle, allowing it to spread to every other part of the wide
world where men can be found inclined to take it.

This declared indifference, but, as I must think, covert real
zeal, for the spread of slavery, I cannot but hate. I hate it because of the monstrous injustice of slavery itself. I hate it because it deprives our republican example of its just influence
in the world; enables the enemies of free institutions with
plausibility to taunt us as hypocrites; causes the real friends of
freedom to doubt our sincerity; and especially because it forces
so many good men among ourselves into an open war with the
very fundamental principles of civil liberty, criticizing the Declaration of Independence, and insisting that there is no right
principle of action but self-interest.

---

[1] Lincoln, *Complete Works*, II, 190-262.

Before proceeding let me say that I think I have no prejudice against the Southern people. They are just what we would be in their situation. If slavery did not now exist among them, they would not introduce it. If it did now exist among us, we should not instantly give it up. This I believe of the masses North and South. Doubtless there are individuals on both sides who would not hold slaves under any circumstances, and others who would gladly introduce slavery anew if it were out of existence. We know that some Southern men do free their slaves, go North and become tip-top Abolitionists, while some Northern ones go South and become most cruel slave-masters.

When Southern people tell us they are no more responsible for the origin of slavery than we are, I acknowledge the fact. When it is said that the institution exists, and that it is very difficult to get rid of it in any satisfactory way, I can understand and appreciate the saying. I surely will not blame them for not doing what I should not know how to do myself. If all earthly power were given me, I should not know what to do as to the existing institution. My first impulse would be to free all the slaves, and send them to Liberia, to their own native land. But a moment's reflection would convince me that whatever of high hope (as I think there is) there may be in this in the long run, its sudden execution is impossible. If they were all landed there in a day, they would all perish in the next ten days; and there are not surplus shipping and surplus money enough to carry them there in many times ten days. What then? Free them all, and keep them among us as underlings? Is it quite certain that this betters their condition? I think I would not hold one in slavery at any rate, yet the point is not clear enough for me to denounce people upon. What next? Free them, and make them politically and socially our equals. My own feelings will not admit of this, and if mine would, we well know that those of the great mass of whites will not. Whether this feeling accords with justice and sound judgment is not the sole question, if indeed it is any part of it. A universal feeling, whether well or ill founded, cannot be safely disregarded. We cannot then make them equals. It does seem to me that systems of gradual emancipation might be adopted, but for their tardiness in this I will not undertake to judge our brethren of the South.

When they remind us of their constitutional rights, I acknowledge them—not grudgingly, but fully and fairly; and I would give them any legislation for the reclaiming of their fugitives which should not in its stringency be more likely to carry a free man into slavery than our ordinary criminal laws are to hang an innocent one.

But all this, to my judgment, furnishes no more excuse for permitting slavery to go into our own free territory than it would for reviving the African slave-trade by law. The law which forbids the bringing of slaves from Africa, and that which has so long forbidden the taking of them into Nebraska, can hardly be distinguished on any moral principle, and the repeal of the former could find quite as plausible excuses as that of the latter.

* * * *

I now come to consider whether the repeal, with its avowed principles, is intrinsically right. I insist that it is not. Take the particular case. A controversy had arisen between the advocates and opponents of slavery, in relation to its establishment within the country we had purchased of France. The southern, and then best, part of the purchase was already in as a slave State. The controversy was settled by also letting Missouri in as a slave State; but with the agreement that within all the remaining part of the purchase, north of a certain line, there should never be slavery. As to what was to be done with the remaining part south of the line, nothing was said; but perhaps the fair implication was, it should come in with slavery if it should so choose. The southern part, except a portion heretofore mentioned, afterward did come in with slavery, as the State of Arkansas. All these many years, since 1820, the northern part had remained a wilderness. At length settlements began in it also. In due course Iowa came in as a free State, and Minnesota was given a territorial government, without removing the slav-

ery restriction. Finally, the sole remaining part north of the
line—Kansas and Nebraska—was to be organized; and it is
proposed, and carried, to blot out the old dividing line of thirty-
four years' standing, and to open the whole of that country to
the intrduction of slavery. Now this, to my mind, is manifestly
unjust. After an angry and dangerous controversy, the parties
made friends by dividing the bone of contention. The one
party first appropriates her own share, beyond all power to be
disturbed in the possession of it, and then seizes the share of
the other party. It is as if two starving men had divided their
only loaf; the one had hastily swallowed his half, and then
grabbed the other's half just as he was putting it to his mouth.

Let me here drop the main argument, to notice what I consider rather an inferior matter. It is argued that slavery will
not go to Kansas and Nebraska, in any event. This is a pallia-
tion, a lullaby. I have some hope that it will not; but let us
not be too confident. As to climate, a glance at the map shows
that there are five slave States—Delaware, Maryland, Virginia,
Kentucky, and Missouri, and also the District of Columbia, all
north of the Missouri Compromise line. The census returns of
1850 show that within these there are eight hundred and sixty-
seven thousand two hundred and seventy-six slaves, being more
than one fourth of all the slaves in the nation.

It is not climate then, that will keep slavery out of these Territories. Is there anything in the peculiar nature of the country?
Missouri adjoins these Territories by her entire western boundary, and slavery is already within every one of her western
counties. I have even heard it said that there are more slaves
in proportion to whites in the northwestern county of Missouri,
than within any other county in the State. Slavery pressed entirely up to the old western boundary of the State, and when
rather recently a part of that boundary at the northwest was
moved out a little farther west, slavery followed on quite up
to the new line. Now when the restriction is removed, what is
to prevent it from going still farther? Climate will not, no
peculiarity of the country will, nothing in nature will. Will

the disposition of the people prevent it? Those nearest the scene are all in favor of the extension. The Yankees who are opposed to it may be most numerous; but, in military phrase, the battle-field is too far from their base of operations.

* * * *

Equal justice to the South, it is said, requires us to consent to the extension of slavery to new countries. That is to say, inasmuch as you do not object to my taking my hog to Nebraska, therefore I must not object to you taking your slave. Now, I admit that this is perfectly logical, if there is no difference between hogs and negroes. But while you thus require me to deny the humanity of the negro, I wish to ask whether you of the South, yourselves, have ever been willing to do as much? It is kindly provided that of all those who come into the world only a small percentage are natural tyrants. That percentage is no larger in the slave States than in the free. The great majority South, as well as North, have human sympathies, of which they can no more divest themselves than they can of their sensibility to physical pain. These sympathies in the bosoms of the Southern people manifest, in many ways, their sense of the wrong of slavery, and their consciousness that, after all, there is humanity in the negro. If they deny this, let me address them a few plain questions. In 1820 you joined the North, almost unanimously, in declaring the African slave-trade piracy, and in annexing to it the punishment of death. Why did you do this? If you did not feel that it was wrong, why did you join in providing that men should be hung for it? The practice was no more than bringing wild negroes from Africa to such as would buy them. But you never thought of hanging men for catching and selling wild horses, wild buffaloes, or wild bears.

* * * *

But one great argument in support of the repeal of the Missouri Compromise is still to come. That argument is "the sacred right of self-government." It seems our distinguished senator has found great difficulty in getting his antagonists, even in the Senate, to meet him fairly on this argument. Some poet has said:

Fools rush in where angels fear to tread.

At the hazard of being thought one of the fools of this quotation, I meet that argument—I rush in—I take that bull by the horns. I trust I understand and truly estimate the right of self-government. My faith in the proposition that each man should do precisely as he pleases with all which is exclusively his own lies at the foundation of the sense of justice there is in me. I extend the principle to communities of men as well as to individuals. I so extend it because it is politically wise, as well as naturally just: politically wise in saving us from broils about matters which do not concern us. Here, or at Washington, I would not trouble myself with the oyster laws of Virginia, or the cranberry laws of Indiana. The doctrine of self-government is right,—absolutely and eternally right,—but it has no just application as here attempted. Or perhaps I should rather say that whether it has such application depends upon whether a negro is not or is a man. If he is not a man, in that case he who is a man may as a matter of self-government do just what he pleases with him.

But if the negro is a man, is it not to that extent a total destruction of self-government to say that he too shall not govern himself? When the white man governs himself, that is self-government; but when he governs himself and also governs another man, that is more than self-government—that is despotism. If the negro is a man, why then my ancient faith teaches me that "all men are created equal," and that there can be no moral right in connection with one man's making a slave of another.

Judge Douglas frequently, with bitter irony and sarcasm, paraphrases our argument by saying: "The white people of Nebraska are good enough to govern themselves, but they are not good enough to govern a few miserable negroes!"

Well! I doubt not that the people of Nebraska are and will

continue to be as good as the average of people elsewhere. I do not say the contrary. What I do say is that no man is good enough to govern another man without that other's consent. I say this is the leading principle, the sheet-anchor of American republicanism. Our Declaration of Independence says:

We hold these truths to be self-evident: That all men are created equal; that they are endowed by their Creator with certain inalienable rights; that among these are life, liberty and the pursuit of happiness. That to secure these rights, governments are instituted among men, DERIVING THEIR JUST POWERS FROM THE CONSENT OF THE GOVERNED.

I have quoted so much at this time merely to show that, according to our ancient faith, the just powers of governments are derived from the consent of the governed. Now the relation of master and slave is *pro tanto* a total violation of this principle. The master not only governs the slave without his consent, but he governs him by a set of rules altogether different from those which he prescribes for himself. Allow all the governed an equal voice in the government, and that, and that only, is self-government.

Let it not be said I am contending for the establishment of political and social equality between the whites and blacks. I have already said the contrary. I am not combating the argument of necessity, arising from the fact that the blacks are already among us; but I am combating what is set up as moral argument for allowing them to be taken where they have never yet been—arguing against the extension of a bad thing, which, where it already exists, we must of necessity manage as we best can.

* * * *

Whether slavery shall go into Nebraska, or other new Territories, is not a matter of exclusive concern to the people who may go there. The whole nation is interested that the best use shall be made of these Territories. We want them for homes of free white people. This they cannot be, to any considerable extent, if slavery shall be planted within them. Slave States are places for poor white people to remove from, not to remove to. New free States are the places for poor people to go to, and better their condition. For this use the nation needs these Territories.

*   *   *   *

Finally, I insist that if there is anything which it is the duty of the whole people to never intrust to any hands but their own, that thing is the preservation and perpetuity of their own liberties and institutions. And if they shall think, as I do, that the extension of slavery endangers them more than any or all other causes, how recreant to themselves if they submit the question, and with it the fate of their country, to a mere handful of men bent only on self-interest. If this question of slavery extension were an insignificant one—one having no power to do harm— it might be shuffled aside in this way; and being, as it is, the great Behemoth of danger, shall the strong grip of the nation be loosened upon him, to intrust him to the hands of such feeble keepers?

I have done with this mighty argument of self-government. Go, sacred thing! Go in peace.

But Nebraska is urged as a great Union-saving measure. Well, I too go for saving the Union. Much as I hate slavery, I would consent to the extension of it rather than see the Union dissolved, just as I would consent to any great evil to avoid a greater one. But when I go to Union-saving, I must believe, at least, that the means I employ have some adaptation to the end. To my mind, Nebraska has no such adaptation.

It hath no relish of salvation in it.

It is an aggravation, rather, of the only one thing which ever endangers the Union. When it came upon us, all was peace and quiet. The nation was looking to the forming of new bonds of union, and a long course of peace and prosperity seemed to lie before us. In the whole range of possibility, there scarcely appears to me to have been anything out of which the slavery agitation could have been revived, except the very project of repealing the Missouri Compromise. Every inch of territory we owned already had a definite settlement of the slavery question, by which all parties were pledged to abide. Indeed, there was no uninhabited country on the continent which we could acquire, if we except some extreme northern regions which are wholly out of the question.

In this state of affairs the Genius of Discord himself could scarcely have invented a way of again setting us by the ears but by turning back and destroying the peace measures of the past. The counsels of that Genius seem to have prevailed. The Missouri Compromise was repealed; and here we are in the midst of a new slavery agitation, such, I think, as we have never seen before. Who is responsible for this? Is it those who resist the measure, or those who causelessly brought it forward and pressed it through, having reason to know, and in fact knowing, it must and would be so resisted? It could not but be expected by its author that it would be looked upon as a measure for the extension of slavery, aggravated by a gross breach of faith.

Argue as you will and long as you will, this is the naked front and aspect of the measure. And in this aspect it could not but produce agitation. Slavery is founded in the selfishness of man's nature—opposition to it in his love of justice. These principles are an eternal antagonism, and when brought into collision so fiercely as slavery extension brings them, shocks and throes and convulsions must ceaselessly follow. Repeal the Missouri Compromise, repeal all compromises, repeal the Declaration of Independence, repeal all past history, you still cannot repeal human nature. It still will be the abundance of man's heart that slavery extension is wrong, and out of the abundance of his heart his mouth will continue to speak.

The structure, too, of the Nebraska bill is very peculiar. The people are to decide the question of slavery for themselves; but when they are to decide, or how they are to decide, or whether, when the question is once decided, it is to remain so or is to be subject to an indefinite succession of new trials, the law does not say. Is it to be decided by the first dozen settlers who arrive there, or is it to await the arrival of a hundred? Is it to be decided by a vote of the people or a vote of the legislature, or, indeed, by a vote of any sort? To these questions the law gives no answer. There is a mystery about this; for when a member proposed to give the legislature express authority to exclude slavery, it was hooted down by the friends of the bill. This fact is worth remembering. Some Yankees in the East are sending emigrants to Nebraska to exclude slavery from it; and, so far as I can judge, they expect the question to be decided by voting in some way or other. But the Missourians are awake, too. They are within a stone's-throw of the contested ground. They hold meetings and pass resolutions, in which not the slightest allusion to voting is made. They resolve that slavery already exists in the Territory; that more shall go there; that they, remaining in Missouri, will protect it, and that Abolitionists shall be hung or driven away. Through all this bowie-knives and six-shooters are seen plainly enough, but never a glimpse of the ballot-box.

And, really, what is the result of all this? Each party within having numerous and determined backers without, is it not probable that the contest will come to blows and bloodshed? Could there be a more apt invention to bring about collision and violence on the slavery question than this Nebraska project is? I do not charge or believe that such was intended by Congress; but if they had literally formed a ring and placed champions within it to fight out the controversy, the fight could be no more likely to come off than it is. And if this fight should begin, is it likely to take a very peaceful, Union-saving turn? Will not the first drop of blood so shed be the real knell of the Union?

The Missouri Compromise ought to be restored. For the sake of the Union, it ought to be restored. We ought to elect a House of Representatives which will vote its restoration. If by any means we omit to do this, what follows? Slavery may or may not be established in Nebraska. But whether it be or not, we shall have repudiated—discarded from the councils of the nation—the spirit of compromise; for who, after this, will ever trust in a national compromise? The spirit of mutual concession —that spirit which first gave us the Constitution, and which has thrice saved the Union—we shall have strangled and cast from us forever. And what shall we have in lieu of it? The South flushed with triumph and tempted to excess; the North, betrayed as they believe, brooding on wrong and burning for revenge. One side will provoke, the other resent. The one will taunt, the other defy; one aggresses, the other retaliates. Already a few in the North defy all constitutional restraints, resist the execution of the fugitive-slave law, and even menace the institution of slavery in the States where it exists. Already a few in the South claim the constitutional right to take and to hold slaves in the free States—demand the revival of the slave-trade—and demand a treaty with Great Britain by which fugitive slaves may be reclaimed from Canada. As yet they are but few on either side. It is a grave question for lovers of the Union, whether the final destruction of the Missouri Compromise, and with it the spirit of all compromise, will or will not embolden and embitter each of these, and fatally increase the number of both.

* * * *

Some men, mostly Whigs, who condemn the repeal of the Missouri Compromise, nevertheless hesitate to go for its restoration, lest they be thrown in company with the Abolitionists. Will they allow me, as an old Whig, to tell them, good-humoredly, that I think this is very silly? Stand with anybody that stands right. Stand with him while he is right, and part with him when he goes wrong. Stand with the Abolitionist in restoring the Missouri Compromise, and stand against him when he attempts to repeal the fugitive-slave law. In the latter case you stand with the Southern disunionist. What of that? You are still right. In both cases you are right. In both cases you expose the dangerous extremes. In both you stand on middle ground, and hold the ship level and steady. In both you are national, and nothing less than national. This is the good old Whig ground. To desert such ground because of any company, is to be less than a Whig—less than a man—less than an American.

I particularly object to the new position which the avowed principle of this Nebraska law gives to slavery in the body politic. I object to it because it assumes that there can be no moral right in the enslaving of one man by another. I object to it as a dangerous dalliance for a free people—a sad evidence that, feeling prosperity, we forget right; that liberty, as a principle, we have ceased to revere. I object to it because the fathers of the republic eschewed and rejected it. The argument of "necessity" was the only argument they ever admitted in favor of slavery; and so far, and so far only, as it carried them did they ever go. They found the institution existing among us, which they could not help, and they cast blame upon the British King for having permitted its introduction. Before the Constitution they prohibited its introduction into the Northwestern Territory, the only country we owned then free from it. At the framing and adoption of the Constitution, they forbore to so much as mention the word "slave" or "slavery" in the whole instrument. In the provision for the recovery of fugitives, the slave is spoken of as a "person held to service or labor." In that prohibiting the abolition of the African slave-trade for twenty years, that trade is spoken of as "the migration or importation of such persons as any of the States now existing shall think proper to admit," etc. These are the only provisions alluding to slavery. Thus the thing is hid away in the Constitution, just as an afflicted man hides away a wen or cancer which he dares not cut out at once, lest he bleed to death,—with the promise, nevertheless, that the cutting may begin at a certain time. Less than this our fathers could not do, and more they would not do. Necessity drove them so far, and further they would not go. But this is not all. The earliest Congress under the Constitution took the same view of slavery. They hedged and hemmed it in to the narrowest limits of necessity.

In 1794 they prohibited an outgoing slave-trade—that is, the taking of slaves from the United States to sell. In 1798 they prohibited the bringing of slaves from Africa into the Mississippi Territory, this Territory then comprising what are now the States of Mississippi and Alabama. This was ten years before they had authority to do the same thing as to the States existing at the adoption of the Constitution. In 1800 they prohibited American citizens from trading in slaves between foreign countries, as, for instance, from Africa to Brazil. In 1803 they passed a law in aid of one or two slave-State laws, in restraint of the internal slave-trade. In 1807, in apparent hot haste, they passed the law, nearly a year in advance,—to take effect the first day of 1808, the very first day the Constitution would permit,—prohibiting the African slave-trade by heavy pecuniary and corporal penalties. In 1820, finding these provisions ineffectual, they declared the slave-trade piracy, and annexed to it the extreme penalty of death. While all this was passing in the General Government, five or six of the original slave States had adopted systems of gradual emancipation, by which the institution was rapidly becoming extinct within their limits. Thus we see that the plain, unmistakable spirit of that age toward slavery was hostility to the principle and toleration only by necessity.

But now it is to be transformed into a "sacred right." Nebraska brings it forth, places it on the highroad to extension and perpetuity, and with a pat on its back says to it, "Go, and God speed you." Henceforth it is to be the chief jewel of the nation—the very figurehead of the ship of state. Little by little, but steadily as man's march to the grave, we have been giving up the old for the new faith. Near eighty years ago we began by declaring that all men are created equal; but now from that beginning we have run down to the other declaration, that for some men to enslave others is a "sacred right of self-government." These principles cannot stand together. They are as opposite as God and Mammon; and whoever holds to the one must despise the other. When Pettit, in connection with his support of the Nebraska bill, called the Declaration of Independence "a self-evident lie," he only did what consistency and candor require all other Nebraska men to do. Of the forty-odd Nebraska Senators who sat present and heard him, no one rebuked him. Nor am I apprised that any Nebraska newspaper, or any Nebraska orator, in the whole nation has ever yet rebuked him. If this had been said among Marion's men, Southerners though they were, what would have become of the man who said it? If this had been said to the men who captured André, the man who said it would probably have been hung sooner than André was. If it had been said in old Independence Hall seventy-eight years ago, the very doorkeeper would have throttled the man and thrust him into the street. Let no one be deceived. The spirit of seventy-six and the spirit of Nebraska are utter antagonisms; and the former is being rapidly displaced by the latter.

Fellow-countrymen, Americans, South as well as North, shall we make no effort to arrest this? Already the liberal party throughout the world expresses the apprehension "that the one retrograde institution in America is undermining the principles of progress, and fatally violating the noblest political system the world ever saw." This is not the taunt of enemies, but the warning of friends. Is it quite safe to disregard it—to despise it? Is there no danger to liberty itself in discarding the earliest practice and first precept of our ancient faith? In our greedy chase to make profit of the negro, let us beware lest we "cancel and tear in pieces" even the white man's charter of freedom.

Our republican robe is soiled and trailed in the dust. Let us repurify it. Let us turn and wash it white in the spirit, if not the blood, of the Revolution. Let us turn slavery from its claims of "moral right" back upon its existing legal rights and its arguments of "necessity." Let us return it to the position our fathers gave it, and there let it rest in peace. Let us readopt the Declaration of Independence, and with it the practices and policy which harmonize with it. Let North and South—let all

Americans—let all lovers of liberty everywhere join in the great and good work. If we do this, we shall not only have saved the Union, but we shall have so saved it as to make and to keep it forever worthy of the saving. We shall have so saved it that the succeeding millions of free, happy people, the world over, shall rise up and call us blessed to the latest generations.

* * * *

KALAMAZOO SPEECH, AUGUST 27, 1856 [1]

This speech has recently been discovered and is not widely known. Lincoln delivered it in the campaign of 1856. John C. Frémont was the Republican presidential candidate and James Buchanan was the Democratic nominee. This was the Republican party's first presidential contest.

FELLOW Countrymen: Under the Constitution of the United States another Presidential contest approaches us. All over this land—that portion, at least, of which I know much—the people are assembling to consider the proper course to be adopted by them. One of the first considerations is to learn what the people differ about. If we ascertain what we differ about, we shall be better able to decide.

The question of slavery, at the present day, should be not only the greatest question, but very nearly the sole question. Our opponents, however, prefer that this should not be the case. To get at this question, I will occupy your attention but a single moment.

The question is simply this: Shall slavery be spread into new territories, or not? This is the naked question. It we should support Fremont successfully in this, it may be charged that we will not be content with restricting slavery in the new territories. If we should charge that James Buchanan, by his platform, is bound to extend slavery into the territories, and that he is in favor of its being thus spread, we should be puzzled to prove it. We believe it, nevertheless.

---

[1] Thomas I. Starr (ed.), *Lincoln's Kalamazoo Address Against Extending Slavery* (Detroit, 1941), 33-46.

By taking the issue as I present it, whether it shall be permitted as an issue, is made up between the parties. Each takes his own stand. This is the question: Shall the Government of the United States prohibit slavery in the [territories of the] United States?

We have been in the habit of deploring the fact that slavery exists among us. We have ever deplored it. Our forefathers did, and they declared, as we have done in later years, the blame rested upon the mother government of Great Britain. We constantly condemn Great Britain for not preventing slavery from coming amongst us. She would not interfere to prevent it, and so individuals were able to introduce the institution without opposition. I have alluded to this, to ask you if this is not exactly the policy of Buchanan and his friends, to place this government in the attitude then occupied by the government of Great Britain—placing the nation in the position to authorize the territories to reproach it, for refusing to allow them to hold slaves.

I would like to ask your attention, any gentleman to tell me when the people of Kansas are going to decide. When are they to do it? I asked that question two years ago—when, and how are [they] to do it? Not many weeks ago, our new Senator from Illinois (Mr. Trumbull), asked Douglas how it could be done. Douglas is a great man—at keeping from answering questions he don't want to answer. He would not answer. He said it was a question for the Supreme Court to decide. In the North, his friends argue that the people can decide it at any time.

The Southerners [Democrats] say there is no power in the people, whatever. We know that from the time that white people have been allowed in the territory, they have brought slaves with them. Suppose the people come up to vote as freely, and with as perfect protection as we could do it here. Will they be at liberty to vote their sentiments? If they can, then all that has ever been said about our provincial ancestors is untrue, and they could have done so, also. We know our Southern friends say that the General Government cannot interfere. The people, say they, have no right to interfere. They could as truly say, "It is amongst us—we cannot get rid of it."

But I am afraid I waste too much time on this point. I take it as an illustration of the principle, that slaves are admitted into the territories. And, while I am speaking of Kansas, how will that operate? Can men vote truly? We will suppose that there are ten men who go into Kansas to settle. Nine of these are opposed to slavery. One has ten slaves. The slaveholder is a good man in other respects: he is a good neighbor, and being a wealthy man, he is enabled to do the others many neighborly kindnesses. They like the man, although they don't like the system by which he holds his fellowmen in bondage. And here let me say, that in intellectual and physical structure, our Southern brethren do not differ from us. They are, like us, subject to passions, and it is only their odious institution of slavery, that makes the breach between us.

These ten men of whom I was speaking, live together three or four years; they intermarry; their family ties are strengthened. And who wonders that in time, the people learn to look upon slavery with complacency? This is the way in which slavery is planted, and gains so firm a foothold. I think this is a strong card that the Nebraska party have played, and won upon, in this game.

I suppose that this crowd are opposed to the admission of slavery into Kansas, yet it is true that in all crowds there are some who differ from the majority. I want to ask the Buchanan men, who are against the spread of slavery, if there be any present, why not vote for the man who is against it? I understand that Mr. Fillmore's position is precisely like Buchanan's. I understand that, by the Nebraska bill, a door has been opened for the spread of slavery in[to] the territories. Examine, if you please, and see if they have ever done any such thing as try to shut the door.

It is true that Fillmore tickles a few of his friends with the notion that he is not the cause of the door being opened. Well;

it brings him into this position: he tries to get both sides, one by denouncing those who opened the door, and the other by hinting that he doesn't care a fig for its being open. If he were President, he would have one side or the other—he would either restrict slavery or not. Of course it would be so. There could be no middle way.

You who hate slavery and love freedom, why not, as Fillmore and Buchanan are on the same ground, vote for Fremont? Why not vote for the man who takes your side of the question? "Well," says Buchanan, "it is none of our business." But is it not *our* business? There are several reasons why I think it is our business. But let us see how it is. Others have urged these reasons before, but they are still of use. By our Constitution we are represented in Congress in proportion to numbers, and in counting the numbers that give us our representatives, three slaves are counted as two people. The State of Maine has six representatives in the lower house of Congress. In strength South Carolina is equal to her. But stop! Maine has *twice as many* white people, and 32,000 to boot! And is that fair? I don't complain of it. This regulation was put in force when the exigencies of the times demanded it, and could not have been avoided. Now, one man in South Carolina is the same as two men here.

Maine should have twice as many men in Congress as South Carolina. It is a fact that any man in South Carolina has more influence and power in Congress today than any two now before me. The same thing is true of all slave States, though it may not be in the same proportion. It is a truth that cannot be denied, that in all the free States no white man is the equal of the white man of the slave States. But this is in the Constitution, and we must stand up to it. The question, then, is, "Have we no interest as to whether the white man of the North shall be the equal of the white man of the South?"

Once when I used this argument in the presence of Douglas, he answered that in the North the black man was counted as a full man, and had an equal vote with the white man, while at the South they were counted as but three-fifths. And Douglas, when he had made this reply, doubtless thought he had forever silenced the objection.

Have we no interest in the free Territories of the United States—that they should be kept open for the homes of free white people? As our Northern States are growing more and more in wealth and population, we are continually in want of an outlet, through which it may pass out to enrich our country. In this we have an interest—a deep and abiding interest. There is another thing, and that is the mature knowledge we have— the greatest interest of all. It is the doctrine, that the people are to be driven from the maxims of our free Government, that despises the spirit which for eighty years has celebrated the anniversary of our national independence.

We are a great empire. We are eighty years old. We stand at once the wonder and admiration of the whole world, and we must enquire what it is that has given us so much prosperity, and we shall understand that to give up that one thing, would be to give up all future prosperity. This cause is that every man can make himself. It has been said that such a race of prosperity has been run nowhere else. We find a people on the Northeast, who have a different government from ours, being ruled by a Queen. Turning to the South, we see a people who, while they boast of being free, keep their fellow beings in bondage. Compare our Free States with either, shall we say here that we have no interest in keeping that principle alive? Shall we say, "Let it be"? No—we have an interest in the maintenance of the principles of the Government, and without this interest, it is worth nothing.

I have noticed in Southern newspapers, particularly the Richmond *Enquirer,* the Southern view of the Free States. They insist that slavery has a right to spread. They defend it upon principle. They insist that their slaves are far better off than Northern freemen. What a mistaken view do these men have of Northern laborers! They think that men are always to remain laborers here—but there is no such class. The man who labored for another last year, this year labors for himself, and next year he will hire others to labor for him. These men don't understand when they think in this manner of Northern free labor. When these reasons can be introduced, tell me not that we have no interest in keeping the territories free for the settlement of free laborers.

I pass, then, from this question. I think we have an ever growing interest in maintaining the free institutions of our country.

It is said that our party is a sectional party. It has been said in high quarters that if Fremont and Dayton were elected the Union would be dissolved. I believe it [that the South does so think]! I believe it! It is a shameful thing that the subject is talked of so much. Did we not have a Southern President and Vice-President at one time? And yet the Union has not yet been dissolved. Why, at this very moment, there is a Northern President and Vice-President. Pierce and King were elected, and King died without ever taking his seat. The Senate elected a Northern man from their own numbers, to perform the duties of the Vice-President. He resigned his seat, however, as soon as he got the job of making a slave State out of Kansas. Was not that a great mistake?

(A voice: "He didn't mean that!")

Then why didn't he speak what he did mean? Why did not he speak what he ought to have spoken? That was the very thing. He should have spoken manly, and we should then have known where to have found him. It is said we expect to elect Fremont by Northern votes. Certainly we do not think the South will elect him. But let us ask the question differently. Does not Buchanan expect to be elected by Southern votes? Fillmore, however, will go out of this contest the most national man we have. He has no prospect of having a single vote on either side of Mason and Dixon's line, to trouble his poor soul about.

We believe that it is right that slavery should not be tolerated in the new territories, yet we cannot get support for this doctrine, except in one part of the country. Slavery is looked upon by men in the light of dollars and cents. The estimated worth of the slaves at the South is $1,000,000,000, and in a very few years, if the institution shall be admitted into the territories, they will have increased fifty percent. in value.

Our adversaries charge Fremont with being an abolitionist. When pressed to show proof, they frankly confess that they can show no such thing. They run off upon the assertion that his supporters are abolitionists. But this they have never attempted to prove. I know of no word in the language that has been used so much as that one, "abolitionist", having no definition. It has no meaning unless taken as designating a person who is abolishing something. If that be its signification, the supporters of Fremont are not abolitionists.

In Kansas all who come there are perfectly free to regulate their own social relations. There has never been a man there who was an abolitionist—for what was there to be abolished? People there had perfect freedom to express what they wished on the subject, when the Nebraska bill was first passed.

Our friends in the South, who support Buchanan, have five disunion men to one at the North. This disunion is a sectional question. Who is to blame for it? Are we? I don't care how you express it.

This government is sought to be put on a new track. Slavery is to be made a ruling element in our government. The question can be avoided in but two ways. By the one, we must submit, and allow slavery to triumph, or, by the other, we must triumph over the black demon. We have chosen the latter manner. If you of the North wish to get rid of this question, you must decide between these two ways—submit and vote for Buchanan, submit and vote that slavery is a just and good thing, and immediately get rid of the question; or unite with us, and help us to triumph. We would all like to have the question done away with, but we cannot submit.

They tell us that we are in company with men who have long been known as abolitionists. What care we how many may feel disposed to labor for our cause? Why do not you, Buchanan men, come in and use your influence to make our party respectable?

How is the dissolution of the Union to be consummated? They tell us that the Union is in danger. Who will divide it? Is it those who make the charge? Are they themselves the persons who wish to see this result? A majority will never dissolve the Union. Can a minority do it?

When this Nebraska bill was first introduced into Congress, the sense of the Democratic party was outraged. That party has ever prided itself, that it was the friend of individual, universal freedom. It was that principle upon which they carried their measures. When the Kansas scheme was conceived, it was natural that this respect and sense should have been outraged.

Now I make this appeal to the Democratic citizens here. Don't you find yourself making arguments in support of these measures, which you never would have made before? Did you ever do it before this Nebraska bill compelled you to do it? If you answer this in the affirmative, see how a whole party has been turned away from their love of liberty!

And now, my Democratic friends, come forward. Throw off these things, and come to the rescue of this great principle of equality. Don't interfere with anything in the Constitution. That must be maintained, for it is the only safeguard of our liberties. And not to Democrats alone do I make this appeal, but to all who love these great and true principles. Come, and keep coming! Strike, and strike again! So sure as God lives, the victory shall be yours.

SPEECH DELIVERED AT SPRINGFIELD, ILLINOIS, AT
THE CLOSE OF THE REPUBLICAN STATE CONVEN-
TION BY WHICH MR. LINCOLN HAD BEEN NAMED
AS THEIR CANDIDATE FOR UNITED STATES
SENATOR, JUNE 16, 1858 [1]

In 1858 the Illinois Republican convention unanimously
nominated Lincoln as the party's candidate for the United
States Senate seat held by Douglas. Lincoln appeared before
the convention to read this speech, which he had prepared
carefully. In it he made his famous "house divided" statement. He devoted a major part of the speech to the Supreme
Court's Dred Scott decision, which declared that neither
Congress nor a territorial legislature could exclude slavery
from a territory. The decision, he said, seemed to be the
result of a conspiracy hatched by outgoing President Franklin
Pierce, incoming President James Buchanan, Chief Justice
Roger B. Taney, and Douglas.

MR. President and Gentlemen of the Convention:
If we could first know where we are, and whither we
are tending, we could better judge what to do, and how to do it.
We are now far into the fifth year since a policy was initiated
with the avowed object and confident promise of putting an
end to slavery agitation. Under the operation of that policy,
that agitation has not only not ceased but has constantly augmented. In my opinion, it will not cease until a crisis shall
have been reached and passed. "A house divided against itself
cannot stand." I believe this government cannot endure permanently half slave and half free. I do not expect the Union
to be dissolved—I do not expect the house to fall—but I do
expect it will cease to be divided. It will become all one thing,
or all the other. Either the opponents of slavery will arrest the
further spread of it, and place it where the public mind shall
rest in the belief that it is in the course of ultimate extinction;
or its advocates will push it forward till it shall become alike
lawful in all the States, old as well as new, North as well as
South.

_____
[1] Lincoln, *Complete Works*, III, 1-15.

Have we no tendency to the latter condition?

Let any one who doubts carefully contemplate that now almost complete legal combination—piece of machinery, so to speak—compounded of the Nebraska doctrine and the Dred Scott decision. Let him consider not only what work the machinery is adapted to do, and how well adapted; but also let him study the history of the construction, and trace, if he can, or rather fail, if he can, to trace the evidences of design and concert of action among its chief architects, from the beginning.

The new year of 1854 found slavery excluded from more than half the States by State constitutions, and from most of the national territory by congressional prohibition. Four days later commenced the struggle which ended in repealing that congressional prohibition. This opened all the national territory to slavery, and was the first point gained.

But, so far, Congress only had acted; and an indorsement by the people, real or apparent, was indispensable to save the point already gained and give chance for more.

This necessity had not been overlooked, but had been provided for, as well as might be, in the notable argument of "squatter sovereignty," otherwise called "sacred right of self-government," which latter phrase, though expressive of the only rightful basis of any government, was so perverted in this attempted use of it as to amount to just this: That if any one man choose to enslave another, no third man shall be allowed to object. That argument was incorporated into the Nebraska bill itself, in the language which follows: "It being the true intent and meaning of this act not to legislate slavery into any Territory or State, nor to exclude it therefrom; but to leave the people thereof perfectly free to form and regulate their domestic institutions in their own way, subject only to the Constitution of the United States." Then opened the roar of loose declamation in favor of "squatter sovereignty" and "sacred right of self-government." "But," said opposition members, "let us amend the bill so as to expressly declare that the people of the Territory may exclude slavery." "Not we," said the friends of the measure; and down they voted the amendment.

While the Nebraska bill was passing through Congress, a law case involving the question of a negro's freedom, by reason of his owner having voluntarily taken him first into a free State and then into a Territory covered by the congressional prohibition, and held him as a slave for a long time in each, was passing through the United States Circuit Court for the District of Missouri; and both Nebraska bill and lawsuit were brought to a decision in the same month of May, 1854. The negro's name was Dred Scott, which name now designates the decision finally made in the case. Before the then next presidential election, the law case came to and was argued in the Supreme Court of the United States; but the decision of it was deferred until after the election. Still, before the election, Senator Trumbull[1] on the floor of the Senate, requested the leading advocate of the Nebraska bill to state his opinion whether the people of a Territory can constitutionally exclude slavery from their limits; and the latter answered: "That is a question for the Supreme Court."

The election came. Mr. Buchanan was elected, and the indorsement, such as it was, secured. That was the second point gained. The indorsement, however, fell short of a clear popular majority by nearly four hundred thousand votes, and so, perhaps, was not overwhelmingly reliable and satisfactory. The outgoing President, in his last annual message, as impressively as possible echoed back upon the people the weight and authority of the indorsement. The Supreme Court met again; did not announce their decision, but ordered a reargument. The presidential inauguration came, and still no decision of the court; but the incoming President in his inaugural address fervently exhorted the people to abide by the forthcoming decision, whatever it might be. Then, in a few days, came the decision.

---

[1] Lyman Trumbull, Republican Senator from Illinois.

* * * *

At length a squabble springs up between the President and the author of the Nebraska bill, on the mere question of fact, whether the Lecompton constitution was or was not, in any just sense, made by the people of Kansas; and in that quarrel the latter declares that all he wants is a fair vote for the people, and that he cares not whether slavery be voted down or voted up. I do not understand his declaration that he cares not whether slavery be voted down or voted up to be intended by him other than as an apt definition of the policy he would impress upon the public mind—the principle for which he declares he has suffered so much, and is ready to suffer to the end. And well may he cling to that principle. If he has any parental feeling, well may he cling to it. That principle is the only shred left of his original Nebraska doctrine. Under the Dred Scott decision "squatter sovereignty" squatted out of existence, tumbled down like temporary scaffolding,—like the mold at the foundry, served through one blast and fell back into loose sand,—helped to carry an election, and then was kicked to the winds. His late joint struggle with the Republicans against the Lecompton constitution involves nothing of the original Nebraska doctrine. That struggle was made on a point—the right of a people to make their own constitution—upon which he and the Republicans have never differed.

The several points of the Dred Scott decision, in connection with Senator Douglas's "care not" policy, constitute the piece of machinery in its present state of advancement. This was the third point gained. The working points of that machinery are:

(1) That no negro slave, imported as such from Africa, and no descendant of such slave, can ever be a citizen of any State, in the sense of that term as used in the Constitution of the United States. This point is made in order to deprive the negro in every possible event of the benefit of that provision of the United States Constitution which declares that "the citizens of each State shall be entitled to all the privileges and immunities of citizens in the several States."

(2) That, "subject to the Constitution of the United States,"

neither Congress nor a territorial legislature can exclude slavery from any United States Territory. This point is made in order that individual men may fill up the Territories with slaves, without danger of losing them as property and thus enhance the chances of permanency to the institution through all the future.

(3) That whether the holding a negro in actual slavery in a free State makes him free as against the holder, the United States courts will not decide, but will leave to be decided by the courts of any slave State the negro may be forced into by the master. This point is made not to be pressed immediately, but, if acquiesced in for a while, and apparently indorsed by the people at an election, than to sustain the logical conclusion that what Dred Scott's master might lawfully do with Dred Scott in the free State of Illinois, every other master may lawfully do with any other one or one thousand slaves in Illinois or in any other free State.

Auxiliary to all this, and working hand in hand with it, the Nebraska doctrine, or what is left of it, is to educate and mold public opinion, at least Northern public opinion, not to care whether slavery is voted down or voted up. This shows exactly where we now are, and partially, also, whither we are tending.

It will throw additional light on the latter, to go back and run the mind over the string of historical facts already stated. Several things will now appear less dark and mysterious than they did when they were transpiring. The people were to be left "perfectly free," "subject only to the Constitution." What the Constitution had to do with it outsiders could not then see. Plainly enough now, it was an exactly fitted niche for the Dred Scott decision to afterward come in, and declare the perfect freedom of the people to be just no freedom at all. Why was the amendment expressly declaring the right of the people voted down? Plainly enough now, the adoption of it would have spoiled the niche for the Dred Scott decision. Why was the court decision held up? Why even a senator's individual opinion withheld till after the presidential election? Plainly enough now, the speaking out then would have damaged the "perfectly free" argument upon which the election was to be carried. Why the outgoing President's felicitation on the indorsement? Why the delay of a reargument? Why the incoming President's advance exhortation in favor of the decision? These things look like the cautious patting and petting of a spirited horse preparatory to mounting him, when it is dreaded that he may give the rider a fall. And why the hasty after-endorsement of the decision by the President and others?

We cannot absolutely know that all these exact adaptations are the result of preconcert. But when we see a lot of framed timbers, different portions of which we know have been gotten out at different times and places and by different workmen,—Stephen, Franklin, Roger, and James, for instance,—and we see these timbers joined together, and see they exactly make the frame of a house or a mill, all the tenons and mortises exactly fitting, and all the lengths and proportions of the different pieces exactly adapted to their respective places, and not a piece too many or too few, not omitting even scaffolding—or, if a single piece be lacking, we see the place in the frame exactly fitted and prepared yet to bring such piece in—in such a case we find it impossible not to believe that Stephen and Franklin and Roger and James all understood one another from the beginning, and all worked upon a common plan or draft drawn up before the first blow was struck.

It should not be overlooked that, by the Nebraska bill, the people of a State as well as Territory were to be left "perfectly free," "subject only to the Constitution." Why mention a State? They were legislating for Territories, and not for or about States. Certainly the people of a State are and ought to be subject to the Constitution of the United States; but why is mention of this lugged into this merely territorial law? Why are the people of a Territory and the people of a State therein lumped together, and their relation to the Constitution therein treated as being precisely the same? While the opinion of the court, by Chief Justice Taney, in the Dred Scott case, and the separate opinions of all the concurring judges, expressly declare that the Constitution of the United States neither permits Congress nor a territorial legislature to exclude slavery from any United States Territory, they all omit to declare whether or not the same Constitution permits a State, or the people of a State, to exclude it. Possibly, this is a mere omission; but who can be quite sure, if McLean or Curtis[1] had sought to get into the opinion a declaration of unlimited power in the people of a State to exclude slavery from their limits, just as Chase and Mace sought to get such declaration, in behalf of the people of a Territory, into the Nebraska bill—I ask, who can be quite sure that it would not have been voted down in the one case as it had been in the other? The nearest approach to the point of declaring the power of a State over slavery is made by Judge Nelson. He approaches it more than once, using the precise idea, and almost the language too, of the Nebraska act. On one occasion his exact language is: "Except in case where the power is restrained by the Constitution of the United States, the law of the State is supreme over the subject of slavery within its jurisdiction." In what cases the power of the States is so restrained by the United States Constitution is left an open question, precisely as the same question as to the restraint on the power of the Territories was left open in the Nebraska act. Put this and that together, and we have another nice little niche, which we may, ere long, see filled with another Supreme Court decision declaring that the Constitution of the United States does not permit a State to exclude slavery from its limits. And this may especially be expected if the doctrine of "care not whether slavery be voted down or voted up" shall gain upon the public mind sufficiently to give promise that such a decision can be maintained when made.

Such a decision is all that slavery now lacks of being alike lawful in all the States. Welcome, or unwelcome, such decision is probably coming, and will soon be upon us, unless the power of the present political dynasty shall be met and

---

[1] Justices McLean and Curtis dissented from the majority opinion.

overthrown. We shall lie down pleasantly dreaming that the people of Missouri are on the verge of making their State free, and we shall awake to the reality instead that the Supreme Court has made Illinois a slave State. To meet and overthrow the power of that dynasty is the work now before all those who would prevent that consummation. That is what we have to do. How can we best do it?

There are those who denounce us openly to their own friends, and yet whisper us softly that Senator Douglas is the aptest instrument there is with which to effect that object. They wish us to infer all from the fact that he now has a little quarrel with the present head of the dynasty; and that he has regularly voted with us on a single point upon which he and we have never differed. They remind us that he is a great man, and that the largest of us are very small ones. Let this be granted. But "a living dog is better than a dead lion." Judge Douglas, if not a dead lion for this work, is at least a caged and toothless one. How can he oppose the advances of slavery? He don't care anything about it. His avowed mission is impressing the "public heart" to care nothing about it. A leading Douglas Democratic newspaper thinks Douglas's superior talent will be needed to resist the revival of the African slave-trade. Does Douglas believe an effort to revive that trade is approaching? He has not said so. Does he really think so? But if it is, how can he resist it? For years he has labored to prove it a sacred right of white men to take negro slaves into the new Territories. Can he possibly show that it is less a sacred right to buy them where they can be bought cheapest? And unquestionably they can be bought cheaper in Africa than in Virginia. He has done all in his power to reduce the whole question of slavery to one of a mere right of property; and as such, how can he oppose the foreign slave-trade? How can he refuse that trade in that "property" shall be "perfectly free," unless he does it as a protection to the home production? And as the home producers will probably not ask the protection, he will be wholly without a ground of opposition.

Senator Douglas holds, we know, that a man may rightfully be wiser today than he was yesterday—that he may rightfully change when he finds himself wrong. But can we, for that reason, run ahead, and infer that he will make any particular change of which he, himself, has given no intimation? Can we safely base our action upon any such vague inference? Now, as ever, I wish not to misrepresent Judge Douglas's position, question his motives, or do aught that can be personally offensive to him. Whenever, if ever, he and we can come together on principle so that our great cause may have assistance from his great ability, I hope to have interposed no adventitious obstacle. But clearly, he is not now with us—he does not pretend to be—he does not promise ever to be.

Our cause, then, must be intrusted to, and conducted by, its own undoubted friends—those whose hands are free, whose hearts are in the work, who do care for the result. Two years ago the Republicans of the nation mustered over thirteen hundred thousand strong. We did this under the single impulse of resistance to a common danger, with every external circumstance against us. Of strange, discordant, and even hostile elements, we gathered from the four winds, and formed and fought the battle through, under the constant hot fire of a disciplined, proud, and pampered enemy. Did we brave all then to falter now?—now, when that same enemy is wavering, dissevered, and belligerent? The result is not doubtful. We shall not fail—if we stand firm, we shall not fail. Wise counsels may accelerate or mistakes delay it, but, sooner or later, the victory is sure to come.

MR. LINCOLN'S REPLY IN THE OTTAWA JOINT DEBATE, AUGUST 21, 1858 [1]

The Illinois Senatorial campaign started out with Lincoln following Douglas around the state and delivering speeches

[1] Lincoln, *Complete Works*, III, 223-257.

in towns where Douglas had spoken. Finally Lincoln, wanting to get Douglas on the same platform with him, challenged the Senator to a series of joint debates. Douglas accepted, and the two met in seven debates, the first of which took place August 21 and the last October 15. They agreed to alternate in opening and closing each debate. The Lincoln-Douglas debates attracted national attention. Douglas was known all over the country, and Lincoln by his ability to stand up to the "Little Giant" enhanced his own reputation tremendously.

The first debate was at Ottawa, and Douglas opened. He launched a barrage of statements intended to put Lincoln on the defensive. He charged that Lincoln had made a deal with disgruntled Democrats and Whigs to break up the two old parties and form an abolition party to be called Republican. He called Lincoln's opposition to the Mexican War. He attacked the "House Divided" speech and accused Lincoln of trying to destroy the Union. He asserted that Lincoln was in favor of Negro equality.

When Lincoln got up to reply, he first read excerpts from his Peoria speech to show that he had never advocated abolitionist doctrines.

NOW, gentlemen, I don't want to read at any great length, but this is the true complexion of all I have ever said in regard to the institution of slavery and the black race. This is the whole of it, and anything that argues me into his idea of perfect social and political equality with the negro is but a specious and fantastic arrangement of words, by which a man can prove a horse-chestnut to be a chestnut horse. I will say here, while upon this subject, that I have no purpose, either directly or indirectly, to interfere with the institution of slavery in the States where it exists. I believe I have no lawful right to do so, and I have no inclination to do so. I have no purpose to introduce political and social equality between the white and the black races. There is a physical difference between the two, which, in my judgment, will probably forever forbid their living together upon the footing of perfect equality; and inasmuch as it becomes a necessity that there must be a difference, I, as well as Judge Douglas, am in favor of the race to which I belong having the superior position. I have never said anything to the contrary, but I hold that, notwithstanding all this, there is no reason in the world why the negro is not entitled to all the natural rights enumerated in the Declaration of Independence—the right to life, liberty, and the pursuit of happiness. I hold that he is as much entitled to these as the white man. I agree with Judge Douglas he is not my equal in many respects—certainly not in color, perhaps not in moral or intellectual endowment. But in the right to eat the bread, without the leave of anybody else, which his own hand earns, he is my equal and the equal of Judge Douglas, and the equal of every living man.

Now I pass on to consider one or two more of these little follies. The judge is woefully at fault about his early friend Lincoln being a "grocery-keeper." I don't know that it would be a great sin if I had been; but he is mistaken. Lincoln never kept a grocery anywhere in the world. It is true that Lincoln did work the latter part of one winter in a little still-house up at the head of a hollow. And so I think my friend, the judge, is equally at fault when he charges me at the time when I was in Congress of having opposed our soldiers who were fighting in the Mexican War. The judge did not make his charge very distinctly, but I tell you what he can prove, by referring to the record. You remember I was an Old Whig, and whenever the Democratic party tried to get me to vote that the war had been righteously begun by the President, I would not do it. But whenever they asked for any money, or land-warrants, or anything to pay the soldiers there, during all that time, I gave the same vote that Judge Douglas did. You can think as you please as to whether that was consistent. Such is the truth; and the judge has the right to make all he can out of it. But when he, by a general charge, conveys the idea that I withheld supplies from the soldiers who were fighting in the Mexican War, or did anything else to hinder the soldiers, he is, to say the least, grossly and altogether mistaken, as a consultation of the records will prove to him.

As I have not used up so much of my time as I had supposed, I will dwell a little longer upon one or two of these
minor topics upon which the judge has spoken. He has read
from my speech in Springfield in which I say that "a house
divided against itself cannot stand." Does the judge say it
can stand? I don't know whether he does or not. The judge
does not seem to be attending to me just now, but I would
like to know if it is his opinion that a house divided against
itself can stand. If he does, then there is a question of
veracity, not between him and me, but between the judge and
an authority of a somewhat higher character.

Now, my friends, I ask your attention to this matter for
the purpose of saying something seriously. I know that the
judge may readily enough agree with me that the maxim
which was put forth by the Saviour is true, but he may allege
that I misapply it; and the judge has a right to urge that in
my application I do misapply it, and then I have a right to
show that I do not misapply it. When he undertakes to say
that because I think this nation, so far as the question of
slavery is concerned, will all become one thing or all the
other, I am in favor of bringing about a dead uniformity in
the various States in all their institutions, he argues erroneously.
The great variety of the local institutions in the States, springing from differences in the soil, differences in the face of the
country, and in the climate, are bonds of union. They do
not make "a house divided against itself," but they make a
house united. If they produce in one section of the country
what is called for by the wants of another section, and this
other section can supply the wants of the first, they are not
matters of discord but bonds of union, true bonds of union.
But can this question of slavery be considered as among these
varieties in the institutions of the country? I leave it to you
to say whether, in the history of our government, this institution of slavery has not always failed to be a bond of union,
and, on the contrary, been an apple of discord and an element
of division in the house. I ask you to consider whether, so

long as the moral constitution of men's minds shall continue to be the same, after this generation and assemblage shall sink into the grave, and another race shall arise with the same moral and intellectual development we have—whether, if that institution is standing in the same irritating position in which it now is, it will not continue an element of division?

If so, then I have a right to say that, in regard to this question, the Union is a house divided against itself; and when the judge reminds me that I have often said to him that the institution of slavery has existed for eighty years in some States, and yet it does not exist in some others, I agree to the fact, and I account for it by looking at the position in which our fathers originally placed it—restricting it from the new Territories where it had not gone, and legislating to cut off its source by the abrogation of the slave-trade, thus putting the seal of legislation against its spread. The public mind did rest in the belief that it was in the course of ultimate extinction. But lately, I think—and in this I charge nothing on the judge's motives—lately, I think, that he, and those acting with him, have placed that institution on a new basis, which looks to the perpetuity and nationalization of slavery. And while it is placed upon this new basis, I say, and I have said, that I believe we shall not have peace upon the question until the opponents of slavery arrest the further spread of it, and place it where the public mind shall rest in the belief that it is in the course of ultimate extinction; or, on the other hand, that its advocates will push it forward until it shall become alike lawful in all the States, old as well as new, North as well as South. Now I believe if we could arrest the spread, and place it where Washington and Jefferson and Madison placed it, it would be in the course of ultimate extinction, and the public mind would, as for eighty years past, believe that it was in the course of ultimate extinction. The crisis would be past, and the institution might be let alone for a hundred years—if it should live so long—in the States where it exists, yet it would be going out of existence in the way best for both the black and the white races. (A voice: "Then do you repudiate popular sovereignty?") Well, then, let us talk about popular sovereignty! What is popular sovereignty? Is it the right of the people to have slavery or not have it, as they see fit, in the Territories? I will state—and I have an able man to watch me—my understanding is that popular sovereignty, as now applied to the question of slavery, does allow the people of a Territory to have slavery if they want to, but does not allow them not to have it if they do not want it. I do not mean that if this vast concourse of people were in a Territory of the United States, any one of them would be obliged to have a slave if he did not want one; but I do say that, as I understand the Dred Scott decision, if any one man wants slaves, all the rest have no way of keeping that one man from holding them.

When I made my speech at Springfield, of which the judge complains, and from which he quotes, I really was not thinking of the things which he ascribes to me at all. I had no thought in the world that I was doing anything to bring about a war between the free and slave States. I had no thought in the world that I was doing anything to bring about a political and social equality of the black and white races. It never occurred to me that I was doing anything or favoring anything to reduce to a dead uniformity all the local institutions of the various States. But I must say, in all fairness to him, if he thinks I am doing something which leads to these bad results, it is none the better that I did not mean it. It is just as fatal to the country, if I have any influence in producing it, whether I intend it or not. But can it be true, that placing this institution upon the original basis—the basis upon which our fathers placed it—can have any tendency to set the Northern and the Southern States at war with one another, or that it can have any tendency to make the people of Vermont raise sugarcane because they raise it in Louisiana, or that it can compel the people of Illinois to cut pine logs on the Grand Prairie, where they will not grow, because they cut pine logs in Maine, where they do grow? The judge says this is a new principle started in regard to this question. Does the judge claim that he is working on the plan of the founders of the government? I think he says in some of his speeches—indeed, I have one here now—that he saw evidence of a policy to allow slavery to be south of a certain line, while north of it should be excluded, and he saw an indisposition on the part of the country to stand upon that policy, and therefore he set about studying the subject upon original principles, and upon original principles he got up the Nebraska bill! I am fighting it upon these "original principles"—fighting it in the Jeffersonian, Washingtonian, and Madisonian fashion.

Now, my friends, I wish you to attend for a little while to one or two others things in that Springfield speech. My main object was to show, so far as my humble ability was capable of showing to the people of this country, what I believed was the truth—that there was a tendency, if not a conspiracy, among those who have engineered this slavery question for the last four or five years, to make slavery perpetual and universal in this nation.

* * * *

When my friend, Judge Douglas, came to Chicago on the 9th of July, this speech having been delivered on the 16th of June, he made an harangue there in which he took hold of this speech of mine, showing that he had carefully read it; and while he paid no attention to this matter at all, but complimented me as being a "kind, amiable, and intelligent gentleman," notwithstanding I had said this, he goes on and deduces, or draws out, from my speech this tendency of mine to set the States at war with one another, to make all the institutions uniform, and set the niggers and white people to marry together. Then, as the judge had complimented me with these pleasant titles (I must confess to my weakness), I was a little "taken," for it came from a great man. I was not very much accustomed to flattery, and it came the sweeter to me. I was rather like the Hoosier with the gingerbread, when he said he reckoned he loved it better than any other man, and got less of it. As the judge had so flattered me, I could not make up my mind that he meant to deal unfairly with me; so I went to work to show him that he misunderstood the whole scope of my speech, and that I really never intended to set the people at war with one another. As an illustration, the next time I met him, which was at Springfield, I used this expression, that I claimed no right under the Constitution, nor had I any inclination, to enter into the slave States and interfere with the institutions of slavery. He says upon that: Lincoln will not enter into the slave States, but will go to the banks of the Ohio, on this side, and shoot over! He runs on, step by step, in the horse-chestnut style of argument, until in the Springfield speech he says, "Unless he shall be successful in firing his batteries, until he shall have extinguished slavery in all the States, the Union shall be dissolved." Now I don't think that was exactly the way to treat "a kind, amiable, intelligent gentleman." I know if I had asked the judge to show when or where it was I had said, that if I didn't succeed in firing into the slave States until slavery should be extinguished, the Union should be dissolved, he could not have shown it. I understand what he would do. He would say, "I don't mean to quote from you, but this was the result of what you say." But I have the right to ask, and I do ask now, did you not put it in such a form that an ordinary reader or listener would take it as an expression from me?

In a speech at Springfield on the night of the 17th, I thought I might as well attend to my business a little, and I recalled his attention as well as I could to this charge of conspiracy to nationalize slavery. I called his attention to the fact that he had acknowledged in my hearing twice that he had carefully read the speech; and, in the language of the lawyers, as he had twice read the speech, and still had put in no plea or answer, I took a default on him. I insisted that I had a right then to renew that charge of conspiracy. Ten days afterward I met the judge at Clinton—that is to say, I was on the ground, but not in the discussion—and heard him make a speech. Then he comes in with his plea to this charge, for the first time, and his plea when put in, as well as I can recollect it amounted to this: that he never had any talk with Judge Taney or the President of the United States with regard to the Dred Scott decision before it was made. I (Lincoln) ought to know that the man who makes a charge without knowing it to be true, falsifies as much as he who knowingly tells a falsehood; and lastly, that he would pronounce the whole thing a falsehood; but he would make no personal application of the charge of falsehood, not because of any regard for the "kind, amiable, intelligent gentleman," but because of his own personal self-respect! I have understood since then (but [turning to Judge Douglas] will not hold the judge to it if he is not willing) that he has broken through the "self-respect," and has got to saying the thing out. The judge nods to me that it is so. It is fortunate for me that I can keep as good-humored as I do, when the judge acknowledges that he has been trying to make a question of veracity with me. I know the judge is a great man, while I am only a small man, but I feel that I have got him. I demur to that plea. I waive all objections that it was not filed till after default was taken, and demur to it upon the merits. What if Judge Douglas never did talk with Chief Justice Taney and the President before the Dred Scott decision was made; does it follow that he could not have had as perfect an understanding without talking as with it? I am not disposed to stand upon my legal advantage. I am disposed to take his denial as being like an answer in chancery, that he neither had any knowledge, information, nor belief in the existence of such a conspiracy. I am disposed to take his answer as being as broad as though he had put it in these words. And now, I ask, even if he had done so, have not I a right to prove it on him, and to offer the evidence of more than two witnesses, by whom to prove it; and if the evidence proves the existence of the conspiracy, does his broad answer, denying all knowledge, information, or belief, disturb the fact? It can only show that he was used by conspirators, and was not a leader of them.

* * * *

Now, my friends, I have but one branch of the subject, in the little time I have left, to which to call your attention, and as I shall come to a close at the end of that branch, it is probable that I shall not occupy quite all the time allotted to me.

Although on these questions I would like to talk twice as long as I have, I could not enter upon another head and discuss it properly without running over my time. I ask the attention of the people here assembled and elsewhere, to the course that Judge Douglas is pursuing every day as bearing upon this question of making slavery national. Not going back to the records, but taking the speeches he makes, the speeches he made yesterday and day before, and makes constantly all over the country—I ask your attention to them.

In the first place, what is necessary to make the institution national? Not war. There is no danger that the people of Kentucky will shoulder their muskets, and, with a young nigger stuck on every bayonet, march into Illinois and force them upon us. There is no danger of our going over there and making war upon them. Then what is necessary for the nationalization of slavery? It is simply the next Dred Scott decision. It is merely for the Supreme Court to decide that no State under the Constitution can exclude it, just as they have already decided that under the Constitution neither Congress nor the territorial legislature can do it. When that is decided and acquiesced in, the whole thing is done. This being true, and this being the way, as I think, that slavery is to be made national, let us consider what Judge Douglas is doing every day to that end. In the first place, let us see what influence he is exerting on public sentiment.

In this and like communities, public sentiment is everything. With public sentiment, nothing can fail; without it, nothing can succeed. Consequently he who molds public sentiment goes deeper than he who enacts statutes or pronounces decisions. He makes statutes and decisions possible or impossible to be executed. This must be borne in mind, as also the additional fact that Judge Douglas is a man of vast influence, so great that it is enough for many men to profess to believe anything when they once find out that Judge Douglas professes to believe it. Consider also the attitude he occupies at the head of a large party—a party which he claims has a majority of all the voters in the country.

This man sticks to a decision which forbids the people of a territory to exclude slavery, and he does so not because he says it is right in itself,—he does not give any opinion on that,—but because it has been decided by the court, and, being decided by the court, he is, and you are, bound to take it in your political action as law—not that he judges at all of its merits, but because a decision of the court is to him a "Thus saith the Lord." He places it on that ground alone, and you will bear in mind that thus committing himself unreservedly to this decision, commits him to the next one just as firmly as to this. He did not commit himself on account of the merit or demerit of the decision, but it is a "Thus saith the Lord." The next decision, as much as this, will be a "Thus saith the Lord." There is nothing that can divert or turn him away from this decision.

It is nothing that I point out to him that his great prototype, General Jackson, did not believe in the binding force of decisions. It is nothing to him that Jefferson did not so believe. I have said that I have often heard him approve of Jackson's course in disregarding the decision of the Supreme Court pronouncing a national bank constitutional. He says I did not hear him say so. He denies the accuracy of my recollection. I say he ought to know better than I, but I will make no question about this thing, though it still seems to me that I heard him say it twenty times. I will tell him though, that he now claims to stand on the Cincinnati platform, which affirms that Congress cannot charter a national bank, in the teeth of that old standing decision that Congress can charter a bank. And I remind him of another piece of history on the question of respect for judicial decisions, and it is a piece of Illinois history, belonging to a time when a large party to which Judge Douglas belonged were displeased with a decision of the Supreme Court of Illinois, because they had decided that a governor could not remove a secretary of state. You will find the whole story in Ford's "History of Illinois," and I know that Judge Douglas will not deny that he was then in favor of over-slaughing that decision by the mode of adding five new judges, so as to vote down the four old ones. Not only so, but it ended in the judge's sitting down on the very bench as one of the five new judges to break down the four old ones. It was in this way precisely that he got his title of judge.

Now, when the judge tells me that men appointed conditionally to sit as members of a court will have to be catechised beforehand upon some subject, I say, "You know, judge; you have tried it." When he says a court of this kind will lose the confidence of all men, will be prostituted and disgraced by such a proceeding, I say, "You know best, judge; you have been through the mill."

But I cannot shake Judge Douglas's teeth loose from the Dred Scott decision. Like some obstinate animal (I mean no disrespect) that will hang on when he has once got his teeth fixed,—you may cut off a leg, or you may tear away an arm, still he will not relax his hold. And so I may point out to the judge, and say that he is bespattered all over, from the beginning of his political life to the present time, with attacks upon judicial decisions,—I may cut off limb after limb of his public record, and strive to wrench from him a single dictum of the court, yet I cannot divert him from it. He hangs to the last to the Dred Scott decision. These things show there is a purpose strong as death and eternity for which he adheres to this decision, and for which he will adhere to all other decisions of the same court. (A Hibernian: "Give us something besides Drid Scott.") Yes; no doubt you want to hear something that don't hurt. Now, having spoken of the Dred Scott decision, one more word and I am done.

Henry Clay,[1] my beau ideal of a statesman, the man for whom I fought all my humble life—Henry Clay once said of a class of men who would repress all tendencies to liberty and ultimate emancipation, that they must, if they would do this, go back to the era of our independence, and muzzle the cannon which thunders its annual joyous return; they must blow out the moral lights around us; they must penetrate the human soul, and eradicate there the love of liberty; and then, and not till then, could they perpetuate slavery in this country! To my thinking, Judge Douglas is, by his example and vast influence, doing that very thing in this community when he says that the negro has nothing in the Declaration of Independence. Henry Clay plainly understood the contrary. Judge Douglas is going back to the era of our Revolution, and to the extent of his ability muzzling the cannon which thunders its annual joyous return. When he invites any people, willing to have slavery, to establish it, he is blowing out the moral lights around us. When he says he "cares not whether slavery is voted down or voted up"—that it is a sacred right of self-government—he is, in my judgment, penetrating the human soul and eradicating the light of reason and the love of liberty in this American people.

And now I will only say that when, by all these means and appliances, Judge Douglas shall succeed in bringing public sentiment to an exact accordance with his own views—when these vast assemblages shall echo back all these sentiments—when they shall come to repeat his views and to avow his principles, and to say all that he says on these mighty questions—then it needs only the formality of the second Dred Scott decision, which he indorses in advance, to make slavery alike lawful in all the States—old as well as new, North as well as South.

---

[1] Henry Clay of Kentucky, one of the leaders of the old Whig party.

My friends, that ends the chapter. The judge can take his half hour.

***

MR. LINCOLN'S OPENING SPEECH IN THE SIXTH JOINT DEBATE, AT QUINCY, OCTOBER 13, 1858 [1]

> In the debates with Douglas are to be found the fullest expressions of Lincoln's views on slavery and the slavery controversy. He presented a clear-cut summary of his position at Quincy, where he opened the debate.

WE have in this nation the element of domestic slavery. It is a matter of absolute certainty that it is a disturbing element. It is the opinion of all the great men who have expressed an opinion upon it, that it is a dangerous element. We keep up a controversy in regard to it. That controversy necessarily springs from difference of opinion, and if we can learn exactly—can reduce to the lowest elements—what that difference of opinion is, we perhaps shall be better prepared for discussing the different systems of policy that we would propose in regard to that disturbing element. I suggest that the difference of opinion, reduced to its lowest terms, is no other than the difference between the men who think slavery a wrong and those who do not think it wrong. The Republican party think it wrong—we think it is a moral, a social, and a political wrong. We think it is a wrong not confining itself merely to the persons or the States where it exists, but that it is a wrong which in its tendency, to say the least, affects the existence of the whole nation. Because we think it wrong, we propose a course of policy that shall deal with it as a wrong. We deal with it as with any other wrong, in so far as we can prevent its growing any larger, and so deal with it that in the run of time there may be some promise of an end to it. We have a due regard to the actual presence of it

---

[1] Lincoln, *Complete Works,* IV, 311-334.

amongst us, and the difficulties of getting rid of it in any satisfactory way, and all the constitutional obligations thrown about it. I suppose that in reference both to its actual existence in the nation, and to our constitutional obligations, we have no right at all to disturb it in the States where it exists, and we profess that we have no more inclination to disturb it than we have the right to do it. We go further than that: we don't propose to disturb it where, in one instance, we think the Constitution would permit us. We think the Constitution would permit us to disturb it in the District of Columbia. Still we do not propose to do that, unless it should be in terms which I don't suppose the nation is very likely soon to agree to—the terms of making the emanicipation gradual and compensating the unwilling owners. Where we suppose we have the constitutional right, we restrain ourselves in reference to the actual existence of the institution and the difficulties thrown about it. We also oppose it as an evil so far as it seeks to spread itself. We insist on the policy that shall restrict it to its present limits. We don't suppose that in doing this we violate anything due to the actual presence of the institution, or anything due to the constitutional guaranties thrown around it.

We oppose the Dred Scott decision in a certain way, upon which I ought perhaps to address you a few words. We do not propose that when Dred Scott has been decided to be a slave by the court, we, as a mob, will decide him to be free. We do not propose that, when any other one, or one thousand, shall be decided by that court to be slaves, we will in any violent way disturb the rights of property thus settled; but we nevertheless do oppose that decision as a political rule, which shall be binding on the voter to vote for nobody who thinks it wrong, which shall be binding on the members of Congress or the President to favor no measure that does not actually concur with the principles of that decision. We do not propose to be bound by it as a political rule in that way, because we think it lays the foundation not merely of enlarging and spreading out what we consider an evil, but it lays the foundation for spreading that evil into the States themselves. We propose so resisting it as to have it reversed if we can, and a new judicial rule established upon this subject.

I will add this, that if there be any man who does not believe that slavery is wrong in the three aspects which I have mentioned, or in any one of them, that man is misplaced and ought to leave us. While, on the other hand, if there be any man in the Republican party who is impatient over the necessity springing from its actual presence, and is impatient of the constitutional guaranties thrown around it, and would act in disregard of these, he too is misplaced, standing with us. He will find his place somewhere else; for we have a due regard, so far as we are capable of understanding them, for all these things. This, gentlemen, as I can give it, is a plain statement of our principles in all their enormity.

I will say now that there is a sentiment in the country contrary to me—a sentiment which holds that slavery is not wrong, and therefore it goes for the policy that does not propose dealing with it as a wrong. That policy is the Democratic policy, and that sentiment is the Democratic sentiment. If there be a doubt in the mind of any one of this vast audience that this is really the central idea of the Democratic party, in relation to this subject, I ask him to bear with me while I state a few things tending, as I think, to prove that proposition. In the first place, the leading man—I think I may do my friend Judge Douglas the honor of calling him such—advocating the present Democratic policy never himself says it is wrong. He has the high distinction, so far as I know, of never having said slavery is either right or wrong. Almost everybody else says one or the other but the judge never does. If there be a man in the Democratic party who thinks it is wrong, and yet clings to that party, I suggest to him in the first place that his leader don't talk as he does, for he never says that it is wrong. In the second place, I suggest to him that if he will examine the policy proposed to be carried forward, he will find that he carefully excludes the idea that there is anything wrong in it. If you will examine the arguments that are made on it, you will find that every one carefully excludes the idea that there is anything wrong in slavery. Perhaps that Democrat who says he is as much opposed to slavery as I am, will tell me that I am wrong about this. I wish him to examine his own course in regard to this matter a moment, and then see if his opinion will not be changed a little. You say it is wrong; but don't you constantly object to anybody else saying so? Do you not constantly argue that this is not the right place to oppose it? You say it must not be opposed in the free States, because slavery is not there; it must not be opposed in the slave States, because it is there; it must not be opposed in politics, because that will make a fuss; it must not be opposed in the pulpit, because it is not religion. Then where is the place to oppose it? There is no suitable place to oppose it. There is no plan in the country to oppose this evil overspreading the continent, which you say yourself is coming. Frank Blair and Gratz Brown tried to get up a system of gradual emancipation in Missouri, had an election in August, and got beat; and you, Mr. Democrat, threw up your hat and hallooed, "Hurrah for Democracy!"

So I say again, that in regard to the arguments that are made, when Judge Douglas says he "don't care whether slavery is voted up or down," whether he means that as an individual expression of sentiment, or only as a sort of statement of his views on national policy, it is alike true to say that he can thus argue logically if he don't see anything wrong in it; but he cannot say so logically if he admits that slavery is wrong. He cannot say that he would as soon see a wrong voted up as voted down. When Judge Douglas says that whoever or whatever community wants slaves, they have a right to have them, he is perfectly logical if there is nothing wrong in the institution; but if you admit that it is wrong, he cannot logically say that anybody has a right to do wrong. When he says that slave property and horse and hog property are alike to be allowed to go into the Territories, upon the principles of equality, he is reasoning truly if there is no difference between them as property; but if the one is property, held rightfully, and the other is wrong, then there is no equality between the right and wrong; so that, turn it in any way you can, in all the arguments sustaining the Democratic policy, and in that policy itself, there is a careful, studied exclusion of the idea that there is anything wrong in slavery. Let us understand this. I am not, just here, trying to prove that we are right and they are wrong. I have been stating where we and they stand, and trying to show what is the real difference between us; and I now can say that whenever we can get the question distinctly stated,—can get all these men who believe that slavery is in some of these respects wrong to stand and act with us in treating it as a wrong,—then, and not till then, I think, will we in some way come to an end of this slavery agitation.

ANNUAL ADDRESS BEFORE THE WISCONSIN STATE AGRICULTURAL SOCIETY, AT MILWAUKEE, WISCONSIN, SEPTEMBER 30, 1859 [1]

This address is Lincoln's most complete statement of the place of labor in the capitalistic system and of his favorite theory that hired labor had no fixed condition in life.

* * * *

THE world is agreed that labor is the source from which human wants are mainly supplied. There is no dispute upon this point. From this point, however, men immediately diverge. Much disputation is maintained as to the best way of applying and controlling the labor element. By some it is assumed that labor is available only in connection with capital —that nobody labors, unless somebody else owning capital,

---

[1] Lincoln, *Complete Works*, V, 236-256.

somehow, by the use of it, induces him to do it. Having assumed this, they proceed to consider whether it is best that capital shall hire laborers, and thus induce them to work by their own consent, or buy them, and drive them to it, without their consent. Having proceeded so far, they naturally conclude that all laborers are naturally either hired laborers or slaves. They further assume that whoever is once a hired laborer, is fatally fixed in that condition for life; and thence again, that his condition is as bad as, or worse than, that of a slave. This is the "mud-sill" theory.[1] But another class of reasoners hold the opinion that there is no such relation between capital and labor as assumed; that there is no such thing as a free man being fatally fixed for life in the condition of a hired laborer; that both these assumptions are false, and all inferences from them groundless. They hold that labor is prior to, and independent of, capital; that, in fact, capital is the fruit of labor, and could never have existed if labor had not first existed; that labor can exist without capital, but that capital could never have existed without labor. Hence they hold that labor is the superior—greatly the superior—of capital.

They do not deny that there is, and probably always will be, a relation between labor and capital. The error, as they hold, is in assuming that the whole labor of the world exists within that relation. A few men own capital; and that few avoid labor themselves, and with their capital hire or buy another few to labor for them. A large majority belong to neither class—neither work for others, nor have others working for them. Even in all our slave States except South Carolina, a majority of the whole people of all colors are neither slaves nor masters. In these free States, a large majority are neither hirers nor hired. Men, with their families—wives, sons and daughters—work for themselves, on their farms, in their houses, and in their shops, taking the whole product to themselves, and asking no favors of capital on the one hand, nor

---

[1] A Southern defender of slavery had declared that unskilled labor, the "mud-sill" type, could only be performed by slaves or by hired workers controlled by the employers.

of hirelings or slaves on the other. It is not forgotten that a considerable number of persons mingle their own labor with capital—that is, labor with their own hands and also buy slaves or hire free men to labor for them; but this is only a mixed, and not a distinct, class. No principle stated is disturbed by the existence of this mixed class. Again, as has already been said, the opponents of the "mud-sill" theory insist that there is not, of necessity, any such thing as the free hired laborer being fixed to that condition for life. There is demonstration for saying this. Many independent men in this assembly doubtless a few years ago were hired laborers. And their case is almost, if not quite, the general rule.

The prudent, penniless beginner in the world labors for wages awhile, saves a surplus with which to buy tools or land for himself, then labors on his own account another while, and at length hires another new beginner to help him. This, say its advocates, is free labor—the just, and generous, and prosperous system, which opens the way for all, gives hope to all, and energy, and progress, and improvement of condition to all. If any continue through life in the condition of the hired laborer, it is not the fault of the system, but because of either a dependent nature which prefers it, or improvidence, folly, or singular misfortune. I have said this much about the elements of labor generally, as introductory to the consideration of a new phase which that element is in process of assuming. The old general rule was that educated people did not perform manual labor. They managed to eat their bread, leaving the toil of producing it to the uneducated. This was not an insupportable evil to the working bees, so long as the class of drones remained very small. But now, especially in these free States, nearly all are educated—quite too nearly all to leave the labor of the uneducated in any wise adequate to the support of the whole. It follows from this that henceforth educated people must labor. Otherwise, education itself would become a positive and intolerable evil. No country can sustain in idleness more than a small percentage of its numbers. The great majority must labor at something productive. From these premises the problem springs, "How can labor and education be the most satisfactorily combined?"

By the "mud-sill" theory it is assumed that labor and education are incompatible, and any practical combination of them impossible. According to that theory, a blind horse upon a tread-mill is a perfect illustration of what a laborer should be —all the better for being blind, that he could not kick understandingly. According to that theory, the education of laborers is not only useless but pernicious and dangerous. In fact, it is, in some sort, deemed a misfortune that laborers should have heads at all. Those same heads are regarded as explosive materials, only to be safely kept in damp places, as far as possible from that peculiar sort of fire which ignites them. A Yankee who could invent a strong-handed man without a head would receive the everlasting gratitude of the "mud-sill" advocates.

But free labor says, "No." Free labor argues that as the Author of man makes every individual with one head and one pair of hands, it was probably intended that heads and hands should cooperate as friends, and that that particular head should direct and control that pair of hands. As each man has one mouth to be fed, and one pair of hands to furnish food, it was probably intended that that particular pair of hands should feed that particular mouth—that each head is the natural guardian, director, and protector of the hands and mouth inseparably connected with it; and that being so, every head should be cultivated and improved by whatever will add to its capacity for performing its charge. In one word, free labor insists on universal education.

I have so far stated the opposite theories of "mud-sill" and "free-labor," without declaring any preference of my own between them. On an occasion like this, I ought not to declare any. I suppose, however, I shall not be mistaken in assuming as a fact that the people of Wisconsin prefer free labor, with its natural companion, education.

This leads to the further reflection that no other human occupation opens so wide a field for the profitable and agreeable combination of labor with cultivated thought, as agriculture. I know nothing so pleasant to the mind as the discovery of anything that is at once new and valuable—nothing that so lightens and sweetens toil as the hopeful pursuit of such discovery. And how vast and how varied a field is agriculture for such discovery! The mind, already trained to thought in the country school, or higher school, cannot fail to find there an exhaustless source of enjoyment. Every blade of grass is a study; and to produce two where there was but one is both a profit and a pleasure. And not grass alone, but soils, seeds, and seasons,—hedges, ditches, and fences—draining, droughts, and irrigation—plowing, hoeing, and harrowing—reaping, mowing, and threshing—saving crops, pests of crops, diseases of crops, and what will prevent or cure them—implements, utensils, and machines, their relative merits, and how to improve them—hogs, horses, and cattle—sheep, goats, and poultry—trees, shrubs, fruits, plants, and flowers—the thousand things of which these are specimens—each a world of study within itself.

In all this, book-learning is available. A capacity and taste for reading gives access to whatever has already been discovered by others. It is the key, or one of the keys, to the already solved problems. And not only so: it gives a relish and facility for successfully pursuing the unsolved ones. The rudiments of science are available, and highly available. Some knowledge of botany assists in dealing with the vegetable world—with all growing crops. Chemistry assists in the analysis of soils, selection and application of manures, and in numerous other ways. The mechanical branches of natural philosophy are ready help in almost everything, but especially in reference to implements and machinery.

The thought recurs that education—cultivated thought—can best be combined with agricultural labor, or any labor, on the principle of thorough work; that careless, half performed, slovenly work makes no place for such combination; and thorough work, again, renders sufficient the smallest quantity of ground to each man; and this, again, conforms to what must occur in a world less inclined to wars and more devoted to the arts of peace than heretofore. Population must increase rapidly, more rapidly than in former times, and ere long the most valuable of all arts will be the art of deriving a comfortable subsistence from the smallest area of soil. No community whose every member possesses this art, can ever be the victim of oppression in any of its forms. Such community will be alike independent of crowned kings, money kings, and land kings.

*   *   *   *

_____

ADDRESS AT COOPER INSTITUTE, NEW YORK, FEBRUARY 27, 1860[1]

In 1860 Lincoln was invited to speak in the East. The address he delivered at Cooper Institute, New York, was perhaps Lincoln's most considered statement of his views on the slavery issue. It has rightly been ranked as one of his greatest pieces of political argumentation. In this speech he made a particular effort to disassociate the Republican party from any connection with abolitionists of the stripe of John Brown.

M R. President and Fellow-Citizens of New York: The facts with which I shall deal this evening are mainly old and familiar; nor is there anything new in the general use I shall make of them. If there shall be any novelty, it will be in the mode of presenting the facts, and the inferences and observations following that presentation. In his speech last autumn at Columbus, Ohio, as reported in the "New-York Times," Senator Douglas said:

Our fathers, when they framed the government under

_____
[1] Lincoln, *Complete Works*, V, 293-328.

which we live, understood this question just as well, and even better, than we do now.

I fully indorse this, and I adopt it as a text for this discourse. I so adopt it because it furnishes a precise and an agreed starting-point for a discussion between Republicans and that wing of the Democracy headed by Senator Douglas. It simply leaves the inquiry: What was the understanding those fathers had of the question mentioned?

What is the frame of government under which we live? The answer must be, "The Constitution of the United States." That Constitution consists of the original, framed in 1787, and under which the present government first went into operation, and twelve subsequently framed amendments, the first ten of which were framed in 1789.

Who were our fathers that framed the Constitution? I suppose the "thirty-nine" who signed the original instrument may be fairly called our fathers who framed that part of the present government. It is almost exactly true to say they framed it, and it is altogether true to say they fairly represented the opinion and sentiment of the whole nation at that time. Their names, being familiar to nearly all, and accessible to quite all, need not now be repeated.

I take these "thirty-nine," for the present, as being "our fathers who framed the government under which we live." What is the question which, according to the text, those fathers understood "just as well, and even better, than we do now"?

It is this: Does the proper division of local from Federal authority, or anything in the Constitution, forbid our Federal Government to control as to slavery in our Federal Territories?

Upon this, Senator Douglas holds the affirmative, and Republicans the negative. This affirmation and denial form an issue; and this issue—this question—is precisely what the text declares our fathers understood "better than we." Let us now inquire whether the "thirty-nine," or any of them, ever acted upon this question; and if they did, how they acted upon it— how they expressed that better understanding. In 1784, three years before the Constitution, the United States then owning the Northwestern Territory, and no other, the Congress of the Confederation had before them the question of prohibiting slavery in that Territory; and four of the "thirty-nine" who afterward framed the Constitution were in that Congress, and voted on that question. Of these, Roger Sherman, Thomas Mifflin, and Hugh Williamson voted for the prohibition, thus showing that, in their understanding, no line dividing local from Federal authority, nor anything else, properly forbade the Federal Government to control as to slavery in Federal territory. The other of the four, James McHenry, voted against the prohibition, showing that for some cause he thought it improper to vote for it.

In 1787, still before the Constitution, but while the convention was in session framing it, and while the Northwestern Territory still was the only Territory owned by the United States, the same question of prohibiting slavery in the Territory again came before the Congress of the Confederation; and two more of the "thirty-nine" who afterward signed the Constitution were in that Congress, and voted on the question. They were William Blount and William Few; and they both voted for the prohibition—thus showing that in their understanding no line dividing local from Federal authority, nor anything else, properly forbade the Federal Government to control as to slavery in Federal territory. This time the prohibition became a law, being part of what is now well known as the ordinance of '87.

The question of Federal control of slavery in the Territories seems not to have been directly before the convention which framed the original Constitution; and hence it is not recorded that the "thirty-nine," or any of them, while engaged on that instrument, expressed any opinion on that precise question.

In 1789, by the first Congress which sat under the Constitution, an act was passed to enforce the ordinance of '87, including the prohibition of slavery in the Northwestern Territory. The bill for this act was reported by one of the "thirty-nine"—Thomas Fitzsimmons, then a member of the House of Representatives from Pennsylvania. It went through all its stages without a word of opposition, and finally passed both branches without ayes and nays, which is equivalent to a unanimous passage. In this Congress there were sixteen of the thirty-nine fathers who framed the original Constitution. They were John Langdon, Nicholas Gilman, Wm. S. Johnson, Roger Sherman, Robert Morris, Thos. Fitzsimmons, William Few, Abraham Baldwin, Rufus King, William Paterson, George Clymer, Richard Bassett, George Read, Pierce Butler, Daniel Carroll and James Madison.

This shows that, in their understanding, no line dividing local from Federal authority, nor anything in the Constitution, properly forbade Congress to prohibit slavery in the Federal territory; else both their fidelity to correct principle, and their oath to support the Constitution, would have constrained them to oppose the prohibition.

Again, George Washington, another of the "thirty-nine," was then President of the United States and as such approved and signed the bill, thus completing its validity as a law, and thus showing that, in his understanding, no line dividing local from Federal authority, nor anything in the Constitution, forbade the Federal Government to control as to slavery in Federal territory.

No great while after the adoption of the original Constitution, North Carolina ceded to the Federal Government the country now constituting the State of Tennessee; and a few years later Georgia ceded that which now constitutes the States of Mississippi and Alabama. In both deeds of cession it was made a condition by the ceding States that the Federal Government should not prohibit slavery in the ceded country. Besides this, slavery was then actually in the ceded country. Under these circumstances, Congress, on taking charge of these countries, did not absolutely prohibit slavery within them. But they did interfere with it—take control of it—even there, to a certain extent. In 1798 Congress organized the Territory of

Mississippi. In the act of organization they prohibited the bringing of slaves into the Territory from any place without the United States, by fine, and giving freedom to slaves so brought. This act passed both branches of Congress without yeas and nays. In that Congress were three of the "thirty-nine" who framed the original Constitution. They were John Langdon, George Read, and Abraham Baldwin. They all probably voted for it. Certainly they would have placed their opposition to it upon record if, in their understanding, any line dividing local from Federal authority, or anything in the Constitution, properly forbade the Federal Government to control as to slavery in Federal territory.

In 1803 the Federal Government purchased the Louisiana country. Our former territorial acquisitions came from certain of our own States; but this Louisiana country was acquired from a foreign nation. In 1804 Congress gave a territorial organization to that part of it which now constitutes the State of Louisiana. New Orleans, lying within that part, was an old and comparatively large city. There were other considerable towns and settlements, and slavery was extensively and thoroughly intermingled with the people. Congress did not, in the Territorial Act, prohibit slavery; but they did interfere with it—take control of it—in a more marked and extensive way than they did in the case of Mississippi. The substance of the provision therein made in relation to slaves was:

1st. That no slave should be imported into the Territory from foreign parts.

2d. That no slave should be carried into it who had been imported into the United States since the first day of May, 1798.

3d. That no slave should be carried into it, except by the owner, and for his own use as a settler; the penalty in all the cases being a fine upon the violator of the law, and freedom to the slave.

This act also was passed without ayes or nays. In the Congress which passed it there were two of the "thirty-nine."

They were Abraham Baldwin and Jonathan Dayton. As stated in the case of Mississippi, it is probable they both voted for it. They would not have allowed it to pass without recording their opposition to it if, in their understanding, it violated either the line properly dividing local from Federal authority, or any provision of the Constitution.

In 1819-20 came and passed the Missouri question. Many votes were taken, by yeas and nays, in both branches of Congress, upon the various phases of the general question. Two of the "thirty-nine"—Rufus King and Charles Pinckney—were members of that Congress. Mr. King steadily voted for slavery prohibition and against all compromises, while Mr. Pinckney as steadily voted against slavery prohibition and against all compromises. By this, Mr. King showed that, in his understanding, no line dividing local from Federal authority, nor anything in the Constitution, was violated by Congress prohibiting slavery in Federal Territory; while Mr. Pinckney, by his votes, showed that, in his understanding, there was some sufficient reason for opposing such prohibition in that case.

The cases I have mentioned are the only acts of the "thirty-nine," or of any of them, upon the direct issue, which I have been able to discover.

To enumerate the persons who thus acted as being four in 1784, two in 1787, seventeen in 1789, three in 1798, two in 1804, and two in 1819-20, there would be thirty of them. But this would be counting John Langdon, Roger Sherman, William Few, Rufus King, and George Read each twice, and Abraham Baldwin three times. The true number of those of the "thirty-nine" whom I have shown to have acted upon the question which, by the text, they understood better than we, is twenty-three, leaving sixteen not shown to have acted upon it in any way.

Here, then, we have twenty-three out of our thirty-nine fathers "who framed the government under which we live," who have, upon their official responsibility and their corporal oaths, acted upon the very question which the text affirms they "understood just as well, and even better, than we do now"; and twenty-one of them—a clear majority of the whole "thirty-nine"—so acting upon it as to make them guilty of gross political impropriety and wilful perjury if, in their understanding, any proper division between local and Federal authority, or anything in the Constitution they had made themselves, and sworn to support, forbade the Federal Government to control as to slavery in the Federal Territories. Thus the twenty-one acted; and, as actions speak louder than words, so actions under such responsibility speak still louder.

Two of the twenty-three voted against congressional prohibition of slavery in the Federal Territories, in the instances in which they acted upon the question. But for what reasons they so voted is not known. They may have done so because they thought a proper division of local from Federal authority, or some provision or principle of the Constitution, stood in the way; or they may, without any such question, have voted against the prohibition on what appeared to them to be sufficient grounds of expediency. No one who has sworn to support the Constitution can conscientiously vote for what he understands to be an unconstitutional measure, however expedient he may think it; but one may and ought to vote against a measure which he deems constitutional if, at the same time, he deems it inexpedient. It, therefore, would be unsafe to set down even the two who voted against the prohibition as having done so because, in their understanding, any proper division of local from Federal authority, or anything in the Constitution, forbade the Federal Government to control as to slavery in Federal territory.

The remaining sixteen of the "thirty-nine," so far as I have discovered, have left no record of their understanding upon the direct question of Federal control of slavery in the Federal Territories. But there is much reason to believe that their understanding upon that question would not have appeared different from that of their twenty-three compeers, had it been manifested at all.

For the purpose of adhering rigidly to the text, I have purposely omitted whatever understanding may have been manifested by any person, however distinguished, other than the thirty-nine fathers who framed the original Constitution; and, for the same reason, I have also omitted whatever understanding may have been manifested by any of the "thirty-nine" even on any other phase of the general question of slavery. If we should look into their acts and declarations on those other phases, as the foreign slave-trade, and the morality and policy of slavery generally, it would appear to us that on the direct question of Federal control of slavery in Federal Territories, the sixteen, if they had acted at all, would probably have acted just as the twenty-three did. Among that sixteen were several of the most noted antislavery men of those times,—as Dr. Franklin, Alexander Hamilton, and Gouverneur Morris,—while there was not one now known to have been otherwise, unless it may be John Rutledge, of South Carolina.

The sum of the whole is that of our thirty-nine fathers who framed the original Constitution, twenty-one—a clear majority of the whole—certainly understood that no proper division of local from Federal authority, nor any part of the Constitution, forbade the Federal Government to control slavery in the Federal Territories; while all the rest had probably the same understanding. Such, unquestionably, was the understanding of our fathers who framed the original Constitution; and the text affirms that they understood the question "better than we."

But, so far, I have been considering the understanding of the question manifested by the framers of the original Constitution. In and by the original instrument, a mode was provided for amending it; and, as I have already stated, the present frame of "the government under which we live" consists of that original, and twelve amendatory articles framed and adopted since. Those who now insist that Federal control of slavery in Federal Territories violates the Constitution, point us to the provisions which they suppose it thus violates; and, as I understand, they all fix upon provisions in these amendatory articles, and not in the original instrument. The Supreme Court, in the Dred Scott case, plant themselves upon the Fifth Amendment, which provides that no person shall be deprived of "life, liberty, or property without due process of law"; while Senator Douglas and his peculiar adherents plant themselves upon the Tenth Amendment, providing that "the powers not delegated to the United States by the Constitution" "are reserved to the States respectively, or to the people."

Now, it so happens that these amendments were framed by the first Congress which sat under the Constitution—the identical Congress which passed the act, already mentioned, enforcing the prohibition of slavery in the Northwestern Territory. Not only was it the same Congress, but they were the identical, same individual men who, at the same session, and at the same time within the session, had under consideration, and in progress toward maturity, these constitutional amendments, and this act prohibiting slavery in all the territory the nation then owned. The constitutional amendments were introduced before, and passed after, the act enforcing the ordinance of '87; so that, during the whole pendency of the act to enforce the ordinance, the constitutional amendments were also pending.

The seventy-six members of that Congress, including sixteen of the framers of the original Constitution, as before stated, were preeminently our fathers who framed that part of "the government under which we live" which is now claimed as forbidding the Federal Government to control slavery in the Federal Territories.

Is it not a little presumptuous in any one at this day to affirm that the two things which that Congress deliberately framed, and carried to maturity at the same time, are absolutely inconsistent with each other? And does not such affirmation become impudently absurd when coupled with the other affirmation, from the same mouth, that those who did the two things alleged to be inconsistent, understood whether they really were inconsistent better than we—better than he who affirms that they are inconsistent?

It is surely safe to assume that the thirty-nine framers of the original Constitution, and the seventy-six members of the Congress which framed the amendments thereto, taken together, do certainly include those who may be fairly called "our fathers who framed the government under which we live." And so assuming, I defy any man to show that any one of them ever, in his whole life, declared that, in his understanding, any proper division of local from Federal authority, or any part of the Constitution, forbade the Federal Government to control as to slavery in the Federal Territories. I go a step further. I defy any one to show that any living man in the whole world ever did, prior to the beginning of the present century (and I might almost say prior to the beginning of the last half of the present century), declare that, in his understanding, any proper division of local from Federal authority, or any part of the Constitution, forbade the Federal Government to control as to slavery in the Federal Territories. To those who now so declare I give not only "our fathers who framed the government under which we live," but with them all other living men within the century in which it was framed, among whom to search, and they shall not be able to find the evidence of a single man agreeing with them.

Now, and here, let me guard a little against being misunderstood. I do not mean to say we are bound to follow implicitly in whatever our fathers did. To do so would be to discard all the lights of current experience—to reject all progress, all improvement. What I do say is that if we would supplant the opinions and policy of our fathers in any case, we should do so upon evidence so conclusive, and argument so clear, that even their great authority, fairly considered and weighed, cannot stand; and most surely not in a case whereof we ourselves declare they understood the question better than we.

If any man at this day sincerely believes that a proper division of local from Federal authority, or any part of the Constitution, forbids the Federal Government to control as to slavery in the Federal Territories, he is right to say so, and to enforce his position by all truthful evidence and fair argument which he can. But he has no right to mislead others, who have less access to history, and less leisure to study it, into the false belief that "our fathers who framed the government under which we live" were of the same opinion—thus substituting falsehood and deception for truthful evidence and fair argument. If any man at this day sincerely believes "our fathers who framed the government under which we live" used and applied principles, in other cases, which ought to have led them to understand that a proper division of local from Federal authority, or some part of the Constitution, forbids the Federal Government to control as to slavery in the Federal Territories, he is right to say so. But he should, at the same time, brave the responsibility of declaring that, in his opinion, he understands their principles better than they did themselves; and especially should he not shirk that responsibility by asserting that they "understood the question just as well, and even better, than we do now."

But enough! Let all who believe that "our fathers who framed the government under which we live understood this question just as well, and even better, than we do now," speak as they spoke, and act as they acted upon it. This is all Republicans ask—all Republicans desire—in relation to slavery. As those fathers marked it, so let it be again marked, as an evil not to be extended, but to be tolerated and protected only because of and so far as its actual presence among us makes that toleration and protection a necessity. Let all the guaranties those fathers gave it be not grudgingly, but fully and fairly, maintained. For this Republicans contend, and with this, so far as I know or believe, they will be content.

And now, if they would listen,—as I suppose they will not, —I would address a few words to the Southern people.

I would say to them: You consider yourselves a reasonable

and a just people; and I consider that in the general qualities of reason and justice you are not inferior to any other people. Still, when you speak of us Republicans, you do so only to denounce us as reptiles, or, at the best, as no better than out-laws. You will grant a hearing to pirates or murderers, but nothing like it to "Black Republicans." In all your contentions with one another, each of you deems an unconditional con-demnation of "Black Republicanism" as the first thing to be attended to. Indeed, such condemnation of us seems to be an indispensable prerequisite—license, so to speak—among you to be admitted or permitted to speak at all. Now can you or not be prevailed upon to pause and to consider whether this is quite just to us, or even to yourselves? Bring forward your charges and specifications, and then be patient long enough to hear us deny or justify.

You say we are sectional. We deny it. That makes an issue; and the burden of proof is upon you. You produce your proof; and what is it? Why, that our party has no existence in your section—gets no votes in your section. The fact is sub-stantially true; but does it prove the issue? If it does, then in case we should, without change of principle, begin to get votes in your section, we should thereby cease to be sectional. You cannot escape this conclusion; and yet, are you willing to abide by it? If you are, you will probably soon find that we have ceased to be sectional, for we shall get votes in your sec-tion this very year. You will then begin to discover, as the truth plainly is, that your proof does not touch the issue. The fact that we get no votes in your section is a fact of your making, and not of ours. And if there be fault in that fact, that fault is primarily yours, and remains so until you show that we repel you by some wrong principle or practice. If we do repel you by any wrong principle or practice, the fault is ours; but this brings you to where you ought to have started —to a discussion of the right or wrong of our principle. If our principle, put in practice, would wrong your section for the benefit of ours, or for any other object, then our principle, and we with it, are sectional, and are justly opposed and denounced as such. Meet us, then, on the question of whether our principle, put in practice, would wrong your section; and so meet us as if it were possible that something may be said on our side. Do you accept the challenge? No! Then you really believe that the principle which "our fathers who framed the government under which we live" thought so clearly right as to adopt it, and indorse it again and again, upon their official oaths, is in fact so clearly wrong as to demand your condemnation without a moment's consideration.

Some of you delight to flaunt in our faces the warning against sectional parties given by Washington in his Farewell Address. Less than eight years before Washington gave that warning, he had, as President of the United States, approved and signed an act of Congress enforcing the prohibition of slavery in the Northwestern Territory, which act embodied the policy of the government upon that subject up to and at the very moment he penned that warning; and about one year after he penned it, he wrote Lafayette that he considered that prohibition a wise measure, expressing in the same connection his hope that we should at some time have a confederacy of free States.

Bearing this in mind, and seeing that sectionalism has since arisen upon this same subject, is that warning a weapon in your hands against us, or in our hands against you? Could Washington himself speak, would he cast the blame of that sectionalism upon us, who sustain his policy, or upon you, who repudiate it? We respect that warning of Washington, and we commend it to you, together with his example pointing to the right application of it.

But you say you are conservative—eminently conservative— while we are revolutionary, destructive, or something of the sort. What is conservatism? Is it not adherence to the old and tried, against the new and untried? We stick to, contend for, the identical old policy on the point in controversy which was adopted by "our fathers who framed the government under which we live"; while you with one accord reject, and scout, and spit upon that old policy, and insist upon substituting something new. True, you disagree among yourselves as to what that substitute shall be. You are divided on new propositions and plans, but you are unanimous in rejecting and denouncing the old policy of the fathers. Some of you are for reviving the foreign slave-trade; some for a congressional slave code for the Territories; some for Congress forbidding the Territories to prohibit slavery within their limits; some for maintaining slavery in the Territories through the judiciary; some for the "gur-reat pur-rinciple" that "if one man would enslave another, no third man should object," fantastically called "popular sovereignty"; but never a man among you is in favor of Federal prohibition of slavery in Federal Territories, according to the practice of "our fathers who framed the government under which we live." Not one of all your various plans can show a precedent or an advocate in the century within which our government originated. Consider, then, whether your claim of conservatism for yourselves, and your charge of destructiveness against us, are based on the most clear and stable foundations.

Again, you say we have made the slavery question more prominent than it formerly was. We deny it. We admit that it is more prominent, but we deny that we made it so. It was not we, but you, who discarded the old policy of the fathers. We resisted, and still resist, your innovation; and thence comes the greater prominence of the question. Would you have that question reduced to its former proportions? Go back to that old policy. What has been will be again, under the same conditions. If you would have the peace of the old times, readopt the precepts and policy of the old times.

You charge that we stir up insurrections among your slaves. We deny it; and what is your proof? Harper's Ferry! John Brown!![1] John Brown was no Republican; and you have failed

[1] John Brown and a small group of abolitionists seized the federal arsenal at Harper's Ferry, Virginia, and tried to instigate a slave rebellion. He was captured and executed.

to implicate a single Republican in his Harper's Ferry enterprise. If any member of our party is guilty in that matter, you know it, or you do not know it. If you do know it, you are inexcusable for not designating the man and proving the fact. If you do not know it, you are inexcusable for asserting it, and especially for persisting in the assertion after you have tried and failed to make the proof. You need not be told that persisting in a charge which one does not know to be true, is simply malicious slander.

Some of you admit that no Republican designedly aided or encouraged the Harper's Ferry affair, but still insist that our doctrines and declarations necessarily lead to such results. We do not believe it. We know we hold no doctrine, and make no declaration, which were not held to and made by "our fathers who framed the government under which we live." You never dealt fairly by us in relation to this affair. When it occurred, some important State elections were near at hand, and you were in evident glee with the belief that, by charging the blame·upon us, you could get an advantage of us in those elections. The elections came, and your expectations were not quite fulfilled. Every Republican man knew that, as to himself at least, your charge was a slander, and he was not much inclined by it to cast his vote in your favor. Republican doctrines and declarations are accompanied with a continual protest against any interference whatever with your slaves, or with you about your slaves. Surely, this does not encourage them to revolt. True, we do, in common with "our fathers who framed the government under which we live," declare our belief that slavery is wrong; but the slaves do not hear us declare even this. For anything we say or do, the slaves would scarcely know there is a Republican party. I believe they would not, in fact, generally know it but for your misrepresentations of us in their hearing. In your political contests among yourselves, each faction charges the other with sympathy with Black Republicanism; and then, to give point to the charge, defines Black Republicanism to simply be insurrection, blood, and thunder among the slaves.

Slave insurrections are no more common now than they were before the Republican party was organized. What induced the Southampton insurrection, twenty-eight years ago, in which at least three times as many lives were lost as at Harper's Ferry? You can scarcely stretch your very elastic fancy to the conclusion that Southampton was "got up by Black Republicanism." In the present state of things in the United States, I do not think a general, or even a very extensive, slave insurrection is possible. The indispensable concert of action cannot be attained. The slaves have no means of rapid communication; nor can incendiary freemen, black or white, supply it. The explosive materials are everywhere in parcels; but there neither are, nor can be supplied, the indispensable connecting trains.

Much is said by Southern people about the affection of slaves for their masters and mistresses; and a part of it, at least, is true. A plot for an uprising could scarcely be devised and communicated to twenty individuals before some one of them, to save the life of a favorite master or mistress, would divulge it. This is the rule; and the slave revolution in Hayti was not an exception to it, but a case occurring under peculiar circumstances. The gunpowder plot of British history, though not connected with slaves, was more in point. In that case, only about twenty were admitted to be secret; and yet one of them, in his anxiety to save a friend, betrayed the plot to that friend, and, by consequence, averted the calamity. Occasional poisonings from the kitchen, and open or stealthy assassinations in the field, and local revolts extending to a score or so, will continue to occur as the natural results of slavery; but no general insurrection of slaves, as I think, can happen in this country for a long time. Whoever much fears, or much hopes, for such an event, will be alike disappointed.

In the language of Mr. Jefferson, uttered many years ago, "It is still in our power to direct the process of emancipation and deportation peaceably, and in such slow degrees, as that the evil will wear off insensibly; and their places be, *pari passu,* filled up by free white laborers. If, on the contrary, it is left to force itself on, human nature must shudder at the prospect held up."

Mr. Jefferson did not mean to say, nor do I, that the power of emancipation is in the Federal Government. He spoke of Virginia; and, as to the power of emancipation, I speak of the slaveholding States only. The Federal Government, however, as we insist, has the power of restraining the extension of the institution—the power to insure that a slave insurrection shall never occur on any American soil which is now free from slavery.

John Brown's effort was peculiar. It was not a slave insurrection. It was an attempt by white men to get up a revolt among slaves, in which the slaves refused to participate. In fact, it was so absurd that the slaves, with all their ignorance, saw plainly enough it could not succeed. That affair, in its philosophy, corresponds with the many attempts, related in history, at the assassination of kings and emperors. An enthusiast broods over the oppression of a people till he fancies himself commissioned by Heaven to liberate them. He ventures the attempt, which ends in little else than his own execution. Orsini's attempt on Louis Napoleon, and John Brown's attempt at Harper's Ferry, were, in their philosophy, precisely the same. The eagerness to cast blame on old England in the one case, and on New England in the other, does not disprove the sameness of the two things.

And how much would it avail you, if you could, by the use of John Brown, Helper's Book,[1] and the like, break up the Republican organization? Human action can be modified to some extent, but human nature cannot be changed. There is a judgment and a feeling against slavery in this nation, which cast at least a million and a half of votes. You cannot destroy that judgment and feeling—that sentiment—by breaking up

---

[1] Hinton R. Helper, a Southerner, had written a book, *The Impending Crisis of the South*, in which he contended that slavery was ruining the South economically. The book enraged the South, and Southern leaders charged that certain Republicans had endorsed the volume to increase its sales.

the political organization which rallies around it. You can scarcely scatter and disperse an army which has been formed into order in the face of your heaviest fire; but if you could, how much would you gain by forcing the sentiment which created it out of the peaceful channel of the ballot-box into some other channel? What would that other channel probably be? Would the number of John Browns be lessened or enlarged by the operation?

But you will break up the Union rather than submit to a denial of your constitutional rights.

That has a somewhat reckless sound; but it would be palliated, if not fully justified, were we proposing, by the mere force of numbers, to deprive you of some right plainly written down in the Constitution. But we are proposing no such thing.

When you make these declarations you have a specific and well-understood allusion to an assumed constitutional right of yours to take slaves into the Federal Territories, and to hold them there as property. But no such right is specifically written in the Constitution. That instrument is literally silent about any such right. We, on the contrary, deny that such a right has any existence in the Constitution, even by implication.

Your purpose, then, plainly stated, is that you will destroy the government, unless you be allowed to construe and force the Constitution as you please, on all points in dispute between you and us. You will rule or ruin in all events.

This, plainly stated, is your language. Perhaps you will say the Supreme Court has decided the disputed constitutional question in your favor. Not quite so. But waiving the lawyer's distinction between dictum and decision, the court has decided the question for you in a sort of way. The court has substantially said, it is your constitutional right to take slaves into the Federal Territories, and to hold them there as property. When I say the decision was made in a sort of way, I mean it was made in a divided court, by a bare majority of the judges, and they not quite agreeing with one another in the reasons for making it; that it is so made as that its avowed supporters disagree with one another about its meaning, and that it was mainly based upon a mistaken statement of fact—the statement in the oponion that "the right of property in a slave is distinctly and expressly affirmed in the Constitution."

An inspection of the Constitution will show that the right of property in a slave is not "distinctly and expressly affirmed" in it. Bear in mind, the judges do not pledge their judicial opinion that such right is impliedly affirmed in the Constitution; but they pledge their veracity that it is "distinctly and expressly" affirmed there—"distinctly," that is, not mingled with anything else—"expressly," that is, in words meaning just that, without the aid of any inference, and susceptible of no other meaning.

If they had only pledged their judicial opinion that such right is affirmed in the instrument by implication, it would be open to others to show that neither the word "slave" nor "slavery" is to be found in the Constitution, nor the word "property" even, in any connection with language alluding to the things slave, or slavery; and that wherever in that instrument the slave is alluded to, he is called a "person"; and wherever his master's legal right in relation to him is alluded to, it is spoken of as "service or labor which may be due"—as a debt payable in service or labor. Also it would be open to show, by contemporaneous history, that this mode of alluding to slaves and slavery, instead of speaking of them, was employed on purpose to exclude from the Constitution the idea that there could be property in man.

To show all this is easy and certain.

When this obvious mistake of the judges shall be brought to their notice, is it not reasonable to expect that they will withdraw the mistaken statement, and reconsider the conclusion based upon it?

And then it is to be remembered that "our fathers who framed the government under which we live"—the men who made the Constitution—decided this same constitutional question in our favor long ago; decided it without division among themselves when making the decision; without division among themselves about the meaning of it after it was made, and, so far as any evidence is left, without basing it upon any mistaken statement of facts.

Under all these circumstances, do you really feel yourselves justified to break up this government unless such a court decision as yours is shall be at once submitted to as a conclusive and final rule of political action? But you will not abide the election of a Republican president! In that supposed event, you say, you will destroy the Union; and then, you say, the great crime of having destroyed it will be upon us! That is cool. A highwayman holds a pistol to my ear, and mutters through his teeth, "Stand and deliver, or I shall kill you, and then you will be a murderer!"

To be sure, what the robber demanded of me—my money—was my own; and I had a clear right to keep it; but it was no more my own than my vote is my own; and the threat of death to me, to extort my money, and the threat of destruction to the Union, to extort my vote, can scarcely be distinguished in principle.

A few words now to Republicans. It is exceedingly desirable that all parts of this great Confederacy shall be at peace, and in harmony one with another. Let us Republicans do our part to have it so. Even though much provoked, let us do nothing through passion and ill temper. Even though the Southern people will not so much as listen to us, let us calmly consider their demands, and yield to them if, in our deliberate view of our duty, we possibly can. Judging by all they say and do, and by the subject and nature of their controversy with us, let us determine, if we can, what will satisfy them.

Will they be satisfied if the Territories be unconditionally surrendered to them? We know they will not. In all their present complaints against us, the Territories are scarcely mentioned. Invasions and insurrections are the rage now. Will it satisfy them if, in the future, we have nothing to do with invasions and insurrections? We know it will not. We so know, because we know we never had anything to do with invasions and insurrections; and yet this total abstaining does not exempt us from the charge and the denunciation.

The question recurs, What will satisfy them? Simply this: we must not only let them alone, but we must somehow convince them that we do let them alone. This, we know by experience, is no easy task. We have been trying to convince them from the very beginning of our organization, but with no success. In all our platforms and speeches we have constantly protested our purpose to let them alone; but this has had no tendency to convince them. Alike unavailing to convince them is the fact that they have never detected a man of us in any attempt to disturb them.

These natural and apparently adequate means all failing, what will convince them? This, and this only: cease to call slavery wrong, and join them in calling it right. And this must be done thoroughly—done in acts as well as in words. Silence will not be tolerated—we must place ourselves avowedly with them. Senator Douglas's new sedition law must be enacted and enforced, suppressing all declarations that slavery is wrong, whether made in politics, in presses, in pulpits, or in private. We must arrest and return their fugitive slaves with greedy pleasure. We must pull down our free-State constitutions. The whole atmosphere must be disinfected from all taint of opposition to slavery, before they will cease to believe that all their troubles proceed from us.

I am quite aware they do not state their case precisely in this way. Most of them would probably say to us, "Let us alone: do nothing to us, and say what you please about slavery." But we do let them alone,—have never disturbed them,—so that, after all, it is what we say which dissatisfies them. They will continue to accuse us of doing, until we cease saying.

I am also aware they have not as yet in terms demanded the overthrow of our free-State constitutions. Yet those constitutions declare the wrong of slavery with more solemn emphasis than do all other sayings against it; and when all these other sayings shall have been silenced, the overthrow of these constitutions will be demanded, and nothing be left to resist the demand. It is nothing to the contrary that they do not demand the whole of this just now. Demanding what they do, and for the reason they do, they can voluntarily stop nowhere short of this consummation. Holding, as they do, that slavery is morally right and socially elevating, they cannot cease to demand a full national recognition of it as a legal right and a social blessing.

Nor can we justifiably withhold this on any ground save our conviction that slavery is wrong. If slavery is right, all words, acts, laws, and constitutions against it are themselves wrong, and should be silenced and swept away. If it is right, we cannot justly object to its nationality—its universality; if it is wrong, they cannot justly insist upon its extension—its enlargement. All they ask we could readily grant, if we thought slavery right; all we ask they could as readily grant, if they thought it wrong. Their thinking it right and our thinking it wrong is the precise fact upon which depends the whole controversy. Thinking it right, as they do, they are not to blame for desiring its full recognition as being right; but thinking it wrong, as we do, can we yield to them? Can we cast our votes with their view, and against our own? In view of our moral, social, and political responsibilities, can we do this?

Wrong as we think slavery is, we can yet afford to let it alone where it is, because that much is due to the necessity arising from its actual presence in the nation; but can we, while our votes will prevent it, allow it to spread into the national Territories, and to overrun us here in these free States? If our sense of duty forbids this, then let us stand by our duty fearlessly and effectively. Let us be diverted by none of those sophistical contrivances wherewith we are so industriously plied and belabored—contrivances such as groping for some middle ground between the right and the wrong: vain as the search for a man who should be neither a living man nor a dead man; such as a policy of "don't care" on a question about which all true men do care; such as Union appeals beseeching true Union men to yield to Disunionists, reversing the divine rule, and calling, not the sinners, but the righteous to repentance; such as invocations to Washington, imploring men to unsay what Washington said and undo what Washington did.

Neither let us be slandered from our duty by false accusations against us, nor frightened from it by menaces of destruction to the government, nor of dungeons to ourselves. Let us have faith that right makes might, and in that faith let us to the end dare to do our duty as we understand it.

LETTER TO GEORGE D. PRENTICE [1]

Prentice, editor of the *Louisville Journal,* was one of many who wrote Lincoln asking that he make a public announcement of his views to dispel the fears felt in the South at the prospect of a Republican victory. Lincoln's answer was typical of his reaction to such requests.

(Private and confidential.)

Springfield, Illinois, October 29, 1860.

MY dear Sir: Yours of the 26th is just received. Your suggestion that I in a certain event shall write a letter setting forth my conservative views and intentions is certainly a very worthy one. But would it do any good? If I were to labor a month I could not express my conservative views and intentions more clearly and strongly than they are expressed in our platform and in my many speeches already in print and before the public. And yet even you, who do occasionally speak of me in terms of personal kindness, give no prominence to these oft-repeated expressions of conservative views and intentions, but busy yourself with appeals to all conservative men to vote for Douglas,—to vote any way which can possibly defeat me,—thus impressing your readers that you think I am the very worst man living. If what I have already said has failed to convince

---

[1] Lincoln, *Complete Works,* VI, 66-67.

you, no repetition of it would convince you. The writing of your letter, now before me, gives assurance that you would publish such a letter from me as you suggest; but, till now, what reason had I to suppose the "Louisville Journal," even, would publish a repetition of that which is already at its command, and which it does not press upon the public attention?

And now, my friend,—for such I esteem you personally,—do not misunderstand me. I have not decided that I will not do substantially what you suggest. I will not forbear from doing so merely on punctilio and pluck. If I do finally abstain, it will be because of apprehension that it would do harm. For the good men of the South—and I regard the majority of them as such—I have no objection to repeat seventy and seven times. But I have bad men to deal with, both North and South; men who are eager for something new upon which to base new misrepresentations; men who would like to frighten me, or at least to fix upon me the character of timidity and cowardice. They would seize upon almost any letter I could write as being an "awful coming down." I intend keeping my eye upon these gentlemen, and to not unnecessarily put any weapons in their hands.

Yours truly,   A. LINCOLN.

(The following indorsement appears on the back:)

(Confidential.)

The within letter was written on the day of its date, and on reflection withheld till now. It expresses the views I still entertain.

A. LINCOLN.

LETTER TO LYMAN TRUMBULL[1]

Lincoln wrote to various Republican members of Congress bidding them stand firm against any compromise on the ex-

[1] Gilbert A. Tracy (ed.), *Uncollected Letters of Abraham Lincoln* (Boston, 1917), 171. This letter was first published in William H. Lambert. "A Lincoln Correspondence," *Century Magazine*, IV (February, 1909), 17.

tension of slavery. Trumbull was a Republican Senator from Illinois.

Private & Confidential

Springfield, Ills. Dec. 10, 1860.

Hon. L. Trumbull.

MY dear Sir: Let there be no compromise on the question of extending slavery. If there be, all our labor is lost, and, ere long, must be done again. The dangerous ground— that into which some of our friends have a hankering to run— is Pop. Sov. Have none of it. Stand firm. The tug has to come, & better now than any time hereafter.

Yours as ever

A. Lincoln.

LETTER TO WILLIAM KELLOGG [1]

Kellogg was a Republican House member from Illinois. He had asked Lincoln what position to take on the compromise measures.

December 11, 1860.

ENTERTAIN no proposition for a compromise in regard to the extension of slavery. The instant you do they have us under again: all our labor is lost, and sooner or later must be done over. Douglas is sure to be again trying to bring in his "popular sovereignty." Have none of it. The tug has to come, and better now than later. You know I think the fugitive-slave clause of the Constitution ought to be enforced —to put it in its mildest form, ought not to be resisted.

[1] Lincoln, *Complete Works*, VI, 77-78.

LETTER TO JOHN A. GILMER [1]

Gilmer was a Congressman from North Carolina. Lincoln considered offering him a place in the cabinet as a conciliatory gesture to the South. In this letter to Gilmer, Lincoln again refused to make a public statement of his views, but he went to considerable pains to assure Gilmer that the administration would not attack any rights of the South guaranteed by the Constitution.

(Strictly confidential)

Springfield, Illinois, December 15, 1860.

MY dear Sir: Yours of the 10th is received. I am greatly disinclined to write a letter on the subject embraced in yours; and I would not do so, even privately as I do, were it not that I fear you might misconstrue my silence. Is it desired that I shall shift the ground upon which I have been elected? I cannot do it. You need only to acquaint yourself with that ground, and press it on the attention of the South. It is all in print and easy of access.

May I be pardoned if I ask whether even you have ever attempted to procure the reading of the Republican platform, or my speeches, by the Southern people? If not, what reason have I to expect that any additional production of mine would meet a better fate? It would make me appear as if I repented for the crime of having been elected, and was anxious to apologize and beg forgiveness. To so represent me would be the principal use made of any letter I might now thrust upon the public. My old record cannot be so used; and that is precisely the reason that some new declaration is so much sought.

Now, my dear sir, be assured that I am not questioning your candor; I am only pointing out that while a new letter would hurt the cause which I think a just one, you can quite as well effect every patriotic object with the old record. Carefully read pages 18, 19, 74, 75, 88, 89, and 267 of the volume of joint debates between Senator Douglas and myself, with the Republican platform adopted at Chicago, and all your

---

[1] Lincoln, *Complete Works*, VI, 79-81.

questions will be substantially answered. I have no thought of recommending the abolition of slavery in the District of Columbia, nor the slave-trade among the slave States, even on the conditions indicated; and if I were to make such recommendation, it is quite clear Congress would not follow it.

As to employing slaves in arsenals and dockyards, it is a thing I never thought of in my recollection, till I saw your letter; and I may say of it precisely as I have said of the two points above.

As to the use of patronage in the slave States, where there are few or no Republicans, I do not expect to inquire for the politics of the appointee, or whether he does or not own slaves. I intend in that matter to accommodate the people in the several localities, if they themselves will allow me to accommodate them. In one word, I never have been, am not now, and probably never shall be in a mood of harassing the people either North or South.

On the territorial question I am inflexible, as you see my position in the book. On that there is a difference between you and us; and it is the only substantial difference. You think slavery is right and ought to be extended; we think it is wrong and ought to be restricted. For this neither has any just occasion to be angry with the other.

As to the State laws, mentioned in your sixth question, I really know very little of them. I never have read one. If any of them are in conflict with the fugitive-slave clause, or any other part of the Constitution, I certainly shall be glad of their repeal; but I could hardly be justified, as a citizen of Illinois, or as President of the United States, to recommend the repeal of a statute of Vermont or South Carolina.

With the assurance of my highest regards, I subscribe myself,

Your obedient servant, A. LINCOLN.

LETTER TO THURLOW WEED [1]

Weed was the boss of the New York Republican machine and the political adviser of William H. Seward, Senator from New York and Republican leader in Congress. Weed was probably trying to get Lincoln's views for the guidance of Seward. Lincoln told Weed that neither the Crittenden Compromise nor popular sovereignty could be accepted as a solution of the issue of slavery and the territories.

Springfield, Illinois, December 17, 1860.

MY dear Sir: Yours of the 11th was received two days ago. Should the convocation of governors of which you speak seem desirous to know my views on the present aspect of things tell them you judge from my speeches that I will be inflexible on the territorial question; that I probably think either the Missouri line extended, or Douglas's and Eli Thayer's popular sovereignty, would lose us everything we gain by the election; that filibustering for all south of us and making slave States of it would follow, in spite of us, in either case; also that I probably think all opposition, real and apparent, to the fugitive-slave clause of the Constitution ought to be withdrawn.

I believe you can pretend to find but little, if anything, in my speeches about secession. But my opinion is, that no State can in any way lawfully get out of the Union without the consent of the others; and that it is the duty of the President and other government functionaries to run the machine as it is.

Truly yours,

A. LINCOLN.

LETTER TO ALEXANDER H. STEPHENS [2]

Stephens was a Georgian who opposed the expediency of secession. This letter was another attempt by Lincoln to

[1] Lincoln, *Complete Works*, VI, 82.
[2] Lincoln, *Complete Works*, VI, 85-86.

privately assure Southern leaders that they need fear no Republican attack upon slavery.

(For your own eye only)

Springfield, Illinois, December 22, 1860.

MY dear Sir: Your obliging answer to my short note is just received, and for which please accept my thanks. I fully appreciate the present peril the country is in, and the weight of responsibility on me. Do the people of the South really entertain fears that a Republican administration would, directly or indirectly, interfere with the slaves, or with them about the slaves? If they do, I wish to assure you, as once a friend, and still, I hope, not an enemy, that there is no cause for such fears. The South would be in no more danger in this respect than it was in the days of Washington. I suppose, however, this does not meet the case. You think slavery is right and ought to be extended, while we think it is wrong and ought to be restricted. That, I suppose, is the rub. It certainly is the only substantial difference between us.

Yours very truly,

A. LINCOLN.

———

FAREWELL ADDRESS AT SPRINGFIELD, ILLINOIS, FEBRUARY 11, 1861 [1]

From the platform of the observation car of the train that was to take him to Washington to become the President of a divided country, Lincoln spoke these moving words to the neighbors who had come to bid him farewell.

MY Friends: No one, not in my situation, can appreciate my feeling of sadness at this parting. To this place, and the kindness of these people, I owe everything. Here I

[1] Lincoln, *Complete Works*, VI, 110-111.

have lived a quarter of a century, and have passed from a young to an old man. Here my children have been born, and one is buried. I now leave, not knowing when or whether ever I may return, with a task before me greater than that which rested upon Washington. Without the assistance of that Divine Being who ever attended him, I cannot succeed. With that assistance, I cannot fail. Trusting in Him who can go with me, and remain with you, and be everywhere for good, let us confidently hope that all will yet be well. To His care commending you, as I hope in your prayers you will commend me, I bid you an affectionate farewell.

ADDRESS IN INDEPENDENCE HALL, PHILADELPHIA, FEBRUARY 22, 1861 [1]

As Lincoln journeyed to Washington to assume the presidency, he spoke at numerous points along the way. These speeches cannot be ranked among his better efforts. He was confused by the crisis of secession, which he had thought would never develop. He was trying to avoid making any definite statements until he could reach Washington and advise with the Republican leaders. Consequently his speeches lacked assurance and authority. At Independence Hall, however, he uttered a classic expression of the importance of democratic America's mission to the world and the consequent necessity of preserving the Union.

MR. Cuyler: I am filled with deep emotion at finding myself standing in this place, where were collected together the wisdom, the patriotism, the devotion to principle, from which sprang the institutions under which we live. You have kindly suggested to me that in my hands is the task of restoring peace to our distracted country. I can say in return, sir, that all the political sentiments I entertain have been drawn, so far as I have been able to draw them, from the sentiments which originated in and were given to the world

---

[1] Lincoln, *Complete Works,* VI, 156-158.

from this hall. I have never had a feeling, politically, that did not spring from the sentiments embodied in the Declaration of Independence. I have often pondered over the dangers which were incurred by the men who assembled here and framed and adopted that Declaration. I have pondered over the toils that were endured by the officers and soldiers of the army who achieved that independence. I have often inquired of myself what great principle or idea it was that kept this Confederacy so long together. It was not the mere matter of separation of the colonies from the motherland, but that sentiment in the Declaration of Independence which gave liberty not alone to the people of this country, but hope to all the world, for all future time. It was that which gave promise that in due time the weights would be lifted from the shoulders of all men, and that all should have an equal chance. This is the sentiment embodied in the Declaration of Independence. Now, my friends, can this country be saved on that basis? If it can, I will consider myself one of the happiest men in the world if I can help to save it. If it cannot be saved upon that principle, it will be truly awful. But if this country cannot be saved without giving up that principle, I was about to say I would rather be assassinated on this spot than surrender it. Now, in my view of the present aspect of affairs, there is no need of bloodshed and war. There is no necessity for it. I am not in favor of such a course; and I may say in advance that there will be no bloodshed unless it is forced upon the government. The government will not use force, unless force is used against it.

My friends, this is wholly an unprepared speech. I did not expect to be called on to say a word when I came here. I supposed I was merely to do something toward raising a flag. I may, therefore, have said something indiscreet. [Cries of "No, no."] But I have said nothing but what I am willing to live by, and, if it be the pleasure of Almighty God to die by.

———

FIRST INAUGURAL ADDRESS, MARCH 4, 1861 [1]

> In the inaugural address, Lincoln announced to the country
> the policy he meant to follow in dealing with the seceded
> states. He thought that if the administration adopted a con-
> ciliatory program the Union could be restored by peaceable
> reconstruction; the seceded states would voluntarily return
> to their allegiance when they saw that the Republicans in-
> tended no attack upon slavery. Hence the inaugural ad-
> dress was an assurance to the South that the government
> would not interfere with slavery in any way. Lincoln's
> purpose was to avoid any overt action and maintain the
> *status quo* until the pro-Union sentiment in the South could
> make its influence felt. Then, he was convinced, the Union
> would be restored.

FELLOW-CITIZENS of the United States: In compliance
with a custom as old as the government itself, I appear
before you to address you briefly, and to take in your presence
the oath prescribed by the Constitution of the United States
to be taken by the President "before he enters on the execution of his office."

I do not consider it necessary at present for me to discuss
those matters of administration about which there is no special
anxiety or excitement.

Apprehension seems to exist among the people of the
Southern States that by the accession of a Republican administration their property and their peace and personal security
are to be endangered. There has never been any reasonable
cause for such apprehension. Indeed, the most ample evidence to the contrary has all the while existed and been open
to their inspection. It is found in nearly all the published
speeches of him who now addresses you. I do but quote
from one of those speeches when I declare that "I have no
purpose, directly or indirectly, to interfere with the institution
of slavery in the States where it exists. I believe I have no
lawful right to do so, and I have no inclination to do so."
Those who nominated and elected me did so with full knowl-

---

[1] Lincoln, *Complete Works*, VI, 169-185.

edge that I had made this and many similar declarations, and had never recanted them.

And, more than this, they placed in the platform for my acceptance, and as a law to themselves and to me, the clear and emphatic resolution which I now read:

Resolved, That the maintenance inviolate of the rights of the States, and especially the right of each State to order and control its own domestic institutions according to its own judgment exclusively, is essential to that balance of power on which the perfection and endurance of our political fabric depend, and we denounce the lawless invasion by armed force of the soil of any State or Territory, no matter under what pretext, as among the gravest of crimes.

I now reiterate these sentiments; and, in doing so, I only press upon the public attention the most conclusive evidence of which the case is susceptible, that the property, peace, and security of no section are to be in any wise endangered by the now incoming administration. I add, too, that all the protection which, consistently with the Constitution and the laws, can be given, will be cheerfully given to all the States when lawfully demanded, for whatever cause—as cheerfully to one section as to another.

There is much controversy about the delivering up of fugitives from service or labor. The clause I now read is as plainly written in the Constitution as any other of its provisions:

No person held to service or labor in one State, under the laws thereof, escaping into another, shall in consequence of any law or regulation therein be discharged from such service or labor, but shall be delivered up on claim of the party to whom such service or labor may be due.

It is scarcely questioned that this provision was intended by those who made it for the reclaiming of what we call fugitive slaves; and the intention of the lawgiver is the law. All members of Congress swear their support to the whole

Constitution—to this provision as much as to any other. To the proposition, then, that slaves whose cases come within the terms of this clause "shall be delivered up," their oaths are unanimous. Now, if they would make the effort in good temper, could they not with nearly equal unanimity frame and pass a law by means of which to keep good that unanimous oath?

There is some difference of opinion whether this clause should be enforced by national or by State authority; but surely that difference is not a very material one. If the slave is to be surrendered, it can be of but little consequence to him or to others by which authority it is done. And should any one in any case be content that his oath shall go unkept on a merely unsubstantial controversy as to how it shall be kept?

Again, in any law upon this subject, ought not all the safeguards of liberty known in civilized and humane jurisprudence to be introduced, so that a free man be not, in any case, surrendered as a slave? And might it not be well at the same time to provide by law for the enforcement of that clause in the Constitution which guarantees that "the citizen of each State shall be entitled to all privileges and immunities of citizens in the several States"?

I take the official oath to-day with no mental reservations, and with no purpose to construe the Constitution or laws by any hypercritical rules. And while I do not choose now to specify particular acts of Congress as proper to be enforced, I do suggest that it will be much safer for all, both in official and private stations, to conform to and abide by all those acts which stand unrepealed, than to violate any of them, trusting to find impunity in having them held to be unconstitutional.

It is seventy-two years since the first inauguration of a President under our National Constitution. During that period fifteen different and greatly distinguished citizens have, in succession, administered the executive branch of the government. They have conducted it through many perils, and generally with great success. Yet, with all this scope of precedent, I now enter upon the same task for the brief constitutional term of four years under great and peculiar difficulty. A disruption of the Federal Union, heretofore only menaced, is now formidably attempted.

I hold that, in contemplation of universal law and of the Constitution, the Union of these States is perpetual. Perpetuity is implied, if not expressed, in the fundamental law of all national governments. It is safe to assert that no government proper ever had a provision in its organic law for its own termination.

Continue to execute all the express provisions of our National Constitution, and the Union will endure forever—it being impossible to destroy it except by some action not provided for in the instrument itself.

Again, if the United States be not a government proper, but an association of States in the nature of contract merely, can it, as a contract, be peaceably unmade by less than all the parties who made it? One party to a contract may violate it —break it, so to speak; but does it not require all to lawfully rescind it?

Descending from these general principles, we find the proposition that, in legal contemplation the Union is perpetual confirmed by the history of the Union itself. The Union is much older than the Constitution. It was formed, in fact, by the Articles of Association in 1774. It was matured and continued by the Declaration of Independence in 1776. It was further matured, and the faith of all the then thirteen States expressly plighted and engaged that it should be perpetual, by the Articles of Confederation in 1778. And, finally, in 1787 one of the declared objects for ordaining and establishing the Constitution was "to form a more perfect Union."

But if the destruction of the Union by one or by a part only of the States be lawfully possible, the Union is less perfect than before the Constitution, having lost the vital element of perpetuity.

It follows from these views that no State upon its own mere motion can lawfully get out of the Union; that resolves and ordinances to that effect are legally void; and that acts of violence, within any State or States, against the authority of the United States, are insurrectionary or revolutionary, according to circumstances.

I therefore consider that, in view of the Constitution and the laws, the Union is unbroken; and to the extent of my ability I shall take care, as the Constitution itself expressly enjoins upon me, that the laws of the Union be faithfully executed in all the States. Doing this I deem to be only a simple duty on my part; and I shall perform it so far as practicable, unless my rightful masters, the American people, shall withhold the requisite means, or in some authoritative manner direct the contrary. I trust this will not be regarded as a menace, but only as the declared purpose of the Union that it will constitutionally defend and maintain itself.

In doing this there needs to be no bloodshed or violence; and there shall be none, unless it be forced upon the national authority. The power confided to me will be used to hold, occupy, and possess the property and places belonging to the government, and to collect the duties and imposts; but beyond what may be necessary for these objects, there will be no invasion, no using of force against or among the people anywhere. Where hostility to the United States, in any interior locality, shall be so great and universal as to prevent competent resident citizens from holding the Federal offices, there will be no attempt to force obnoxious strangers among the people for that object. While the strict legal right may exist in the government to enforce the exercise of these offices, the attempt to do so would be so irritating, and so nearly impracticable withal, that I deem it better to forego for the time the uses of such offices.

The mails, unless repelled, will continue to be furnished in all parts of the Union. So far as possible, the people everywhere shall have that sense of perfect security which is most favorable to calm thought and reflection. The course here indicated will be followed unless current events and experience shall show a modification or change to be proper, and in every case and exigency my best discretion will be exercised according to circumstances actually existing, and with a view and a hope of a peaceful solution of the national troubles and the restoration of fraternal sympathies and affections.

That there are persons in one section or another who seek to destroy the Union at all events, and are glad of any pretext to do it, I will neither affirm nor deny; but if there be such, I need address no word to them. To those, however, who really love the Union may I not speak?

Before entering upon so grave a matter as the destruction of our national fabric, with all its benefits, its memories, and its hopes, would it not be wise to ascertain precisely why we do it? Will you hazard so desperate a step while there is any possibility that any portion of the ills you fly from have no real existence? Will you, while the certain ills you fly to are greater than all the real ones you fly from—will you risk the commission of so fearful a mistake?

All profess to be content in the Union if all constitutional rights can be maintained. Is it true, then, that any right, plainly written in the Constitution, has been denied? I think not. Happily the human mind is so constituted that no party can reach to the audacity of doing this. Think, if you can, of a single instance in which a plainly written provision of the Constitution has ever been denied. If by the mere force of numbers a majority should deprive a minority of any clearly written constitutional right, it might, in a moral point of view, justify revolution—certainly would if such a right were a vital one. But such is not our case. All the vital rights of minorities and of individuals are so plainly assured to them by affirmations and negations, guarantees and prohibitions, in the Constitution, that controversies never arise concerning them. But no organic law can ever be framed with a provision specifically applicable to every question which may occur in practical administration.

No foresight can anticipate, nor any document of reasonable length contain, express provisions for all possible questions. Shall fugitives from labor be surrendered by national or by State authority? The Constitution does not expressly say. *May* Congress prohibit slavery in the Territories? The Constitution does not expressly say. *Must* Congress protect slavery in the Territories? The Constitution does not expressly say.

From questions of this class spring all our constitutional controversies, and we divide upon them into majorities and minorities. If the minority will not acquiesce, the majority must, or the government must cease. There is no other alternative; for continuing the government is acquiescence on one side or the other.

If a minority in such case will secede rather than acquiesce, they make a precedent which in turn will divide and ruin them; for a minority of their own will secede from them whenever a majority refuses to be controlled by such minority. For instance, why may not any portion of a new confederacy a year or two hence arbitrarily secede again, precisely as portions of the present Union now claim to secede from it? All who cherish disunion sentiments are now being educated to the exact temper of doing this.

Is there such perfect identity of interests among the States to compose a new Union, as to produce harmony only, and prevent renewed secession?

Plainly, the central idea of secession is the essence of anarchy. A majority held in restraint by constitutional checks and limitations, and always changing easily with deliberate changes of popular opinions and sentiments, is the only true sovereign of a free people. Whoever rejects it does, of necessity, fly to anarchy or to despotism. Unanimity is impossible; the rule of a minority, as a permanent arrangement, is wholly inadmissible; so that, rejecting the majority principle, anarchy or despotism in some form is all that is left.

I do not forget the position, assumed by some, that constitutional questions are to be decided by the Supreme Court;

nor do I deny that such decisions must be binding, in any case, upon the parties to a suit, as to the object of that suit, while they are also entitled to very high respect and consideration in all parallel cases by all other departments of the government. And while it is obviously possible that such decision may be erroneous in any given case, still the evil effect following it, being limited to that particular case, with the chance that it may be overruled and never become a precedent for other cases, can better be borne than could the evils of a different practice.

At the same time, the candid citizen must confess that if the policy of the government, upon vital questions affecting the whole people, is to be irrevocably fixed by decisions of the Supreme Court, the instant they are made, in ordinary litigation between parties in personal actions, the people will have ceased to be their own rulers, having to that extent practically resigned their government into the hands of that eminent tribunal. Nor is there in this view any assault upon the court or the judges. It is a duty from which they may not shrink to decide cases properly brought before them, and it is no fault of theirs if others seek to turn their decisions to political purposes.

One section of our country believes slavery is right, and ought to be extended, while the other believes it is wrong, and ought not to be extended. This is the only substantial dispute. The fugitive-slave clause of the Constitution, and the law for the suppression of the foreign slave-trade, are each as well enforced, perhaps, as any law can ever be in a community where the moral sense of the people imperfectly supports the law itself. The great body of the people abide by the dry legal obligation in both cases, and a few break over in each. This, I think, cannot be perfectly cured; and it would be worse in both cases after the separation of the sections than before. The foreign slave-trade, now imperfectly suppressed, would be ultimately revived, without restriction, in one section, while fugitive slaves, now only partially surrendered, would not be surrendered at all by the other.

Physically speaking, we cannot separate. We cannot re-move our respective sections from each other, nor build an impassable wall between them. A husband and wife may be divorced, and go out of the presence and beyond the reach of each other; but the different parts of our country cannot do this. They cannot but remain face to face, and intercourse, either amicable or hostile, must continue between them. Is it possible, then, to make that intercourse more advantageous or more satisfactory after separation than before? Can aliens make treaties easier than friends can make laws? Can treaties be more faithfully enforced between aliens than laws can among friends? Suppose you go to war, you cannot fight always; and when, after much loss on both sides, and no gain on either, you cease fighting, the identical old questions as to terms of intercourse are again upon you.

This country, with its institutions, belongs to the people who inhabit it. Whenever they shall grow weary of the existing government, they can exercise their constitutional right of amending it, or their revolutionary right to dismember or overthrow it. I cannot be ignorant of the fact that many worthy and patriotic citizens are desirous of having the Na-tional Constitution amended. While I make no recommenda-tion of amendments, I fully recognize the rightful authority of the people over the whole subject, to be exercised in either of the modes prescribed in the instrument itself; and I should, under existing circumstances, favor rather than oppose a fair opportunity being afforded the people to act upon it. I will venture to add that to me the convention mode seems prefer-able, in that it allows amendments to originate with the people themselves, instead of only permitting them to take or reject propositions originated by others not specially chosen for the purpose, and which might not be precisely such as they would wish to either accept or refuse. I understand a proposed amendment to the Constitution—which amendment, however, I have not seen—has passed Congress, to the effect that the Federal Government shall never interfere with the domestic institutions of the States, including that of persons held to service. To avoid misconstruction of what I have said, I depart from my purpose not to speak of particular amendments so far as to say that, holding such a provision to now be implied constitutional law, I have no objection to its being made express and irrevocable.

The chief magistrate derives all his authority from the people, and they have conferred none upon him to fix terms for the separation of the States. The people themselves can do this also if they choose; but the executive, as such, has nothing to do with it. His duty is to administer the present government, as it came to his hands, and to transmit it, unimpaired by him, to his successor.

Why should there not be a patient confidence in the ultimate justice of the people? Is there any better or equal hope in the world? In our present differences is either party without faith of being in the right? If the Almighty Ruler of Nations, with his eternal truth and justice, be on your side of the North, or on yours of the South, that truth and that justice will surely prevail by the judgment of this great tribunal of the American people.

By the frame of the government under which we live, this same people have wisely given their public servants but little power for mischief; and have, with equal wisdom, provided for the return of that little to their own hands at very short intervals. While the people retain their virtue and vigilance, no administration, by any extreme of wickedness or folly, can very seriously injure the government in the short space of four years.

My countrymen, one and all, think calmly and well upon this whole subject. Nothing valuable can be lost by taking time. If there be an object to hurry any of you in hot haste to a step which you would never take deliberately, that object will be frustrated by taking time; but no good object can be frustrated by it. Such of you as are now dissatisfied, still have the old Constitution unimpaired, and, on the sensitive point,

the laws of your own framing under it; while the new admin-
istraion will have no immediate power, if it would, to change
either. If it were admitted that you who are dissatisfied hold
the right side in the dispute, there still is no single good reason
for precipitate action. Intelligence, patriotism, Christianity,
and a firm reliance on Him who has never yet forsaken this
favored land, are still competent to adjust in the best way all
our present difficulty.

In your hands, my dissatisfied fellow-countrymen, and not
in mine, is the momentous issue of civil war. The government
will not assail you. You can have no conflict without being
yourselves the aggressors. You have no oath registered in
heaven to destroy the government, while I shall have the most
solemn one to "preserve, protect, and defend it."

I am loath to close. We are not enemies, but friends. We
must not be enemies. Though passion may have strained, it
must not break our bonds of affection. The mystic chords of
memory, stretching from every battle-field and patriot grave to
every living heart and hearthstone all over this broad land,
will yet swell the chorus of the Union when again touched,
as surely they will be, by the better angels of our nature.

MESSAGE TO CONGRESS IN SPECIAL SESSION, JULY 4, 1861 [1]

When Lincoln sent this message to Congress, all hopes of
conciliation and compromise had passed. War was a grim
reality. Consequently this was a war message. It revealed
Lincoln's determination to restore the Union at any cost.
He realized now that slavery was not the issue that had
caused secession but that the South was contending for
independence. In this message he argued powerfully for the
right of the federal government to exercise sovereign power.
If the government was not sovereign, he said, then the
American Union, the world's greatest democracy, could be

[1] Lincoln, *Complete Works,* VI, 297-325.

wrapped up and put away on some forgotten shelf reserved for experiments that had failed. He defined the purposes of the war: this was a people's war, a struggle to maintain democratic government.

FELLOW-CITIZENS of the Senate and House of Representatives: Having been convened on an extraordinary occasion, as authorized by the Constitution, your attention is not called to any ordinary subject of legislation.

At the beginning of the present presidential term, four months ago, the functions of the Federal Government were found to be generally suspended within the several States of South Carolina, Georgia, Alabama, Mississippi, Louisiana, and Florida, excepting only those of the Post-office Department.

Within these States all the forts, arsenals, dockyards, custom-houses, and the like, including the movable and stationary property in and about them, had been seized, and were held in open hostility to this government, excepting only Forts Pickens, Taylor, and Jefferson, on and near the Florida coast, and Fort Sumter, in Charleston Harbor, South Carolina. The forts thus seized had been put in improved condition, new ones had been built, and armed forces had been organized and were organizing, all avowedly with the same hostile purpose.

The forts remaining in the possession of the Federal Government in and near these States were either besieged or menaced by warlike preparations, and especially Fort Sumter was nearly surrounded by well-protected hostile batteries, with guns equal in quality to the best of its own, and outnumbering the latter as perhaps ten to one. A disproportionate share of the Federal muskets and rifles had somehow found their way into these States, and had been seized to be used against the government. Accumulations of the public revenue lying within them had been seized for the same object. The navy was scattered in distant seas, leaving but a very small part of it within the immediate reach of the government. Officers of the Federal army and navy had resigned in great numbers; and of those resigning a large proportion had taken up arms against the government. Simultaneously, and in connection with all this, the purpose to sever the Federal Union was openly avowed. In accordance with this purpose, an ordinance had been adopted in each of these States, declaring the States respectively to be separated from the National Union. A formula for instituting a combined government of these States had been promulgated; and this illegal organization, in the character of confederate States, was already invoking recognition, aid, and intervention from foreign powers.

Finding this condition of things, and believing it to be an imperative duty upon the incoming executive to prevent, if possible, the consummation of such attempt to destroy the Federal Union, a choice of means to that end became indispensable. This choice was made and was declared in the inaugural address. The policy chosen looked to the exhaustion of all peaceful measures before a resort to any stronger ones. It sought only to hold the public places and property not already wrested from the government, and to collect the revenue, relying for the rest on time, discussion, and the ballot-box. It promised a continuance of the mails, at government expense, to the very people who were resisting the government; and it gave repeated pledges against any disturbance to any of the people, or any of their rights. Of all that which a President might constitutionally and justifiably do in such a case, everything was forborne without which it was believed possible to keep the government on foot.

On the 5th of March (the present incumbent's first full day in office), a letter of Major Anderson, commanding at Fort Sumter, written on the 28th of February and received at the War Department on the 4th of March, was by that department placed in his hands. This letter expressed the professional opinion of the writer that reinforcements could not be thrown into that fort within the time for his relief, rendered necessary by the limited supply of provisions, and with a view of holding possession of the same, with a force of less than twenty thousand good and well-disciplined men. This opinion was concurred in by all the officers of his command, and their memoranda on the subject were made inclosures of Major Anderson's letter. The whole was immediately laid before Lieutenant-General Scott, was at once concurred with Major Anderson in opinion. On reflection, however, he took full time, consulting with other officers, both of the army and the navy, and at the end of four days came reluctantly but decidedly to the same conclusion as before. He also stated at the same time that no such sufficient force was then at the control of the government, or could be raised and brought to the ground within the time when the provisions in the fort would be exhausted. In a purely military point of view, this reduced the duty of the administration in the case to the mere matter of getting the garrison safely out of the fort.

It was believed, however, that to so abandon that position, under the circumstances, would be utterly ruinous; that the necessity under which it was to be done would not be fully understood; that by many it would be construed as a part of a voluntary policy; that at home it would discourage the friends of the Union, embolden its adversaries, and go far to insure to the latter a recognition abroad; that, in fact, it would be our national destruction consummated. This could not be allowed. Starvation was not yet upon the garrison, and ere it would be reached Fort Pickens might be reinforced. This last would be a clear indication of policy; and would better enable the country to accept the evacuation of Fort Sumter as a military necessity. An order was at once directed to be sent for the landing of the troops from the steamship *Brooklyn* into Fort Pickens. This order could not go by land, but must take the longer and slower route by sea. The first return news from the order was received just one week before the fall of Fort Sumter. The news itself was that the officer commanding the *Sabine*, to which vessel the troops had been transferred from the *Brooklyn*, acting upon some *quasi* armistice of the late administration (and of the existence of which the present administration, up to the time the order was despatched, had only too vague and uncertain rumors to fix attention), had refused to land the troops. To now reinforce Fort Pickens before a crisis would be reached at Fort Sumter was impossible—rendered so by the near exhaustion of provisions in the latter-named fort. In precaution against such a conjuncture, the government had, a few days before, commenced preparing an expedition as well adapted as might be to relieve Fort Sumter, which expedition was intended to be ultimately used, or not, according to circumstances. The strongest anticipated case for using it was now presented, and it was resolved to send it forward. As had been intended in this contingency, it was also resolved to notify the governor of South Carolina that he might expect an attempt would be made to provision the fort; and that, if the attempt should not be resisted, there would be no effort to throw in men, arms, or ammunition, without further notice, or in case of an attack upon the fort. This notice was accordingly given; whereupon the fort was attacked and bombarded to its fall, without even awaiting the arrival of the provisioning expedition.

It is thus seen that the assault upon and reduction of Fort Sumter was in no sense a matter of self-defense on the part of the assailants. They well knew that the garrison in the fort could by no possibility commit aggression upon them. They knew—they were expressly notified—that the giving of bread to the few brave and hungry men of the garrison was all which would on that occasion be attempted, unless themselves, by resisting so much, should provoke more. They knew that this government desired to keep the garrison in the fort, not to assail them, but merely to maintain visible possession, and thus to preserve the Union from actual and immediate dissolution—trusting, as hereinbefore stated, to time, discussion, and the ballot-box for final adjustment; and they assailed and reduced the fort for precisely the reverse object—to drive out the visible authority of the Federal Union, and thus force it to immediate dissolution. That this was their object the executive well understood; and having said to them in the inaugural address, "You can have no conflict without being yourselves the aggressors," he took pains not only to keep this declaration good, but also to keep the case so free from the power of ingenious sophistry that the world should not be able to misunderstand it. By the affair at Fort Sumter, with its surrounding circumstances, that point was reached. Then and thereby the assailants of the government began the conflict of arms, without a gun in sight or in expectancy to return their fire, save only the few in the fort sent to that harbor years before for their own protection, and still ready to give that protection in whatever was lawful. In this act, discarding all else, they have forced upon the country the distinct issue, "immediate dissolution or blood."

And this issue embraces more than the fate of these United States. It presents to the whole family of man the question whether a constitutional republic or democracy—a government of the people by the same people—can or cannot maintain its territorial integrity against its own domestic foes. It presents the question whether discontented individuals, too few in numbers to control administration according to organic law in any case, can always, upon the pretenses made in this case, or on any other pretenses, or arbitrarily without any pretense, break up their government, and thus practically put an end to free government upon the earth. It forces us to ask: "Is there, in all republics, this inherent and fatal weakness?" "Must a government, of necessity, be too strong for the liberties of its own people, or too weak to maintain its own existence?"

So viewing the issue, no choice was left but to call out the war power of the government; and so to resist force employed for its destruction, by force for its preservation.

The call was made, and the response of the country was most gratifying, surpassing in unanimity and spirit the most sanguine expectation. Yet none of the States commonly called slave States, except Delaware, gave a regiment through regular State organization. A few regiments have been organized within some others of those States by individual enterprise, and received into the government service. Of course the seceded States, so called (and to which Texas had been joined about the time of the inaugaration), gave no troops to the cause of the Union. The border States, so called, were not uniform in their action, some of them being almost for the Union, while in others—as Virginia, North Carolina, Tennessee, and Arkansas—the Union sentiment was nearly repressed and silenced. The course taken in Virginia was the most remarkable—perhaps the most important. A convention elected by the people of that State to consider this very question of disrupting the Federal Union was in session at the capital of Virginia when Fort Sumter fell. To this body the people had chosen a large majority of professed Union men. Almost immediately after the fall of Sumter, many members of that majority went over to the original disunion minority, and with them adopted an ordinance for withdrawing the State from the Union. Whether this change was wrought by their great approval of the assault upon Sumter, or their great resentment at the government's resistance to that assault, is not definitely known. Although they submitted the ordinance for ratification to a vote of the people, to be taken on a day then somewhat more than a month distant, the convention and the legislature (which was also in session at the same time and place), with leading men of the State not members of either, immediately commenced acting as if the State were already out of the Union. They pushed military preparations vigorously forward all over the State. They seized the United States armory at Harper's Ferry, and the navy-yard at Gosport, near Norfolk. They received—perhaps invited—into their State large bodies of troops, with their war-like appointments, from the so-called seceded States. They formally entered into a treaty of temporary alliance and cooperation with the so-called "Confederate States," and sent members to their congress at Montgomery. And, finally, they permitted the insurrectionary government to be transferred to their capital at Richmond.

The people of Virginia have thus allowed this giant insurrection to make its nest within her borders; and this government has no choice left but to deal with it where it finds it. And it has the less regret as the loyal citizens have, in due form, claimed its protection. Those loyal citizens this government is bound to recognize and protect, as being Virginia.

In the border States, so-called,—in fact, the Middle States,—there are those who favor a policy which they call "armed neutrality"; that is, an arming of those States to prevent the Union forces passing one way, or the disunion the other, over their soil. This would be disunion completed. Figuratively speaking, it would be the building of an impassable wall along the line of separation—and yet not quite an impassable one, for under the guise of neutrality it would tie the hands of Union men and freely pass supplies from among them to the insurrectionists, which it could not do as an open enemy. At a stroke it would take all the trouble off the hands of secession, except only what proceeds from the external blockade. It would do for the disunionists that which, of all things, they most desire—feed them well, and give them disunion without a struggle of their own. It recognizes no fidelity to the Constitution, no obligation to maintain the Union; and while very many who have favored it are doubtless loyal citizens, it is, nevertheless, very injurious in effect.

Recurring to the action of the government, it may be stated that at first a call was made for 75,000 militia; and, rapidly following this, a proclamation was issued for closing the ports of the insurrectionary districts by proceedings in the nature of blockade. So far all was believed to be strictly legal. At this point the insurrectionists announced their purpose to enter upon the practice of privateering.

Other calls were made for volunteers to serve for three years, unless sooner discharged, and also for large additions to the regular army and navy. These measures, whether strictly legal or not, were ventured upon, under what appeared to be a popular demand and a public necessity; trusting then, as now, that Congress would readily ratify them. It is believed that nothing has been done beyond the constitutional competency of Congress.

Soon after the first call for militia, it was considered a duty to authorize the commanding general in proper cases, according to his discretion, to suspend the privilege of the writ of *habeas corpus,* or, in other words, to arrest and detain, without resort to the ordinary processes and forms of laws, such individuals as he might deem dangerous to the public safety. This authority has purposely been exercised but very sparingly. Nevertheless, the legality and propriety of what has been done under it are questioned, and the attention of the country has been called to the proposition that one who has sworn to "take care that the laws be faithfully executed" should not himself violate them. Of course some consideration was given to the questions of power and propriety before this matter was acted upon. The whole of the laws which were required to be faithfully executed were being resisted and failing of execution in nearly one-third of the States. Must they be allowed to finally fail of execution, even had it been perfectly clear that by the use of the means necessary to their execution some single law, made in such extreme tenderness of the citizen's liberty that, practically, it relieves more of the guilty than of the innocent, should to a very limited extent be violated? To state the question more directly, are all the laws but one to go unexecuted, and the government itself go to pieces lest that one be violated? Even in such a case, would not the official oath be broken if the government should be overthrown, when it was believed that disregarding the single law would tend to preserve it? But it was not believed that this question was presented. It was not believed that any law was violated. The provision of the Constitution that "the privilege of the writ of *habeas corpus* shall not be suspended, unless when, in cases of rebellion or invasion, the public safety may require it," is equivalent to a provision—is a provision—that such privilege may be suspended when, in case of rebellion or invasion, the public safety does require it. It was decided that we have a case of rebellion, and that the public safety does require the qualified suspension of the privilege of the writ which was autho'rized to be made. Now it is insisted that Congress, and not the executive, is vested with this power. But the Constitution itself is silent as to which or who is to exercise the power; and as the provision was plainly made for a dangerous emergency, it cannot be believed the framers of the instrument intended that in every case the danger should run its course until Congress could be called together, the very assembling of which might be prevented, as was intended in this case, by the rebellion.

No more extended argument is now offered, as an opinion at some length will probably be presented by the attorney-general. Whether there shall be any legislation upon the subject, and if any, what, is submitted entirely to the better judgment of Congress.

The forbearance of this government had been so extraordinary and so long continued as to lead some foreign nations to shape their action as if they supposed the early destruction of our National Union was probable. While this, on discovery, gave the executive some concern, he is now happy to say that the sovereignty and rights of the United States are now everywhere practically respected by foreign powers; and a general sympathy with the country is manifested throughout the world.

The reports of the Secretaries of the Treasury, War, and the Navy will give the information in detail deemed necessary and convenient for your deliberation and action; while the executive and all the departments will stand ready to supply omissions, or to communicate new facts considered important for you to know.

It is now recommended that you give the legal means for making this contest a short and decisive one: that you place at the control of the government for the work at least four hundred thousand men and $400,000,000. That number of men is about one tenth of those of proper ages within the regions where, apparently, all are willing to engage; and the sum is less than a twenty-third part of the money value owned by the men who seem ready to devote the whole. A debt of $600,000,000 now is a less sum per head than was the debt of our Revolution when we came out of that struggle; and the money value in the country now bears even a greater proportion to what it was then than does the population. Surely each man has as strong a motive now to preserve our liberties as each had then to establish them.

A right result at this time will be worth more to the world than ten times the men and ten times the money. The evidence reaching us from the country leaves no doubt that the material for the work is abundant, and that it needs only the hand of legislation to give it legal sanction, and the hand of the executive to give it practical shape and efficiency. One of the greatest perplexities of the government is to avoid receiving troops faster than it can provide for them. In a word, the people will save their government if the government itself will do its part only indifferently well.

It might seem, at first thought, to be of little difference whether the present movement at the South be called "secession" or "rebellion." The movers, however, well understand the difference. At the beginning they knew they could never raise their treason to any respectable magnitude by any name which implies violation of law. They knew their people possessed as much of moral sense, as much of devotion to law and order, and as much pride in and reverence for the history and government of their common country as any other civilized and patriotic people. They knew they could make no advancement directly in the teeth of these strong and noble sentiments. Accordingly, they commenced by an insidious debauching of the public mind. They invented an ingenious sophism which, if conceded, was followed by perfectly logical steps, through all the incidents, to the complete destruction of the Union. The sophism itself is that any State of the Union may consistently with the National Constitution, and therefore lawfully and peacefully, withdraw from the Union without the consent of the Union or of any other State. The little disguise that the supposed right is to be exercised only for just cause, themselves to be the sole judges of its justice, is too thin to merit any notice.

With rebellion thus sugar-coated they have been drugging the public mind of their section for more than thirty years, and until at length they have brought many good men to a willingness to take up arms against the government the day after some assemblage of men have enacted the farcical pretense of taking their State out of the Union, who could have been brought to no such thing the day before.

This sophism derives much, perhaps the whole, of its currency from the assumption that there is some omnipotent and sacred supremacy pertaining to a State—to each State of our Federal Union. Our States have neither more nor less power than that reserved to them in the Union by the Constitution —no one of them ever having been a State out of the Union. The original ones passed into the Union even before they cast off their British colonial dependence; and the new ones each came into the Union directly from a condition of dependence, excepting Texas. And even Texas, in its temporary independence, was never designated a State. The new ones only took the designation of States on coming into the Union, while that name was first adopted for the old ones in and by the Declaration of Independence. Therein the "United Colonies" were declared to be "free and independent States"; but even then the object plainly was not to declare their independence of one another or of the Union, but directly the contrary, as their mutual pledge and their mutual action before, at the time, and afterward, abundantly show. The express plighting of faith by each and all of the original thirteen in the Articles of Confederation, two years later, that the Union shall be perpetual, is most conclusive. Having never been States either in substance or in name outside of the Union, whence this magical omnipotence of "State Rights," asserting a claim of power to lawfully destroy the Union itself? Much is said about the "sovereignty" of the States; but the word even is not in the National Constitution, nor, as is believed, in any of the State constitutions. What is "sovereignty" in the political sense of the term? Would it be far wrong to define it "a political community without a political superior"? Tested by this, no one of our States except Texas ever was a sovereignty. And even Texas gave up the character on coming into the Union; by which act she acknowledged the Constitution of the United States, and the laws and treaties of the United States made in pursuance of the Constitution, to be for her the supreme law of the land. The States have their status in the Union, and they have no other legal status. If they break from this, they can only do so against law and by revolution. The Union, and not themselves separately, procured their independence and their liberty. By conquest or purchase the Union gave each of them whatever of independence or liberty it has. The Union is older than any of the States, and, in fact, it created them as States. Originally some dependent colonies made the Union, and, in turn, the Union threw off their old dependence for them, and made them States, such as they are. Not one of them ever had a State constitution independent of the Union. Of course, it is not forgotten that all the new States framed their constitutions before they entered the Union —nevertheless, dependent upon and preparatory to coming into the Union.

Unquestionably the States have the powers and rights reserved to them in and by the National Constitution; but among these surely are not included all conceivable powers, however mischievous or destructive, but, at most, such only as were known in the world at the time as governmental powers; and certainly a power to destroy the government itself had never been known as a governmental, as a merely administrative power. This relative matter of national power and State rights, as a principle, is no other than the principle of generality and locality. Whatever concerns the whole should be confided to the whole—to the General Government; while whatever concerns only the State should be left exclusively to the State. This is all there is of original principle about it. Whether the National Constitution in defining boundaries between the two has applied the principle with exact accuracy, is not to be questioned. We are all bound by that defining, without question.

What is now combated is the position that secession is consistent with the Constitution—is lawful and peaceful. It is not contended that there is any express law for it; and nothing should ever be implied as law which leads to unjust or absurd consequences. The nation purchased with money the countries out of which several of these States were formed. Is it just that they shall go off without leave and without refunding? The nation paid very large sums (in the aggregate, I believe, nearly a hundred millions) to relieve Florida of the aboriginal tribes. Is it just that she shall now be off without consent or without making any return? The nation is now in debt for money applied to the benefit of these so-called seceding States in common with the rest. Is it just either that creditors shall go unpaid or the remaining States pay the whole? A part of the present national debt was contracted to pay the old debts of Texas. Is it just that she shall leave and pay no part of this herself?

Again, if one State may secede, so may another; and when all shall have seceded, none is left to pay the debts. Is this quite just to creditors? Did we notify them of this sage view of ours when we borrowed their money?

If we now recognize this doctrine by allowing the seceders to go in peace, it is difficult to see what we can do if others choose to go or to extort terms upon which they will promise to remain.

The seceders insist that our Constitution admits of secession. They have assumed to make a national constitution of their own, in which of necessity they have either discarded or retained the right of secession as they insist it exists in ours. If they have discarded it, they thereby admit that on principle it ought not to be in ours. If they have retained it by their own construction of ours, they show that to be consistent they must secede from one another whenever they shall find it the easiest way of settling their debts, or effecting any other selfish or unjust object. The principle itself is one of disintegration, and upon which no government can possibly endure.

If all the States save one should assert the power to drive that one out of the Union, it is presumed the whole class of seceder politicians would at once deny the power and denounce the act as the greatest outrage upon State rights. But suppose that precisely the same act, instead of being called "driving the one out," should be called "the seceding of the others from that one," it would be exactly what the seceders claim to do, unless, indeed, they make the point that the one, because it is a minority, may rightfully do what the others, because they are a majority, may not rightfully do. These politicians are subtle and profound on the rights of minorities. They are not partial to that power which made the Constitution and speaks from the preamble called itself "We, the People."

It may well be questioned whether there is to-day a majority of the legally qualified voters of any State, except perhaps South Carolina, in favor of disunion. There is much reason to believe that the Union men are the majority in many, if not in every other one, of the so-called seceded States. The contrary has not been demonstrated in any one of them. It is ventured to affirm this even of Virginia and Tennessee; for the result of an election held in military camps, where the bayonets are all on one side of the question voted upon, can scarcely be considered as demonstrating popular sentiment. At such an election, all that large class who are at once for the Union and against coercion would be coerced to vote against the Union.

It may be affirmed without extravagance that the free institutions we enjoy have developed the powers and improved the condition of our whole people beyond any example in the world. Of this we now have a striking and an impressive illustration. So large an army as the government has now on foot was never before known, without a soldier in it but who has taken his place there of his own free choice. But more than this, there are many single regiments whose members, one and another, possess full practical knowledge of all the arts, sciences, professions, and whatever else, whether useful or elegant, is known in the world; and there is scarcely one from which there could not be selected a President, a cabinet, a congress, and perhaps a court, abundantly competent to administer the government itself. Nor do I say this is not true also in the army of our late friends, now adversaries in this contest; but if it is, so much better the reason why the government which has conferred such benefits on both them and us should not be broken up. Whoever in any section proposes to abandon such a government would do well to consider in deference to what principle it is that he does it—what better he is likely to get in its stead—whether the substitute will give, or be intended to give, so much of good to the people? There are some foreshadowings on this subject. Our adversaries have adopted some declarations of independence in which, unlike the good old one, penned by Jefferson, they omit the words "all men are created equal." Why? They have adopted a temporary national constitution, in the preamble of which, unlike our good old one, signed by Washington, they omit "We, the People," and substitute, "We, the deputies of the sovereign and independent States." Why? Why this deliberate pressing out of view the rights of men and the authority of the people?

This is essentially a people's contest. On the side of the Union it is a struggle for maintaining in the world that form and substance of government whose leading object is to elevate the condition of men—to lift artificial weights from all shoulders; to clear the paths of laudable pursuit for all; to afford all an unfettered start, and a fair chance in the race of life. Yielding to partial and temporary departures, from necessity, this is the leading object of the government for whose existence we contend.

I am most happy to believe that the plain people understand and appreciate this. It is worthy of note that while in this, the government's hour of trial, large numbers of those in the army and navy who have been favored with the offices have resigned and proved false to the hand which had pampered them, not one common soldier or common sailor is known to have deserted his flag.

Great honor is due to those officers who remained true, despite the example of their treacherous associates; but the greatest honor, and most important fact of all, is the unamimous firmness of the common soldiers and common sailors. To the last man, so far as known, they have successfully resisted the traitorous efforts of those whose commands, but an hour before, they obeyed as absolute law. This is the patriotic instinct of the plain people. They understand, without an argument, that the destroying of the government which was made by Washington means no good to them.

Our popular government has often been called an experiment. Two points in it our people have already settled—the successful establishing and the successful administering of it. One still remains—its successful maintenance against a formidable internal attempt to overthrow it. It is now for them to demonstrate to the world that those who can fairly carry an election can also suppress a rebellion; that ballots are the rightful and peaceful successors of bullets; and that when ballots have fairly and constitutionally decided, there can be no successful appeal back to bullets; that there can be no successful appeal, except to ballots themselves, at succeeding elections. Such will be a great lesson of peace: teaching men that what they cannot take by an election, neither can they take it by a war; teaching all the folly of being the beginners of a war.

Lest there be some uneasiness in the minds of candid men as to what is to be the course of the government toward the Southern States after the rebellion shall have been suppressed, the executive deems it proper to say it will be his purpose then, as ever, to be guided by the Constitution and the laws; and that he probably will have no different understanding of the powers and duties of the Federal Government relatively to the rights of the States and the people, under the Constitution, than that expressed in the inaugural address.

He desires to preserve the government, that it may be administered for all as it was administered by the men who made it. Loyal citizens everywhere have the right to claim this of their government, and the government has no right to withhold or neglect it. It is not perceived that in giving it there is any coercion, any conquest, or any subjugation, in any just sense of those terms.

The Constitution provides, and all the States have accepted the provision, that "the United States shall guarantee to every State in this Union a republican form of government." But if a State may lawfully go out of the Union, having done so, it may also discard the republican form of government; so that to prevent its going out is an indispensable means to the end of maintaining the guarantee mentioned; and when an end is lawful and obligatory, the indispensable means to it are also lawful and obligatory.

It was with the deepest regret that the executive found the duty of employing the war power in defense of the government forced upon him. He could but perform this duty or surrender the existence of the government. No compromise by public servants could, in this case, be a cure; not that compromises are not often proper, but that no popular government can long survive a marked precedent that those who carry an election can only save the government from immediate destruction by giving up the main point upon which the people gave the election. The people themselves, and not their servants, can safely reverse their own deliberate decisions.

As a private citizen the executive could not have consented that these institutions shall perish; much less could he, in betrayal of so vast and so sacred a trust as the free people have confided to him. He felt that he had no moral right to shrink, nor even to count the chances of his own life in what might follow. In full view of his great responsibility he has, so far, done what he has deemed his duty. You will now, according to your own judgment, perform yours.

He sincerely hopes that your views and your actions may so accord with his, as to assure all faithful citizens who have been disturbed in their rights of a certain and speedy restoration to them, under the Constitution and the laws.

And having thus chosen our course, without guile and with pure purpose, let us renew our trust in God, and go forward without fear and with manly hearts.

ABRAHAM LINCOLN.

LETTER TO GENERAL JOHN C. FRÉMONT [1]

Frémont was the commander of the Western Department, with headquarters in St. Louis. Lincoln had appointed him to this important post largely for political reasons. Frémont had been the Republican party's first presidential candidate in 1856, and he had a large following among the radical Republicans. In the West Frémont accomplished little of military importance, but he stirred up a prime political storm. On August 30 he issued a proclamation establishing martial law in his district and emancipating the slaves of those persons who had joined the Confederacy. This violated Lincoln's announced policy of conducting the war for the sole purpose of restoring the Union. Lincoln knew it would lose the government the support of many conservatives. He asked Frémont, in this letter, to modify the proclamation. The general refused, and on September 11 Lincoln ordered the proclamation revoked.

[1] Lincoln, *Complete Works*, VI, 350-351.

Washington, D. C., September 2, 1861.

MY dear Sir: Two points in your proclamation of August 30 give me some anxiety:

First. Should you shoot a man, according to the proclamation, the Confederates would very certainly shoot our best men in their hands in retaliation; and so, man for man, indefinitely. It is, therefore, my order that you allow no man to be shot under the proclamation without first having my approbation or consent.

Second. I think there is great danger that the closing paragraph, in relation to the confiscation of property and the liberating slaves of traitorous owners, will alarm our Southern Union friends and turn them against us; perhaps ruin our rather fair prospect for Kentucky. Allow me, therefore, to ask that you will, as of your own motion, modify that paragraph so as to conform to the first and fourth sections of the act of Congress entitled, "An act to confiscate property used for insurrectionary purposes," approved August 6, 1861, and a copy of which act I herewith send you.[1]

This letter is written in a spirit of caution, and not of censure. I send it by special messenger, in order that it may certainly and speedily reach you.

Yours very truly,

A. LINCOLN.

———

LETTER TO ORVILLE H. BROWNING [2]

Many people protested against Lincoln's action in overruling Frémont. Among them was Browning, United States Senator from Illinois and a close friend of Lincoln's. The President's reply to Browning was a masterful summation of his war policy and his views on slavery. He revoked the

[1] The first confiscation act provided for the confiscation of slaves who were employed as military laborers in the Confederacy.
[2] Lincoln, *Complete Works*, VI, 357-361.

proclamation because it would have alienated certain groups whose support was necessary to save the Union; he was opposed to destroying slavery in a violent, irregular manner.

(Private and confidential.)

Executive Mansion, September 22, 1861.

MY dear Sir: Yours of the 17th is just received; and coming from you, I confess it astonishes me. That you should object to my adhering to a law which you had assisted in making and presenting to me less than a month before is odd enough. But this is a very small part. General Frémont's proclamation as to confiscation of property and the liberation of slaves is purely political and not within the range of military law or necessity. If a commanding general finds a necessity to seize the farm of a private owner for a pasture, an encampment, or a fortification, he has the right to do so, and to so hold it as long as the necessity lasts; and this is within military law, because within military necessity. But to say the farm shall no longer belong to the owner, or his heirs forever, and this as well when the farm is not needed for military purposes as when it is, is purely political, without the savor of military law about it. And the same is true of slaves. If the general needs them, he can seize them and use them; but when the need is past, it is not for him to fix their permanent future condition. That must be settled according to laws made by law-makers, and not by military proclamations. The proclamation in the point in question is simply "dictatorship." It assumes that the general may do anything he pleases—confiscate the lands and free the slaves of loyal people, as well as of disloyal ones. And going the whole figure, I have no doubt, would be more popular with some thoughtless people than that which has been done! But I cannot assume this reckless position, nor allow others to assume it on my responsibility.

You speak of it as being the only means of saving the government. On the contrary, it is itself the surrender of the government. Can it be pretended that it is any longer the Government of the United States—any government of constitution and laws—wherein a general or a president may make permanent rules of property by proclamation? I do not say Congress might not with propriety pass a law on the point, just such as General Frémont proclaimed. I do not say I might not, as a member of Congress, vote for it. What I object to is, that I, as President, shall expressly or impliedly seize and exercise the permanent legislative functions of the government.

So much as to principle. Now as to policy. No doubt the thing was popular in some quarters, and would have been more so if it had been a general declaration of emancipation. The Kentucky legislature would not budge till that proclamation was modified; and General Anderson telegraphed me that on the news of General Frémont having actually issued deeds of manumission, a whole company of our volunteers threw down their arms and disbanded. I was so assured as to think it probable that the very arms we had furnished Kentucky would be turned against us. I think to lose Kentucky is nearly the same as to lose the whole game. Kentucky gone, we cannot hold Missouri, nor, as I think, Maryland. These all against us, and the job on our hands is too large for us. We would as well consent to separation at once, including the surrender of this capital. On the contrary, if you will give up your restlessness for new positions, and back me manfully on the grounds upon which you and other kind friends gave me the election and have approved in my public documents, we shall go through triumphantly. You must not understand I took my course on the proclamation because of Kentucky. I took the same ground in a private letter to General Frémont before I heard from Kentucky.

You think I am inconsistent because I did not also forbid General Frémont to shoot men under the proclamation. I understand that part to be within military law, but I also think, and so privately wrote General Frémont, that it is impolitic in this, that our adversaries have the power, and will certainly exercise it, to shoot as many of our men as we shoot of theirs.

I did not say this in the public letter, because it is a subject I prefer not to discuss in the hearing of our enemies.

There has been no thought of removing General Frémont on any ground connected with his proclamation, and if there has been any wish for his removal on any ground, our mutual friend Sam. Glover can probably tell you what it was. I hope no real necessity for it exists on any ground.

Your friend, as ever,

A. LINCOLN.

————

ANNUAL MESSAGE TO CONGRESS, DECEMBER 3, 1861 [1]

Lincoln's first annual message to Congress was mainly a review of events since the beginning of war and a justification of the measures he had taken to defeat the Confederacy. It contained two noteworthy pronouncements. He reemphasized that the war was one for the restoration of the Union and he warned the radical Republicans against any extreme measures designed to turn it into an abolitionist crusade. He repeated his earlier declaration that this was a people's war —a war to preserve the rights of labor against an overweening slavocracy.

FELLOW-CITIZENS of the Senate and House of Representatives: In the midst of unprecedented political troubles we have cause of great gratitude to God for unusual good health and most abundant harvests.

You will not be surprised to learn that, in the peculiar exigencies of the times, our intercourse with foreign nations has been attended with profound solicitude, chiefly turning upon our own domestic affairs.

A disloyal portion of the American people have, during the whole year, been engaged in an attempt to divide and destroy the Union. A nation which endures factious domestic division

---

[1] Lincoln, *Complete Works,* VII, 28-60.

is exposed to disrespect abroad; and one party, if not both, is sure, sooner or later, to invoke foreign intervention. Nations thus tempted to interfere are not always able to resist the counsels of seeming expediency and ungenerous ambition, although' measures adopted under such influences seldom fail to be unfortunate and injurious to those adopting them.

The disloyal citizens of the United States who have offered the ruin of our country in return for the aid and comfort which they have invoked abroad, have received less patronage and encouragement than they probably expected. If it were just to suppose, as the insurgents have seemed to assume, that foreign nations in this case, discarding all moral, social, and treaty obligations, would act solely and selfishly for the most speedy restoration of commerce, including, especially, the acquisition of cotton, those nations appear as yet not to have seen their way to their object more directly or clearly through the destruction than through the preservation of the Union. If we could dare to believe that foreign nations are actuated by no higher principle than this, I am quite sure a sound argument could be made to show them that they can reach their aim more readily and easily by aiding to crush this rebellion than by giving encouragement to it.

The principal lever relied on by the insurgents for exciting foreign nations to hostility against us, as already intimated, is the embarrassment of commerce. Those nations, however, not improbably saw from the first that it was the Union which made as well our foreign as our domestic commerce. They can scarcely have failed to perceive that the effort for disunion produces the existing difficulty; and that one strong nation promises more durable peace and a more extensive, valuable, and reliable commerce than can the same nation broken in hostile fragments.

It is not my purpose to review our discussions with foreign states, because, whatever might be their wishes or dispositions, the integrity of our country and the stability of our government mainly depend, not upon them, but on the loyalty, virtue, patriotism, and intelligence of the American people. The correspondence itself, with the usual reservations, is herewith submitted.

I venture to hope it will appear that we have practised prudence and liberality toward foreign powers, averting causes of irritation, and with firmness maintaining our own rights and honor.

Since, however, it is apparent that here, as in every other State, foreign dangers necessarily attend domestic difficulties, I recommend that adequate and ample measures be adopted for maintaining the public defenses on every side. While under this general recommendation provision for defending our sea-coast line readily occurs to the mind, I also in the same connection ask the attention of Congress to our great lakes and rivers. It is believed that some fortifications and depots of arms and munitions, with harbor and navigation improvements, all at well-selected points upon these, would be of great importance to the national defense and preservation. I ask attention to the views of the Secretary of War, expressed in his report upon the same general subject.

* * * *

The operations of the treasury during the period which has elapsed since your adjournment have been conducted with signal success. The patriotism of the people has placed at the disposal of the government the large means demanded by the public exigencies. Much of the national loan has been taken by citizens of the industrial classes whose confidence in their country's faith, and zeal for their country's deliverance from present peril, have induced them to contribute to the support of the government the whole of their limited acquisitions. This fact imposes peculiar obligations to economy in disbursement and energy in action.

The revenue from all sources, including loans, for the financial year ending on the 30th June, 1861, was $86,835,900.27, and the expenditures for the same period, including payments on account of the public debt, were $84,578,834.47; leaving a balance in the treasury, on the 1st July, of $2,257,065.80. For the first quarter of the financial year ending on the 30th September, 1861, the receipts from all sources, including the balance of 1st of July, were $102,532,509.27, and the expenses $98,239,733.09; leaving a balance on the 1st October, 1861, of $4,292,776.18.

Estimates for the remaining three quarters of the year, and for the financial year 1863, together with his views of ways and means for meeting the demands contemplated by them, will be submitted to Congress by the Secretary of the Treasury. It is gratifying to know that the expenditures made necessary by the rebellion are not beyond the resources of the loyal people, and to believe that the same patriotism which has thus far sustained the government will continue to sustain it till peace and union shall again bless the land.

I respectfully refer to the report of the Secretary of War for information respecting the numerical strength of the army, and for recommendations having in view an increase of its efficiency and the well-being of the various branches of the service intrusted to his care. It is gratifying to know that the patriotism of the people has proved equal to the occasion, and that the number of troops tendered greatly exceeds the force which Congress authorized me to call into the field.

I refer with pleasure to those portions of his report which make allusion to the creditable degree of discipline already attained by our troops, and to the excellent sanitary condition of the entire army.

The recommendation of the secretary for an organization of the militia upon a uniform basis is a subject of vital importance to the future safety of the country, and is commended to the serious attention of Congress.

The large addition to the regular army, in connection with the defection that has so considerably diminished the number of its officers, gives peculiar importance to his recommendation for increasing the corps of cadets to the greatest capacity of the Military Academy.

* * * *

The report of the Secretary of the Navy presents in detail the operations of that branch of the service, the activity and energy which have characterized its administration, and the results of measures to increase its efficiency and power. Such have been the additions, by construction and purchase, that it may almost be said a navy has been created and brought into service since our difficulties commenced.

Besides blockading our extensive coast, squadrons larger than ever before assembled under our flag have been put afloat and performed deeds which have increased our naval renown.

I would invite special attention to the recommendation of the secretary for a more perfect organization of the navy by introducing additional grades in the service.

The present organization is defective and unsatisfactory, and the suggestions submitted by the department will, it is believed, if adopted, obviate the difficulties alluded to, promote harmony, and increase the efficiency of the navy.

* * * *

One of the unavoidable consequences of the present insurrection is the entire suppression, in many places, of all the ordinary means of administering civil justice by the officers, and in the forms of existing law. This is the case, in whole or in part, in all the insurgent States; and as our armies advance upon and take possession of parts of those States, the practical evil becomes more apparent. There are no courts nor officers to whom the citizens of other States may apply for the enforcement of their lawful claims against citizens of the insurgent States; and there is a vast amount of debt constituting such claims. Some have estimated it as high as $200,000,000, due, in large part, from insurgents in open rebellion to loyal citizens who are, even now, making great sacrifices in the discharge of their patriotic duty to support the government.

Under these circumstances, I have been urgently solicited to establish, by military power, courts to administer summary justice in such cases. I have thus far declined to do it, not because I had any doubt that the end proposed—the collection of the debts—was just and right in itself, but because I have been unwilling to go beyond the pressure of necessity in the unusual exercise of power. But the powers of Congress, I suppose, are equal to the anomalous occasion, and therefore I refer the whole matter to Congress, with the hope that a plan may be devised for the administration of justice in all such parts of the insurgent States and Territories as may be under the control of this government, whether by a voluntary return to allegiance and order, or by the power of our arms; this, however, not to be a permanent institution, but a temporary substitute, and to cease as soon as the ordinary courts can be reestablished in peace.

It is important that some more convenient means should be provided, if possible, for the adjustment of claims against the government, especially in view of their increased number by reason of the war. It is as much the duty of government to render prompt justice against itself, in favor of citizens, as it is to administer the same between private individuals. The investigation and adjudication of claims in their nature belong to the judicial department; besides, it is apparent that the attention of Congress will be more than usually engaged, for some time to come, with great national questions. It was intended, by the organization of the Court of Claims, mainly to remove this branch of business from the halls of Congress; but while the court has proved to be an effective and valuable means of investigation, it in great degree fails to effect the object of its creation for want of power to make its judgments final.

Fully aware of the delicacy, not to say the danger, of the subject, I commend to your careful consideration whether this power of making judgments final may not properly be given to the court, reserving the right of appeal on questions of law to the Supreme Court, with such other provisions as experience may have shown to be necessary.

* * * *

Under and by virtue of the act of Congress entitled "An act to confiscate property used for insurrectionary purposes," approved August 6, 1861, the legal claims of certain persons to the labor and service of certain other persons have become forfeited; and numbers of the latter, thus liberated, are already dependent on the United States, and must be provided for in some way. Besides this, it is not impossible that some of the States will pass similar enactments for their own benefit respectively, and by operation of which persons of the same class will be thrown upon them for disposal. In such case I recommend that Congress provide for accepting such persons from such States, according to some mode of valuation, in lieu, *pro tanto,* of direct taxes, or upon some other plan to be agreed on with such States respectively; that such persons, on such acceptance by the General Government, be at once deemed free; and that, in any event, steps be taken for colonizing both classes (or the one first mentioned, if the other shall not be brought into existence) at some place or places in a climate congenial to them. It might be well to consider, too, whether the free colored people already in the United States could not, so far as individuals may desire, be included in such colonization.

To carry out the plan of colonization may involve the acquiring of territory, and also the appropriation of money beyond that to be expended in the territorial acquisition. Having practised the acquisition of territory for nearly sixty years, the question of constitutional power to do so is no longer an open one with us. The power was questioned at first by Mr. Jefferson, who, however, in the purchase of Louisiana, yielded his scruples on the plea of great expediency. If it be said that the only legitimate object of acquiring territory is to furnish homes for white men, this measure effects that object; for the emigration of colored men leaves additional room for white men remaining or coming here. Mr. Jefferson, however, placed the importance of procuring Louisiana more on political and commercial grounds than on providing room for population.

On this whole proposition, including the appropriation of money with the acquisition of territory, does not the expediency amount to absolute necessity—that without which the government itself cannot be perpetuated.

The war continues. In considering the policy to be adopted for suppressing the insurrection, I have been anxious and careful that the inevitable conflict for this purpose shall not degenerate into a violent and remorseless revolutionary struggle. I have, therefore, in every case thought it proper to keep the integrity of the Union prominent as the primary object of the contest on our part, leaving all questions which are not of vital military importance to the more deliberate action of the legislature.

In the exercise of my best discretion I have adhered to the blockade of the ports held by the insurgents, instead of putting in force, by proclamation, the law of Congress enacted at the last session for closing those ports.

So, also, obeying the dictates of prudence as well as the obligations of law, instead of transcending I have adhered to the act of Congress to confiscate property used for insurrectionary purposes. If a new law upon the same subject shall be proposed, its propriety will be duly considered. The Union must be preserved; and hence all indispensable means must be employed. We should not be in haste to determine that radical and extreme measures, which may reach the loyal as well as the disloyal, are indispensable.

The inaugural address at the beginning of the administration, and the message to Congress at the late special session, were both mainly devoted to the domestic controversy out of which the insurrection and consequent war have sprung. Nothing now occurs to add or subtract, to or from, the principles or general purposes stated and expressed in those documents.

The last ray of hope for preserving the Union peaceably expired at the assault upon Fort Sumter; and a general review of what has occurred since may not be unprofitable. What was painfully uncertain then is much better defined and more distinct now; and the progress of events is plainly in the right direction. The insurgents confidently claimed a strong support from north of Mason and Dixon's line; and the friends of the Union were not free from apprehension on the point. This, however, was soon settled definitely, and on the right side. South of the line, noble little Delaware led off right from the first. Maryland was made to seem against the Union. Our soldiers were assaulted, bridges were burned, and railroads torn up within her limits, and we were many days, at one time, without the ability to bring a single regiment over her soil to the capital. Now her bridges and railroads are repaired and open to the government; she already gives seven regiments to the cause of the Union and none to the enemy; and her people, at a regular election, have sustained the Union by a larger majority and a larger aggregate vote than they ever before gave to any candidate or any question. Kentucky, too, for some time in doubt, is now decidedly, and, I think, unchangeably, ranged on the side of the Union. Missouri is comparatively quiet, and, I believe, cannot again be overrun by the insurrectionists. These three States of Maryland, Kentucky, and Missouri, neither of which would promise a single soldier at first, have now an aggregate of not less than forty thousand in the field for the Union, while of their citizens certainly not more than a third of that number, and they of doubtful whereabouts and doubtful existence, are in arms against it. After a somewhat bloody struggle of months, winter closes on the Union people of western Virginia, leaving them masters of their own country.

An insurgent force of about 1500, for months dominating the narrow peninsular region constituting the counties of Accomac and Northampton, and known as the eastern shore of Virginia, together with some contiguous parts of Maryland, have laid down their arms, and the people there have renewed their allegiance to and accepted the protection of the old flag. This leaves no armed insurrectionist north of the Potomac or east of the Chesapeake.

Also we have obtained a footing at each of the isolated points, on the southern coast, of Hatteras, Port Royal, Tybee Island, near Savannah, and Ship Island; and we likewise have some general accounts of popular movements in behalf of the Union in North Carolina and Tennessee.

These things demonstrate that the cause of the Union is advancing steadily and certainly southward.

Since your last adjournment Lieutenant-General Scott[1] has retired from the head of the army. During his long life the nation has not been unmindful of his merit; yet, on calling to mind how faithfully, ably, and brilliantly he has served the country from a time far back in our history when few of the now living had been born, and thenceforward continually, I cannot but think we are still his debtors. I submit, therefore, for your consideration what further mark of recognition is due to him and to ourselves as a grateful people.

With the retirement of General Scott came the executive duty of appointing in his stead a general-in-chief of the army. It is a fortunate circumstance that neither in council nor country was there, so far as I know, any difference of opinion as to the proper person to be selected. The retiring chief repeatedly expressed his judgment in favor of General McClellan for the position, and in this the nation seemed to give a unanimous concurrence. The designation of General McClellan is, therefore, in considerable degree the selection of the country as well as of the executive, and hence there is better reason to hope there will be given him the confidence and cordial support thus by fair implication promised, and without which he cannot with so full efficiency serve the country.

It has been said that one bad general is better than two good ones; and the saying is true, if taken to mean no more than that an army is better directed by a single mind, though inferior, than by two superior ones at variance and crosspurposes with each other.

And the same is true in all joint operations wherein those

---

[1] Winfield Scott.

engaged can have none but a common end in view, and can differ only as to the choice of means. In a storm at sea no one on board can wish the ship to sink; and yet not infrequently all go down together because too many will direct, and no single mind can be allowed to control.

It continues to develop that the insurrection is largely, if not exclusively, a war upon the first principle of popular government—the rights of the people. Conclusive evidence of this is found in the most grave and maturely considered public documents as well as in the general tone of the insurgents. In those documents we find the abridgment of the existing right of suffrage and the denial to the people of all right to participate in the selection of public officers except the legislative, boldly advocated, with labored arguments to prove that large control of the people in government is the source of all political evil. Monarchy itself is sometimes hinted at as a possible refuge from the power of the people.

In my present position I could scarcely be justified were I to omit raising a warning voice against this approach of returning despotism.

It is not needed nor fitting here that a general argument should be made in favor of popular institutions; but there is one point, with its connections, not so hackneyed as most others, to which I ask a brief attention. It is the effort to place capital on an equal footing with, if not above, labor, in the structure of government. It is assumed that labor is available only in connection with capital; that nobody labors unless somebody else, owning capital, somehow by the use of it induces him to labor. This assumed, it is next considered whether it is best that capital shall hire laborers, and thus induce them to work by their own consent, or buy them, and drive them to it without their consent. Having proceeded thus far, it is naturally concluded that all laborers are either hired laborers or what we call slaves. And, further, it is assumed that whoever is once a hired laborer is fixed in that condition for life.

Now, there is no such relation between capital and labor as

assumed, nor is there any such thing as a free man being fixed for life in the condition of a hired laborer. Both these assumptions are false, and all inferences from them are groundless.

Labor is prior to, and independent of, capital. Capital is only the fruit of labor, and could never have existed if labor had not first existed. Labor is the superior of capital, and deserves much the higher consideration. Capital has its rights, which are as worthy of protection as any other rights. Nor is it denied that there is, and probably always will be, a relation between labor and capital producing mutual benefits. The error is assuming that the whole labor of the community exists within that relation. A few men own capital, and that few avoid labor themselves, and with their capital hire or buy another few to labor for them. A large majority belong to neither class—neither work for others nor have others working for them. In most of the Southern States a majority of the whole people, of all colors, are neither slaves nor masters; while in the Northern a large majority are neither hirers nor hired. Men with their families—wives, sons, and daughters—work for themselves, on their farms, in their houses, and in their shops taking the whole product to themselves, and asking no favors of capital on the one hand, nor of hired laborers or slaves on the other. It is not forgotten that a considerable number of persons mingle their own labor with capital—that is, they labor with their own hands and also buy or hire others to labor for them; but this is only a mixed and not a distinct class. No principle stated is disturbed by the existence of this mixed class.

Again, as has already been said, there is not, of necessity, any such thing as the free hired laborer being fixed to that condition for life. Many independent men everywhere in these States, a few years back in their lives, were hired laborers. The prudent, penniless beginner in the world labors for wages awhile, saves a surplus with which to buy tools or land for himself, then labors on his own account another while, and at length hires another new beginner to help him. This is the just and generous and prosperous system which opens the way to all—gives hope to all, and consequent energy and progress and improvement of condition to all. No men living are more worthy to be trusted than those who toil up from poverty— none less inclined to take or touch aught which they have not honestly earned. Let them beware of surrendering a political power which they already possess, and which, if surrendered, will surely be used to close the door of advancement against such as they, and to fix new disabilities and burdens upon them, till all of liberty shall be lost.

From the first taking of our national census to the last are seventy years; and we find our population at the end of the period eight times as great as it was at the beginning. The increase of those other things which men deem desirable has been even greater. We thus have, at one view, what the popular principle, applied to government, through the machinery of the States and the Union, has produced in a given time; and also what, if firmly maintained, it promises for the future. There are already among us those who, if the Union be preserved, will live to see it contain 250,000,000. The struggle of to-day is not altogether for to-day—it is for a vast future also. With a reliance on Providence all the more firm and earnest, let us proceed in the great task which events have devolved upon us.

ABRAHAM LINCOLN.

Washington, December 3, 1861.

———

LETTER TO GENERAL GEORGE B. McCLELLAN [1]

After the Union disaster at Manassas in July, 1861, Lincoln called McClellan to Washington to take command of the eastern army. Later the President made McClellan general-in-chief of all the armies. McClellan was a superb organizer and a brilliant military engineer. His faults were an over-developed sense of caution and an overwhelming sense of his own importance. In addition he was a Democrat, and he

---

[1] Lincoln, *Complete Works*, VII, 93-94.

aroused the undying enmity of the radical Republicans, who had no mind to see a general of Democratic antecedents win the war. McClellan worked out a plan to attack Richmond from the east, a route where the preponderant Union sea power could be used to advantage and which would place the army on a short land line to the Confederate capital. Lincoln the layman feared the results of this plan. He wanted to move the army southward from Washington toward Richmond, always keeping it between the Confederate and the Union capital. His proposal would have necessitated the maintenance of a long supply line and it gave the Confederate army a wide area in which to maneuver. Most authorities now think McClellan's plan was the better one. In this letter Lincoln voiced his objections to McClellan's plan.

Executive Mansion, February 3, 1862.

MY dear Sir: You and I have distinct and different plans for a movement of the Army of the Potomac—yours to be down the Chesapeake, up the Rappahannock to Urbana, and across land to the terminus of the railroad on the York River; mine to move directly to a point on the railroad southwest of Manassas.

If you will give me satisfactory answers to the following questions, I shall gladly yield my plan to yours.

First. Does not your plan involve a greatly larger expenditure of time and money than mine?

Second. Wherein is a victory more certain by your plan than mine?

Third. Wherein is a victory more valuable by your plan than mine?

Fourth. In fact, would it not be less valuable in this, that it would break no great line of the enemy's communications, while mine would?

Fifth. In case of disaster, would not a retreat be more difficult by your plan than mine?

Yours truly,

ABRAHAM LINCOLN.

MESSAGE TO CONGRESS RECOMMENDING COMPEN-
SATED EMANCIPATION, MARCH 6, 1862 [1]

> Lincoln was convinced that the best way to accomplish the
> abolition of slavery was by voluntary state action, with the
> federal government providing financial compensation. He
> hoped to get such a plan started in the loyal slave states,
> but these states took no action on his proposal.

FELLOW-CITIZENS of the Senate and House of Representatives: I recommend the adoption of a joint resolution
by your honorable bodies, which shall be substantially as
follows:

Resolved, That the United States ought to cooperate with
any State which may adopt gradual abolishment of slavery,
giving to such State pecuniary aid, to be used by such State,
in its discretion, to compensate for the inconveniences, public
and private, produced by such change of system.

If the proposition contained in the resolution does not meet
the approval of Congress and the country, there is the end; but
if it does command such approval, I deem it of importance that
the States and people immediately interested should be at once
distinctly notified of the fact, so that they may begin to consider
whether to accept or reject it. The Federal Government would
find its highest interest in such a measure, as one of the most
efficient means of self-preservation. The leaders of the existing
insurrection entertain the hope that this government will ultimately be forced to acknowledge the independence of some
part of the disaffected region, and that all the slave States north
of such part will then say, "The Union for which we have
struggled being already gone, we now choose to go with the
Southern section." To deprive them of this hope substantially
ends the rebellion; and the initiation of emancipation com-
pletely deprives them of it as to all the States initiating it. The
point is not that all the States tolerating slavery would very
soon, if at all, initiate emancipation; but that while the offer

---

[1] Lincoln, *Complete Works,* VII, 112-115.

is equally made to all, the more Northern shall, by such initiation, make it certain to the more Southern that in no event will the former ever join the latter in their proposed confederacy. I say "initiation" because, in my judgment, gradual and not sudden emancipation is better for all. In the mere financial or pecuniary view, any member of Congress, with the census tables and treasury reports before him, can readily see for himself how very soon the current expenditures of this war would purchase, at fair valuation, all the slaves in any named State. Such a proposition on the part of the General Government sets up no claim of a right by Federal authority to interfere with slavery within State limits, referring, as it does, the absolute control of the subject in each case to the State and its people immediately interested. It is proposed as a matter of perfectly free choice with them.

In the annual message, last December, I thought fit to say, "The Union must be preserved, and hence all indispensable means must be employed." I said this not hastily, but deliberately. War has been made, and continues to be, an indispensable means to this end. A practical reacknowledgment of the national authority would render the war unnecessary, and it would at once cease. If, however, resistance continues, the war must also continue; and it is impossible to foresee all the incidents which may attend and all the ruin which may follow it. Such as may seem indispensable, or may obviously promise great efficiency, toward ending the struggle, must and will come.

The proposition now made, though an offer only, I hope it may be esteemed no offense to ask whether the pecuniary consideration tendered would not be of more value to the States and private persons concerned than are the institution and property in it, in the present aspect of affairs?

While it is true that the adoption of the proposed resolution would be merely initiatory and not within itself a practical measure, it is recommended in the hope that it would soon lead to important practical results. In full view of my great responsibility to my God and to my country, I earnestly beg the attention of Congress and the people to the subject.

ABRAHAM LINCOLN.

LETTER TO HENRY J. RAYMOND [1]

In this letter to Henry J. Raymond, editor of the *New York Times,* Lincoln argued for compensated emancipation as a device to shorten the war.

(Private.)

Executive Mansion, March 9, 1862.

MY dear Sir: I am grateful to the New York journals, and not less so to the "Times" than to others, for their kind notices of the late special message to Congress.

Your paper, however, intimates that the proposition, though well intentioned, must fail on the score of expense. I do hope you will reconsider this. Have you noticed the facts that less than one half day's cost of this war would pay for all the slaves in Delaware at $400 per head—that eighty-seven days' cost of this war would pay for all in Delaware, Maryland, District of Columbia, Kentucky, and Missouri at the same price? Were those States to take the step, do you doubt that it would shorten the war more than eighty-seven days, and thus be an actual saving of expense?

Please look at these things and consider whether there should not be another article in the "Times."

Yours very truly,

A. LINCOLN.

---

[1] Lincoln, *Complete Works,* VII, 119.

LETTER TO GENERAL GEORGE B. McCLELLAN [1]

> With great reluctance, Lincoln permitted McClellan to start his movement to attack Richmond from the east. The President feared that while McClellan was operating at such a distance from Washington the Confederates would seize the opportunity to take the capital. Therefore he stipulated to McClellan that an adequate force must be left to defend Washington. After McClellan departed for the field the radical Republicans, led by Secretary of War Edwin M. Stanton and the Congressional Committee on the Conduct of the War, came to Lincoln with stories that McClellan had not obeyed instructions, that the city was open to capture. They deceived Lincoln. Actually McClellan had placed 65,000 men in and around the approaches to Washington. Lincoln decided more men were needed to hold the city. First he withdrew General Louis Blenker's division of 10,000 from McClellan's army and followed this by ordering General Irvin McDowell's corps of 30,000 to remain near Washington. Thus McClellan lost a good part of his army. The radicals, who wanted him to fail, were jubilant.
>
> In this letter Lincoln rebuked McClellan for leaving Washington undefended. He also urged the general, who had edged cautiously toward Richmond, to hasten his progress.

Washington, April 9, 1862.

MY dear Sir: Your despatches, complaining that you are not properly sustained, while they do not offend me, do pain me very much.

Blenker's division was withdrawn from you before you left here, and you knew the pressure under which I did it, and, as I thought, acquiesced in it—certainly not without reluctance.

After you left I ascertained that less than 20,000 unorganized men, without a single field-battery, were all you designed to be left for the defense of Washington and Manassas Junction, and part of this even was to go to General Hooker's old position; General Bank's corps, once designed for Manassas Junction, was divided and tied up on the line of Winchester and Strasburg, and could not leave it without again exposing

---

[1] Lincoln, *Complete Works*, VII, 141-143.

the upper Potomac and the Baltimore and Ohio Railroad. This presented (or would present, when McDowell and Sumner should be gone) a great temptation to the enemy to turn back from the Rappahannock and sack Washington. My explicit order that Washington should, by the judgment of all the commanders of corps, be left entirely secure, had been neglected. It was precisely this that drove me to detain McDowell.

I do not forget that I was satisfied with your arrangement to leave Banks at Manassas Junction; but when that arrangement was broken up and nothing was substituted for it, of course I was not satisfied. I was constrained to substitute something for it myself.

And now allow me to ask, do you really think I should permit the line from Richmond *via* Manassas Junction to this city to be entirely open, except what resistance could be presented by less than 20,000 unorganized troops? This is a question which the country will not allow me to evade.

There is a curious mystery about the number of the troops now with you. When I telegraphed you on the 6th, saying you had over 100,000 with you, I had just obtained from the Secretary of War a statement, taken as he said from your own returns, making 108,000 then with you and *en route* to you. You now say you will have but 85,000 when all *en route* to you shall have reached you. How can this discrepancy of 23,000 be accounted for?

As to General Wool's command, I understand it is doing for you precisely what a like number of your own would have to do if that command was away.[1] I suppose the whole force which has gone forward to you is with you by this time; and if so, I think it is the precise time for you to strike a blow. By delay the enemy will relatively gain upon you—that is, he will gain faster by fortifications and reinforcements than you can by reinforcements alone.

And once more let me tell you it is indispensable to you that

---

[1] Wool commanded Fortress Monroe, which was in the region where McClellan was operating but was not under his command.

you strike a blow. I am powerless to help this. You will do me the justice to remember I always insisted that going down the bay in search of a field, instead of fighting at or near Manassas, was only shifting and not surmounting a difficulty; that we would find the same enemy and the same or equal intrenchments at either place. The country will not fail to note —is noting now—that the present hesitation to move upon an intrenched enemy is but the story of Manassas repeated.[1]

I beg to assure you that I have never written you or spoken to you in greater kindness of feeling than now, nor with a fuller purpose to sustain you, so far as in my most anxious judgment I consistently can; but you must act.

Yours very truly,

A. LINCOLN.

——

LETTER TO GENERAL GEORGE B. McCLELLAN [2]

Over the protests of McClellan, Lincoln had ordered the Army of the Potomac organized into corps, and had designated as corps commanders Generals Irvin McDowell, E. V. Sumner, Samuel P. Heintzelman, and E. D. Keyes. These officers were not friendly to McClellan; he had wanted the appointments to go to certain favorites of his like Fitz-John Porter and William B. Franklin. After McClellan started his campaign, he asked Lincoln for permission to suspend the corps organization. Lincoln consented, but he warned McClellan that the latter's opposition to the corps system was arousing criticism which could not be disregarded.

Fort Monroe, Virginia, May 9, 1862.

MY dear Sir: I have just assisted the Secretary of War in framing part of a despatch to you relating to army corps, which despatch of course will have reached you before this will.

[1] Lincoln refers to McClellan's refusal to attack the Confederates at Manassas in the previous year.
[2] Lincoln, *Complete Works*, VII, 156-157.

I wish to say a few words to you privately on this subject. I ordered the army corps organization not only on the unanimous opinion of the twelve generals whom you had selected and assigned as generals of division, but also on the unanimous opinion of every military man I could get an opinion from (and every modern military book), yourself only excepted. Of course I did not on my own judgment pretend to understand the subject. I now think it indispensable for you to know how your struggle against it is received in quarters which we cannot entirely disregard. It is looked upon as merely an effort to pamper one or two pets and to persecute and degrade their supposed rivals. I have had no word from Sumner, Heintzelman, or Keyes. The commanders of these corps are of course the three highest officers with you, but I am constantly told that you have no consultation or communication with them; that you consult and communicate with nobody but General Fitz-John Porter and perhaps General Franklin. I do not say these complaints are true or just, but at all events it is proper you should know of their existence. Do the commanders of corps disobey your orders in anything?

When you relieved General Hamilton of his command the other day, you thereby lost the confidence of at least one of your best friends in the Senate. And here let me say, not as applicable to you personally, that senators and representatives speak of me in their places as they please without question, and that officers of the army must cease addressing insulting letters to them for taking no greater liberty with them.

But to return. Are you strong enough—are you strong enough, even with my help—to set your foot upon the necks of Sumner, Heintzelman, and Keyes all at once? This is a practical and very serious question for you.

The success of your army and the cause of the country are the same, and of course I only desire the good of the cause.

Yours truly,

A. LINCOLN.

PROCLAMATION REVOKING GENERAL HUNTER'S ORDER OF MILITARY EMANCIPATION, MAY 19, 1862 [1]

Emulating Frémont, General David Hunter issued on May 9 a proclamation freeing the slaves in his military district. Again Lincoln overruled an impetuous general, and for the same reason that he had revoked Frémont's proclamation. The President realized, however, that Hunter's action was a reflection of the increasing sentiment in the country for the destruction of slavery. So he made another, and fruitless, appeal to the loyal slave states to take up compensated emancipation before it was too late.

BY THE PRESIDENT OF THE UNITED STATES OF AMERICA:

A Proclamation.

WHEREAS there appears in the public prints what purports to be a proclamation of Major-General Hunter, in the words and figures following, to wit:

(General Orders No. 11.)

Headquarters Department of the South,

Hilton Head, Port Royal, S. C., May 9, 1862.

The three States of Georgia, Florida, and South Carolina, comprising the military department of the South, having deliberately declared themselves no longer under the protection of the United States of America, and having taken up arms against the said United States, it became a military necessity to declare martial law. This was accordingly done on the 25th day of April, 1862. Slavery and martial law in a free country are altogether incompatible; the persons in these three States—Georgia, Florida, and South Carolina—heretofore held as slaves, are therefore declared forever free.

By command of Major-General D. Hunter:

(Official.)   Ed. W. Smith,

Acting Assistant Adjutant-General.

---

[1] Lincoln, *Complete Works*, VII, 170-173.

And whereas the same is producing some excitement and misunderstanding: therefore,

I, Abraham Lincoln, President of the United States, proclaim and declare that the Government of the United States had no knowledge, information, or belief of an intention on the part of General Hunter to issue such a proclamation; nor has it yet any authentic information that the document is genuine. And further, that neither General Hunter, nor any other commander or person, has been authorized by the Government of the United States to make a proclamation declaring the slaves of any State free; and that the supposed proclamation now in question, whether genuine or false, is altogether void as far as respects such a declaration.

I further make known that, whether it be competent for me, as commander-in-chief of the army and navy, to declare the slaves of any State or States free, and whether, at any time, in any case, it shall have become a necessity indispensable to the maintenance of the government to exercise such supposed power, are questions which, under my responsibility, I reserve to myself, and which I cannot feel justified in leaving to the decision of commanders in the field. These are totally different questions from those of police regulations in armies and camps. On the sixth day of March last, by special message, I recommended to Congress the adoption of a joint resolution, to be substantially as follows:

> Resolved, That the United States ought to cooperate with any State which may adopt gradual abolishment of slavery, giving to such State pecuniary aid, to be used by such State, in its discretion, to compensate for the inconvenience, public and private, produced by such change of system.

The resolution, in the language above quoted, was adopted by large majorities in both branches of Congress, and now stands an authentic, definite, and solemn proposal of the nation to the States and people most immediately interested in the subject-matter. To the people of those States I now earnestly appeal. I do not argue—I beseech you to make arguments for yourselves. You cannot, if you would, be blind to the signs of the times. I beg of you a calm and enlarged consideration of them, ranging, if it may be, far above personal and partizan politics. This proposal makes common cause for a common object, casting no reproaches upon any. It acts not the Pharisee. The change it contemplates would come gently as the dews of heaven, not rending or wrecking anything. Will you not embrace it? So much good has not been done, by one effort, in all past time, as in the providence of God it is now your high privilege to do. May the vast future not have to lament that you have neglected it.

In witness whereof, I have hereunto set my hand and caused the seal of the United States to be affixed.

> Done at the city of Washington, this nineteenth day of May, in the year of our Lord one thousand eight hundred and sixty-two, and of the independence of the United States the eighty-sixth.

> ABRAHAM LINCOLN.

TELEGRAM TO GENERAL GEORGE B. McCLELLAN [1]

> When Lincoln sent this telegram, the Confederate army under Robert E. Lee was pushing McClellan back from Richmond. McClellan was retreating but he was doing so in an orderly manner. He wanted reenforcements to hold his ground and assume the offensive again. Lincoln did not think McClellan could succeed even with more troops; and in his kindly way the President tried to console the general for the failure of the attack upon Richmond and to intimate gently that help would not be forthcoming.

War Department, June 28, 1862.

MAJOR-GENERAL McClellan: Save your army, at all events. Will send reinforcements as fast as we can. Of

---

[1] Lincoln, *Complete Works*, VII, 239-240.

course they cannot reach you today, to-morrow, or next day. I have not said you were ungenerous for saying you needed reinforcements. I thought you were ungenerous in assuming that I did not send them as fast as I could. I feel any misfortune to you and your army quite as keenly as you feel it yourself. If you have had a drawn battle, or a repulse, it is the price we pay for the enemy not being in Washington. We protected Washington, and the enemy concentrated on you. Had we stripped Washington, he would have been upon us before the troops could have gotten to you. Less than a week ago you notified us that reinforcements were leaving Richmond to come in front of us. It is the nature of the case, and neither you nor the government is to blame. Please tell at once the present condition and aspect of things.

A. LINCOLN.

TELEGRAM TO GENERAL GEORGE B. McCLELLAN [1]

> McClellan again asked for reenforcements. This time Lincoln told him bluntly that no more troops could be sent. McClellan would have to hold on as best as he could or retreat. Eventually Lincoln decided to remove McClellan's army from its position and bring it back near Washington. John Pope succeeded McClellan as commander. In August Pope suffered a crushing defeat at the second battle of Manassas.

War Department, Washington, July 1, 1862.
3:30 P.M.

MAJOR-GENERAL George B. McClellan: It is impossible to reinforce you for your present emergency. If we had a million of men, we could not get them to you in time. We have not the men to send. If you are not strong enough to face the enemy, you must find a place of security, and wait, rest, and repair. Maintain your ground if you can, but save the army

---

[1] Lincoln, *Complete Works*, VII, 253.

at all events, even if you fall back to Fort Monroe. We still have strength enough in the country, and will bring it out.

A. LINCOLN.

———

APPEAL TO FAVOR COMPENSATED EMANCIPATION, READ BY THE PRESIDENT TO BORDER-STATE REPRESENTATIVES, JULY 12, 1862 [1]

> This personal appeal to the Congressmen of the loyal slave states was Lincoln's last attempt to secure compensated emancipation by state action. He told his hearers that unless they adopted his scheme the radicals would succeed in forcing some drastic action against slavery. His appeal fell on deaf ears. Reluctantly Lincoln resolved, in this same month, to issue an emancipation proclamation.

GENTLEMEN: After the adjournment of Congress, now very near, I shall have no opportunity of seeing you for several months. Believing that you of the border States hold more power for good than any other equal number of members, I feel it a duty which I cannot justifiably waive to make this appeal to you. I intend no reproach or complaint when I assure you that, in my opinion, if you all had voted for the resolution in the gradual-emancipation message of last March, the war would now be substantially ended. And the plan therein proposed is yet one of the most potent and swift means of ending it. Let the States which are in rebellion see definitely and certainly that in no event will the States you represent ever join their proposed confederacy, and they cannot much longer maintain the contest. But you cannot divest them of their hope to ultimately have you with them so long as you show a determination to perpetuate the institution within your own States. Beat them at elections, as you have overwhelmingly done, and, nothing daunted, they still claim you as their own. You and I know what the lever of their power is. Break that lever before

---

[1] Lincoln, *Complete Works*, VII, 270-274.

their faces, and they can shake you no more forever. Most of you have treated me with kindness and consideration, and I trust you will not now think I improperly touch what is exclusively your own, when, for the sake of the whole country, I ask, Can you, for your States, do better than to take the course I urge? Discarding punctilio and maxims adapted to more manageable times, and looking only to the unprecedentedly stern facts of our case, can you do better in any possible event? You prefer that the constitutional relation of the States to the nation shall be practically restored without disturbance of the institution; and if this were done, my whole duty in this respect, under the Constitution and my oath of office, would be performed. But it is not done, and we are trying to accomplish it by war. The incidents of the war cannot be avoided. If the war continues long, as it must if the object be not sooner attained, the institution in your States will be extinguished by mere friction and abrasion—by the mere incidents of the war. It will be gone, and you will have nothing valuable in lieu of it. Much of its value is gone already. How much better for you and for your people to take the step which at once shortens the war and secures substantial compensation for that which is sure to be wholly lost in any other event! How much better to thus save the money which else we sink forever in the war! How much better to do it while we can, lest the war ere long render us pecuniarily unable to do it! How much better for you as seller, and the nation as buyer, to sell out and buy out that without which the war could never have been, than to sink both the things to be sold and the price of it in cutting one another's throats! I do not speak of emancipation at once, but of a decision at once to emancipate gradually. Room in South America for colonization can be obtained cheaply and in abundance, and when numbers shall be large enough to be company and encouragement for one another, the freed people will not be so reluctant to go.

I am pressed with a difficulty not yet mentioned—one which threatens division among those who, united, are none too strong. An instance of it is known to you. General Hunter is an honest man. He was, and I hope still is, my friend. I valued him none the less for his agreeing with me in the general wish that all men everywhere could be free. He proclaimed all men free within certain States, and I repudiated the proclamation. He expected more good and less harm from the measure than I could believe would follow. Yet, in repudiating it, I gave dissatisfaction, if not offense, to many whose support the country cannot afford to lose. And this is not the end of it. The pressure in this direction is still upon me, and is increasing. By conceding what I now ask, you can relieve me, and, much more, can relieve the country, in this important point. Upon these considerations I have again begged your attention to the message of March last. Before leaving the capital, consider and discuss it among yourselves. You are patriots and statesmen, and as such I pray you consider this proposition, and at the least commend it to the consideration of your States and people. As you would perpetuate popular government for the best people in the world, I beseech you that you do in no wise omit this. Our common country is in great peril, demanding the loftiest views and boldest action to bring it speedy relief. Once relieved, its form of government is saved to the world, its beloved history and cherished memories are vindicated, and its happy future fully assured and rendered inconceivably grand. To you, more than to any others, the privilege is given to assure that happiness and swell that grandeur, and to link your own names therewith forever.

LETTER TO HORACE GREELEY [1]

On August 19, 1862, Horace Greeley, editor of the radical *New York Tribune*, published in his paper an appeal to Lincoln entitled "The Prayer of Twenty Millions." Greeley demanded that Lincoln make emancipation one of the aims

[1] Lincoln, *Complete Works*, VIII, 15-16.

of the war. Although Lincoln had already determined to issue an emancipation proclamation, he had kept his purpose secret. This public letter to Greeley was one of Lincoln's finest statements of his purpose to save the Union by any means.

Executive Mansion,

Washington, August 22, 1862.

DEAR Sir: I have just read yours of the 19th, addressed to myself through the New York "Tribune." If there be in it any statements or assumptions of fact which I may know to be erroneous, I do not now and here, controvert them. If there be in it any inferences which I may believe to be falsely drawn, I do not, now and here, argue against them. If there be perceptible in it an impatient and dictatorial tone, I waive it in deference to an old friend whose heart I have always supposed to be right.

As to the policy I "seem to be pursuing," as you say, I have not meant to leave any one in doubt.

I would save the Union. I would save it the shortest way under the Constitution. The sooner the national authority can be restored, the nearer the Union will be "the Union as it was." If there be those who would not save the Union unless they could at the same time save slavery, I do not agree with them. If there be those who would not save the Union unless they could at the same time destroy slavery, I do not agree with them. My paramount object in this struggle is to save the Union, and is not either to save or to destroy slavery. If I could save the Union without freeing any slave, I would do it; and if I could save it by freeing all the slaves, I would do it; and if I could save it by freeing some and leaving others alone, I would also do that. What I do about slavery and the colored race, I do because I believe it helps to save the Union; and what I forbear, I forbear because I do not believe it would help to have the Union. I shall do less whenever I shall believe what I am doing hurts the cause, and I shall do more whenever I shall believe doing more will help the cause. I shall try to correct errors when shown to be errors, and I shall adopt new views so fast as they shall appear to be true views.

I have here stated my purpose according to my view of official duty; and I intend no modification of my oft-expressed personal wish that all men everywhere could be free. Yours,

A. LINCOLN.

————

REPLY TO A COMMITTEE FROM THE RELIGIOUS DENOMINATIONS OF CHICAGO, ASKING THE PRESIDENT TO ISSUE A PROCLAMATION OF EMANCIPATION, SEPTEMBER 13, 1862 [1]

> In this remarkable statement, Lincoln presented telling arguments against the practicality of an emancipation proclamation. Yet nine days later he issued one. This document affords evidence that Lincoln was extremely reluctant to resort to war-time emancipation and did so only to prevent the radicals from seizing the initiative.

THE subject presented in the memorial is one upon which I have thought much for weeks past, and I may even say for months. I am approached with the most opposite opinions and advice, and that by religious men who are equally certain that they represent the divine will. I am sure that either the one or the other class is mistaken in that belief, and perhaps in some respects both. I hope it will not be irreverent for me to say that if it is probable that God would reveal his will to others on a point so connected with my duty, it might be supposed he would reveal it directly to me; for, unless I am more deceived in myself that I often am, it is my earnest desire to know the will of Providence in this matter. And if I can learn what it is, I will do it.

These are not, however, the days of miracles, and I suppose it will be granted that I am not to expect a direct revelation.

---

[1] Lincoln, *Complete Works*, VIII, 28-33.

I must study the plain physical facts of the case, ascertain what is possible, and learn what appears to be wise and right.

The subject is difficult, and good men do not agree. For instance, the other day four gentlemen of standing and intelligence from New York called as a delegation on business connected with the war; but, before leaving, two of them earnestly beset me to proclaim general emancipation, upon which the other two at once attacked them. You know also that the last session of Congress had a decided majority of anti-slavery men, yet they could not unite on this policy. And the same is true of the religious people. Why, the rebel soldiers are praying with a great deal more earnestness, I fear, than our own troops, and expecting God to favor their side; for one of our soldiers who had been taken prisoner told Senator Wilson[1] a few days since that he met with nothing so discouraging as the evident sincerity of those he was among in their prayers. But we will talk over the merits of the case.

What good would a proclamation of emancipation from me do, especially as we are now situated? I do not want to issue a document that the whole world will see must necessarily be inoperative, like the Pope's bull against the comet. Would my word free the slaves, when I cannot even enforce the Constitution in the rebel States? Is there a single court, or magistrate, or individual that would be influenced by it there? And what reason is there to think it would have any greater effect upon the slaves than the late law of Congress, which I approved, and which offers protection and freedom to the slaves of rebel masters who come within our lines? Yet I cannot learn that that law has caused a single slave to come over to us. And suppose they could be induced by a proclamation of freedom from me to throw themselves upon us, what should we do with them? How can we feed and care for such a multitude? General Butler[2] wrote me a few days since that he was issuing more rations to the slaves who have rushed to him than to all the

---

[1] Henry Wilson of Massachusetts.
[2] Benjamin F. Butler, in command at New Orleans.

white troops under his command. They eat, and that is all; though it is true General Butler is feeding the whites also by the thousand, for it nearly amounts to a famine there. If, now, the pressure of the war should call off our forces from New Orleans to defend some other point, what is to prevent the masters from reducing the blacks to slavery again? For I am told that whenever the rebels take any black prisoners, free or slave, they immediately auction them off. They did so with those they took from a boat that was aground in the Tennessee River a few days ago. And then I am very ungenerously attacked for it! For instance, when, after the late battles at and near Bull Run, an expedition went out from Washington under a flag of truce to bury the dead and bring in the wounded, and the rebels seized the blacks who went along to help, and sent them into slavery, Horace Greeley said in his paper the government would do nothing about it. What could I do?

Now, then, tell me, if you please, what possible result of good would the issuing of such a proclamation as you desire? Understand, I raise no objections against it on legal or constitutional grounds; for, as commander-in-chief of the army and navy, in time of war I suppose I have a right to take any measure which may best subdue the enemy; nor do I urge objections of a moral nature, in view of possible consequences of insurrection and massacre at the South.

I view this matter as a practical war measure, to be decided on according to the advantages or disadvantages it may offer to the suppression of the rebellion.

I admit that slavery is the root of the rebellion, or at least its *sine qua non*. The ambition of politicians may have instigated them to act, but they would have been impotent without slavery as their instrument. I will also concede that emancipation would help us in Europe, and convince them that we are incited by something more than ambition. I grant, further, that it would help somewhat at the North, though not so much, I fear, as you and those you represent imagine. Still some additional strength would be added in that way to the war, and then, unquestionably, it would weaken the rebels by drawing off their laborers, which is of great importance; but I am not sure we could do much with the blacks. If we were to arm them, I fear that in a few weeks the arms would be in the hands of the rebels; and, indeed, thus far we have not had arms enough to equip our white troops. I will mention another thing, though it meet only your scorn and contempt. There are fifty thousand bayonets in the Union armies from the border slave States. It would be a serious matter if, in consequence of a proclamation such as you desire, they should go over to the rebels. I do not think they all would—not so many, indeed, as a year ago, or six months ago—not so many to-day as yesterday. Every day increases their Union feeling. They are also getting their pride enlisted, and want to beat the rebels.

Let me say one thing more: I think you should admit that we already have an important principle to rally and unite the people, in the fact that constitutional government is at stake. This is a fundamental idea going down about as deep as anything.

Do not misunderstand me because I have mentioned these objections. They indicate the difficulties that have thus far prevented my action in some such way as you desire. I have not decided against a proclamation of liberty to the slaves, but hold the matter under advisement; and I can assure you that the subject is on my mind, by day and night, more than any other. Whatever shall appear to be God's will, I will do. I trust that in the freedom with which I have canvassed your views I have not in any respect injured your feelings.

PRELIMINARY EMANCIPATION PROCLAMATION, SEPTEMBER 22, 1862 [1]

> Lincoln had laid aside his emancipation in July, waiting for a military victory before making it public. On September 17

[1] Lincoln, *Complete Works*, VIII, 36-41.

McClellan defeated Lee at Antietam. Thereupon Lincoln issued the proclamation. It was a warning to the seceded states that unless they returned to their allegiance by January 1, he would declare their slaves free. Presumably, if they did return, the proclamation would not be issued.

BY THE PRESIDENT OF THE UNITED STATES OF AMERICA:

A Proclamation.

I Abraham Lincoln, President of the United States of America, and commander-in-chief of the army and navy thereof, do hereby proclaim and declare that hereafter, as heretofore, the war will be prosecuted for the object of practically restoring the constitutional relation between the United States and each of the States, and the people thereof, in which States that relation is or may be suspended or disturbed.

That it is my purpose, upon the next meeting of Congress, to again recommend the adoption of a practical measure tendering pecuniary aid to the free acceptance or rejection of all slave States, so called, the people whereof may not then be in rebellion against the United States, and which States may then have voluntarily adopted, or thereafter may voluntarily adopt, immediate or gradual abolishment of slavery within their respective limits; and that the effort to colonize persons of African descent with their consent upon this continent or elsewhere, with the previously obtained consent of the governments existing there, will be continued.

That on the first day of January, in the year of our Lord one thousand eight hundred and sixty-three, all persons held as slaves within any State or designated part of a State the people whereof shall then be in rebellion against the United States, shall be then, thenceforward, and forever free; and the Executive Government of the United States, including the military and naval authority thereof, will recognize and maintain the freedom of such persons, and will do no act or acts to repress such persons, or any of them, in any efforts they may make for their actual freedom.

That the Executive will, on the first day of January aforesaid, by proclamation designate the States and parts of States, if any, in which the people thereof, respectively shall then be in rebellion against the United States; and the fact that any State or the people thereof, shall on that day be in good faith represented in the Congress of the United States by members chosen thereto at elections wherein a majority of the qualified voters of such State shall have participated, shall, in the absence of strong countervailing testimony, be deemed conclusive evidence that such State, and the people thereof, are not then in rebellion against the United States.

That attention is hereby called to an act of Congress entitled "An act to make an additional article of war," approved March 13, 1862, and which act is in the words and figure following:

Be it enacted by the Senate and House of Representatives of the United States of America in Congress assembled, That hereafter the following shall be promulgated as an additional article of war, for the government of the army of the United States, and shall be obeyed and observed as such:

ARTICLE —. All officers or persons in the military or naval service of the United States are prohibited from employing any of the forces under their respective commands for the purpose of returning fugitives from service or labor who may have escaped from any persons to whom such service or labor is claimed to be due; and any officer who shall be found guilty by a court martial of violating this article shall be dismissed from the service.

SEC. 2. And be it further enacted, That this act shall take effect from and after its passage.

Also to the ninth and tenth sections of an act entitled "An act to suppress insurrections, to punish treason and rebellion, to seize and confiscate property of rebels, and for other purposes," approved July 17, 1862, and which sections are in the words and figures following:

SEC. 9. And be it further enacted, That all slaves of persons who shall hereafter be engaged in rebellion against the Government of the United States, or who shall in any way give aid or comfort thereto, escaping from such persons and taking refuge within the lines of the army; and all slaves captured from such persons or deserted by them, and coming under the control of the Government of the United States; and all slaves of such persons found on (or) being within any place occupied by rebel forces and afterwards occupied by the forces of the United States, shall be deemed captives of war, and shall be forever free of their servitude, and not again held as slaves.

SEC. 10. And be it further enacted, That no slave escaping into any State, Territory, or the District of Columbia, from any other State, shall be delivered up, or in any way impeded, or hindered of his liberty except for crime, or some offense against the laws, unless the person claiming said fugitive shall first make oath that the person to whom the labor or services of such fugitive is alleged to be due is his lawful owner, and has not borne arms against the United States in the present rebellion, nor in any way given aid and comfort thereto; and no person engaged in the military or naval service of the United States shall, under any pretense whatever, assume to decide on the validity of the claim of any person to the service or labor of any other person, or surrender up any such person to the claimant, on pain of being dismissed from the service.

And I do hereby enjoin upon and order all persons engaged in the military and naval service of the United States to observe, obey, and enforce, within their respective spheres of service, the act and sections above recited.

And the Executive will in due time recommend that all citizens of the United States who shall have remained loyal thereto throughout the rebellion shall (upon the restoration of the constitutional relation between the United States and their respective States and people, if that relation shall have been suspended or disturbed) be compensated for all losses by acts of the United States, including the loss of slaves.

In witness whereof, I have hereunto set my hand and caused the seal of the United States to be affixed.

Done at the city of Washington, this twenty-second day of September, in the year of our Lord, one thousand eight hundred and sixty-two, and of the independence of the United States the eighty-seventh.

ABRAHAM LINCOLN.

————

LETTER TO GENERAL GEORGE B. McCLELLAN [1]

After Pope's failure at Manassas, Lincoln had reappointed McClellan to the eastern command. McClellan took over at a critical moment. The Confederates under Lee were about to invade Maryland. At Antietam McClellan met Lee and forced him to retreat. Lincoln thought McClellan had lost an opportunity to end the war by smashing Lee with a vigorous pursuit. Then the President became impatient because McClellan did not advance rapidly into Virginia. In this letter he criticized McClellan for being too cautious. In November he removed McClellan from command.

Executive Mansion

Washington, D. C., October 13, 1862.

MY dear Sir: You remember my speaking to you of what I called your over-cautiousness. Are you not over-cautious when you assume that you cannot do what the enemy is constantly doing? Should you not claim to be at least his equal in prowess, and act upon the claim? As I understand, you telegraphed General Halleck[2] that you cannot subsist your army at Winchester unless the railroad from Harper's Ferry to that point be put in working order. But the enemy does now subsist his army at Winchester, at a distance nearly twice as great from railroad transportation as you would have to do without the railroad last named. He now wagons from Culpeper Court House, which is just about twice as far as you would

---

[1] Lincoln, *Complete Works*, VIII, 57-61.
[2] Henry W. Halleck, Lincoln's military adviser.

have to do from Harper's Ferry. He is certainly not more than half as well provided with wagons as you are. I certainly should be pleased for you to have the advantage of the railroad from Harper's Ferry to Winchester, but it wastes all the remainder of autumn to give it to you, and in fact ignores the question of time, which cannot and must not be ignored. Again, one of the standard maxims of war, as you know, is to "operate upon the enemy's communications as much as possible without exposing your own." You seem to act as if this applies against you, but cannot apply in your favor. Change positions with the enemy, and think you not he would break your communication with Richmond within the next twenty-four hours? You dread his going into Pennsylvania; but if he does so in full force, he gives up his communications to you absolutely, and you have nothing to do but to follow and ruin him. If he does so with less than full force, fall upon and beat what is left behind all the easier. Exclusive of the water-line, you are now nearer Richmond than the enemy is by the route that you can and he must take. Why can you not reach there before him, unless you admit that he is more than your equal on a march? His route is the arc of a circle, while yours is the chord. The roads are as good on yours as on his. You know I desired, but did not order you to cross the Potomac below, instead of above, the Shenandoah and Blue Ridge. My idea was that this would at once menace the enemy's communications, which I would seize if he would permit.

If he should move northward, I would follow him closely, holding his communications. If he should prevent our seizing his communications and move toward Richmond, I would press closely to him, fight him if a favorable opportunity should present, and at least try to beat him to Richmond on the inside track. I say "try"; if we never try, we shall never succeed. If he makes a stand at Winchester, moving neither north nor south, I would fight him there, on the idea that if we cannot beat him when he bears the wastage of coming to us, we never can when we bear the wastage of going to him. This

proposition is simple truth, and is too important to be lost sight
of for a moment. In coming to us he tenders us an advantage
which we should not waive. We should not so operate as to
merely drive him away. As we must beat him somewhere or
fail finally, we can do it, if at all, easier near to us than far
away. If we cannot beat the enemy where he now is, we never
can, he again being within the intrenchments of Richmond.

Recurring to the idea of going to Richmond on the inside
track, the facility of supplying from the side away from the
enemy is remarkable, as it were, by the different spokes of a
wheel extending from the hub toward the rim, and this whether
you move directly by the chord or on the inside arc, hugging
the Blue Ridge more closely. The chord-line, as you see, carries
you by Aldie, Hay Market, and Fredericksburg; and you see
how turnpikes, railroads, and finally the Potomac, by Aquia
Creek, meet you at all points from Washington; the same, only
the lines lengthened a little if you press closer to the Blue Ridge
part of the way.

The gaps through the Blue Ridge I understand to be about
the following distances from Harper's Ferry, to wit: Vestal's,
5 miles; Gregory's, 13; Snicker's, 18; Ashby's, 28; Manassas,
38; Chester, 45; and Thornton's, 53. I should think it prefer-
able to take the route nearest the enemy, disabling him to make
an important move without your knowledge, and compelling
him to keep his forces together for dread of you. The gaps
would enable you to attack if you should wish. For a great part
of the way you would be practically between the enemy and
both Washington and Richmond, enabling us to spare you the
greatest number of troops from here. When at length running
for Richmond ahead of him enables him to move this way, if
he does so, turn and attack him in rear. But I think he should
be engaged long before such point is reached. It is all easy if
our troops march as well as the enemy, and it is unmanly to
say they cannot do it. This letter is in no sense an order.

Yours truly,

A. LINCOLN.

LETTER TO GOVERNOR GEORGE F. SHEPLEY [1]

Shepley was military governor of Louisiana, where Lincoln was anxious to get a reconstructed, loyal state government established. In this letter he warned Shepley against the error of permitting northern men not citizens of the state to take over the control of the reconstruction movement.

Executive Mansion,

Washington, November 21, 1862.

DEAR Sir: Dr. Kennedy, bearer of this, has some apprehension that Federal officers not citizens of Louisiana may be set up as candidates for Congress in that State. In my view there could be no possible object in such an election. We do not particularly need members of Congress from there to enable us to get along with legislation here. What we do want is the conclusive evidence that respectable citizens of Louisiana are willing to be members of Congress and to swear support of the Constitution, and that other respectable citizens there are willing to vote for them and send them. To send a parcel of Northern men here as representatives, elected, as would be understood (and perhaps really so), at the point of the bayonet, would be disgusting and outrageous; and were I a member of Congress here, I would vote against admitting any such man to a seat.

Yours very truly,

A. LINCOLN.

———

LETTER TO GENERAL CARL SCHURZ [2]

Schurz was a Republican political leader who had entered the army. He criticized Lincoln for giving important military commands to Democrats, whose hearts were not in the war. Lincoln's reply was a masterful demolition of Schurz's

[1] Lincoln, *Complete Works*, VIII, 79.
[2] Lincoln, *Complete Works*, VIII, 84-87.

case and a gentle rebuke to Schurz, whose own military career had not been too successful.

Executive Mansion

Washington, November 24, 1862.

MY dear Sir: I have just received and read your letter of the 20th. The purport of it is that we lost the late elections and the Administration is failing because the war is unsuccessful, and that I must not flatter myself that I am not justly to blame for it. I certainly know that if the war fails, the Administration fails, and that I will be blamed for it, whether I deserve it or not. And I ought to be blamed if I could do better. You think I could do better; therefore you blame me already. I think I could not do better; therefore I blame you for blaming me. I understand you now to be willing to accept the help of men who are not Republicans, provided they have "heart in it." Agreed. I want no others. But who is to be the judge of hearts, or of "heart in it"? If I must discard my own judgment and take yours, I must also take that of others; and by the time I should reject all I should be advised to reject, I should have none left, Republicans or others—not even yourself. For be assured, my dear sir, there are men who have "heart in it" that think you are performing your part as poorly as you think I am performing mine. I certainly have been dissatisfied with the slowness of Buell and McClellan; but before I relieved them I had great fears I should not find successors to them who would do better; and I am sorry to add that I have seen little since to relieve those fears.

I do not see the prospect of any more rapid movements. I fear we shall at last find out that the difficulty is in our case rather than in particular generals. I wish to disparage no one —certainly not those who sympathize with me; but I must say I need success more than I need sympathy, and that I have not seen the so much greater evidence of getting success from my sympathizers than from those who are denounced as the contrary. It does seem to me that in the field the two classes have been very much alike in what they have done and what they have failed to do. In sealing their faith with their blood, Baker and Lyon and Bohlen and Richardson, Republicans, did all that men could do; but did they any more than Kearny and Stevens and Reno and Mansfield, none of whom were Republicans, and some at least of whom have been bitterly and repeatedly denounced to me as secession sympathizers? I will not perform the ungrateful task of comparing cases of failure.

In answer to your question, "Has it not been publicly stated in the newspapers, and apparently proved as a fact, that from the commencement of the war the enemy was continually supplied with information by some of the confidential subordinates of as important an officer as Adjutant-General Thomas?" I must say "No" as far as my knowledge extends. And I add that if you can give any tangible evidence upon the subject, I will thank you to come to this city and do so.

Very truly your friend,

A. LINCOLN.

———

ANNUAL MESSAGE TO CONGRESS, DECEMBER 1, 1862 [1]

This is undoubtedly Lincoln's best message to Congress. Certainly it is a more finished literary production than any of the other messages. The last paragraph is one of the finest things he ever wrote. The message contains two noteworthy pieces of writing: the moving plea for compensated emancipation and the description of the country as a physical entity, in which Lincoln aimed to give "imaginative reality to the national ideal."

FELLOW-CITIZENS of the Senate and House of Representatives: Since your last annual assembling another year of health and bountiful harvest has passed; and while it has not pleased the Almighty to bless us with a return of peace, we can

[1] Lincoln, *Complete Works*, VIII, 93-131.

but press on, guided by the best light he gives us, trusting that in his own good time and wise way all will yet be well.

*   *   *   *

On the 22d day of September last a proclamation was issued by the Executive, a copy of which is herewith submitted. In accordance with the purpose expressed in the second paragraph of that paper, I now respectfully recall your attention to what may be called "compensated emancipation."

A nation may be said to consist of its territory, its people, and its laws. The territory is the only part which is of certain durability. "One generation passeth away, and another generation cometh, but the earth abideth forever." It is of the first importance to duly consider and estimate this ever-enduring part. That portion of the earth's surface which is owned and inhabited by the people of the United States is well adapted to be the home of one national family, and it is not well adapted for two or more. Its vast extent and its variety of climate and productions are of advantage in this age for one people, whatever they might have been in former ages. Steam, telegraphs, and intelligence have brought these to be an advantageous combination for one united people.

In the inaugural address I briefly pointed out the total inadequacy of disunion as a remedy for the differences between the people of the two sections.

*   *   *   *

There is no line, straight or crooked, suitable for a national boundary upon which to divide. Trace through, from east to west, upon the line between the free and slave country, and we shall find a little more than one third of its length are rivers, easy to be crossed, and populated, or soon to be populated, thickly upon both sides; while nearly all its remaining length are merely surveyors' lines, over which people may walk back and forth without any consciousness of their presence. No part of this line can be made any more difficult to pass by writing it down on paper or parchment as a national boundary. The fact of separation, if it comes, gives up on the part of the seceding section the fugitive-slave clause along with all other constitutional obligations upon the section seceded from, while I should expect no treaty stipulation would be ever made to take its place.

But there is another difficulty. The great interior region, bounded east by the Alleghanies, north by the British dominions, west by the Rocky Mountains, and south by the line along which the culture of corn and cotton meets, and which includes part of Virginia, part of Tennessee, all of Kentucky, Ohio, Indiana, Michigan, Wisconsin, Illinois, Missouri, Kansas, Iowa, Minnesota, and the Territories of Dakota, Nebraska, and part of Colorado, already has above ten millions of people, and will have fifty millions within fifty years if not prevented by any political folly or mistake. It contains more than one third of the country owned by the United States—certainly more than one million of square miles. Once half as populous as Massachusetts already is, it would have more than seventy-five millions of people. A glance at the map shows that, territorially speaking, it is the great body of the republic. The other parts are but marginal borders to it, the magnificent region sloping west from the Rocky Mountains to the Pacific being the deepest and also the richest in undeveloped resources. In the production of provisions, grains, grasses, and all which proceed from them, this great interior region is naturally one of the most important in the world. Ascertain from the statistics the small proportion of the region which has, as yet, been brought into cultivation, and also the large and rapidly increasing amount of its products, and we shall be overwhelmed with the magnitude of the prospect presented; and yet this region has no seacoast, touches no ocean anywhere. As part of one nation, its people now find, and may forever find, their way to Europe by New York, to South America and Africa by New Orleans, and to Asia by San Francisco. But separate our common country into two nations as designed by the present rebellion, and every man of this great interior region is thereby cut off from some one or more of these outlets—not, perhaps, by a physical barrier, but by embarrassing and onerous trade regulations.

And this is true wherever a dividing or boundary line may be fixed. Place it between the now free and slave country, or place it south of Kentucky or north of Ohio, and still the truth remains that none south of it can trade to any port or place north of it, and none north of it can trade to any port or place south of it, except upon terms dictated by a government foreign to them. These outlets, east, west, and south, are indispensable to the well-being of the people inhabiting, and to inhabit, this vast interior region. Which of the three may be the best is no proper question. All are better than either; and all of right belong to that people and to their successors forever. True to themselves, they will not ask where a line of separation shall be, but will vow rather that there shall be no such line. Nor are the marginal regions less interested in these communications to and through them to the great outside world. They, too, and each of them, must have access to this Egypt of the West without paying toll at the crossing of any national boundary.

Our national strife springs not from our permanent part, not from the land we inhabit, not from our national homestead. There is no possible severing of this but would multiply, and not mitigate, evils among us. In all its adaptations and aptitudes it demands union and abhors separation. In fact, it would ere long force reunion, however much of blood and treasure the separation might have cost.

Our strife pertains to ourselves—to the passing generations of men; and it can without convulsion be hushed forever with the passing of one generation.

In this view I recommend the adoption of the following resolution and articles amendatory to the Constitution of the United States:

"Resolved by the Senate and House of Representatives of the United States of America in Congress assembled (two-thirds of both houses concurring), That the following articles be proposed to the legislatures (or conventions) of the several States as amendments to the Constitution of the United States, all or any of which articles when ratified by three fourths of the said legislatures (or conventions) to be valid as part or parts of the said Constitution, viz.:

"Article —.

"Every state wherein slavery now exists which shall abolish the same therein at any time or times before the first day of January in the year of our Lord one thousand and nine hundred, shall receive compensation from the United States as follows, to wit:

"The President of the United States shall deliver to every such State bonds of the United States, bearing interest at the rate of   per cent. per annum, to an amount equal to the aggregate sum of   for each slave shown to have been therein by the eighth census of the United States, said bonds to be delivered to such State by instalments, or in one parcel at the completion of the abolishment, accordingly as the same shall have been gradual or at one time within such State; and interest shall begin to run upon any such bond only from the proper time of its delivery as aforesaid. Any State having received bonds as aforesaid, and afterward reintroducing or tolerating slavery therein, shall refund to the United States the bonds so received, or the value thereof, and all interest paid thereon.

"Article —.

"All slaves who shall have enjoyed actual freedom by the chances of the war at any time before the end of the rebellion, shall be forever free; but all owners of such who shall not have been disloyal shall be compensated for them at the same rates as are provided for States adopting abolishment of slavery, but in such way that no slave shall be twice accounted for.

"Article —.

"Congress may appropriate money and otherwise provide

for colonizing free colored persons, with their own consent, at any place or places without the United States."

I beg indulgence to discuss these proposed articles at some length. Without slavery the rebellion could never have existed; without slavery it could not continue.

Among the friends of the Union there is great diversity of sentiment and of policy in regard to slavery and the African race amongst us. Some would perpetuate slavery; some would abolish it suddenly and without compensation; some would abolish it gradually, and with compensation; some would remove the freed people from us, and some would retain them with us; and there are yet other minor diversities. Because of these diversities we waste much strength in struggles among ourselves. By mutual concession we should harmonize and act together. This would be compromise; but it would be compromise among the friends, and not with the enemies of the Union. These articles are intended to embody a plan of such mutual concessions. If the plan shall be adopted, it is assumed that emancipation will follow at least in several of the States.

As to the first article, the main points are: first, the emancipation; secondly, the length of time for consummating it—thirty-seven years; and, thirdly, the compensation.

The emancipation will be unsatisfactory to the advocates of perpetual slavery; but the length of time should greatly mitigate their dissatisfaction. The time spares both races from the evils of sudden derangement—in fact, from the necessity of any derangement; while most of those whose habitual course of thought will be disurbed by the measure will have passed away before its consummation. They will never see it. Another class will hail the prospect of emancipation, but will deprecate the length of time. They will feel that it gives too little to the now living slaves. But it really gives them much. It saves them from the vagrant destitution which must largely attend immediate emancipation in localities where their numbers are very great; and it gives the inspiring assurance that their posterity shall be free forever. The plan leaves to each State choosing to act under it to abolish slavery now, or at the end of the century, or at any intermediate time, or by degrees extending over the whole or any part of the period; and it obliges no two States to proceed alike. It also provides for compensation, and generally the mode of making it. This, it would seem, must further mitigate the dissatisfaction of those who favor perpetual slavery, and especially of those who are to receive the compensation. Doubtless some of those who are to pay, and not to receive, will object. Yet the measure is both just and economical. In a certain sense the liberation of slaves is the destruction of property—property acquired by descent or by purchase, the same as any other propetry. It is no less true for having been often said, that the people of the South are not more responsible for the original introduction of this property than are the people of the North; and when it is remembered how unhesitatingly we all use cotton and sugar and share the profits of dealing in them, it may not be quite safe to say that the South has been more responsible than the North for its continuance. If, then, for a common object this property is to be sacrificed, is it not just that it be done at a common charge?

And if, with less money, or money more easily paid, we can preserve the benefits of the Union by this means than we can by the war alone, is it not also economical to do it? Let us consider it then. Let us ascertain the sum we have expended in the war since compensated emancipation was proposed last March, and consider whether, if that measure had been promptly accepted by even some of the slave States, the same sum would not have done more to close the war than has been otherwise done. If so, the measure would save money, and in that view would be a prudent and economical measure. Certainly it is not so easy to pay something as it is to pay nothing; but it is easier to pay a large sum than it is to pay a larger one. And it is easier to pay any sum when we are able, than it is to pay it before we are able. The war requires large sums, and requires them at once. The aggregate sum necessary for compensated emancipation of course would be large. But it would require no ready cash, nor the bonds even, any faster than the emancipation progresses. This might not, and probably would not, close before the end of the thirty-seven years. At that time we shall probably have 100,000,000 of people to share the burden, instead of 31,000,000 as now. And not only so, but the increase of our population may be expected to continue for a long time after that period as rapidly as before, because our territory will not have become full. I do not state this inconsiderately. At the same ratio of increase which we have maintained, on an average, from our first national census of 1790 until that of 1860, we should in 1900 have a population of 103,208,415. And why may we not continue that ratio far beyond that period? Our abundant room—our broad national homestead—is our ample resource. Were our territory as limited as are the British Isles, very certainly our population could not expand as stated. Instead of receiving the foreign-born as now, we should be compelled to send part of the native-born away. But such is not our condition.

*   *   *   *

The proposed emancipation would shorten the war, perpetuate peace, insure this increase of population, and proportionately the wealth of the country. With these, we should pay all the emancipation would cost, together with our other debt, easier than we should pay our other debt without it. If we had allowed our old national debt to run at six per cent. per annum simple interest, from the end of our Revolutionary struggle until to-day, without paying anything on either principal or interest, each man of us would owe less upon that debt now than each man owed upon it then; and this because our increase of men, through the whole period, has been greater than six per cent.—has run faster than the interest upon the debt. Thus, time alone relieves a debtor nation, so long as its population increases faster than unpaid interest accumulates on its debt.

This fact would be no excuse for delaying payment of what

is justly due; but it shows the great importance of time in this connection—the great advantage of a policy by which we shall not have to pay, until we number a hundred millions, what by a different policy we would have to pay now, when we number but thirty-one millions. In a word, it shows that a dollar will be much harder to pay for the war than will be a dollar for emancipation on the proposed plan. And then the latter will cost no blood, no precious life. It will be a saving of both.

As to the second article, I think it would be impracticable to return to bondage the class of persons therein contemplated. Some of them doubtless, in the property sense, belong to loyal owners; and hence provision is made in this article for compensating such.

The third article relates to the future of the freed people. It does not oblige, but merely authorizes, Congress to aid in colonizing such as may consent. This sought not to be regarded as objectionable, on the one hand or on the other, inasmuch as it comes to nothing unless by the mutual consent of the people to be deported, and the American voters through their representatives in Congress. I cannot make it better known than it already is, that I strongly favor colonization. And yet I wish to say there is an objection urged against free colored persons remaining in the country which is largely imaginary, if not sometimes malicious.

It is insisted that their presence would injure and displace white labor and white laborers. If there ever could be a proper time for mere catch arguments, that time surely is not now. In times like the present, men should utter nothing for which they would not willingly be responsible through time and in eternity. Is it true, then, that colored people can displace any more white labor by being free than by remaining slaves? If they stay in their old places, they jostle no white laborers; if they leave their old places, they leave them open to white laborers. Logically, there is neither more nor less of it. Emancipation, even without deportation, would probably enhance the wages of white labor, and very surely would not reduce them.

Thus, the customary amount of labor would still have to be performed; the freed people would surely not do more than their old proportion of it, and very probably for a time would do less, leaving an increased part to white laborers, bringing their labor into greater demand, and consequently enhancing the wages of it. With deportation, even to a limited extent, enhanced wages to white labor is mathematically certain. Labor is like any other commodity in the market—increase the demand for it, and you increase the price of it. Reduce the supply of black labor by colonizing the black labor out of the country and by precisely so much you increase the demand for, and wages of, white labor.

But it is dreaded that the freed people will swarm forth and cover the whole land? Are they not already in the land? Will liberation make them any more numerous? Equally distributed among the whites of the whole country, and there would be but one colored to seven whites. Could the one in any way greatly disturb the seven? There are many communities now having more than one free colored person to seven whites, and this without any apparent consciousness of evil from it. The District of Columbia, and the States of Maryland and Delaware, are all in this condition. The District has more than one free colored to six whites; and yet in its frequent petitions to Congress I believe it has never presented the presence of free colored persons as one of its grievances. But why should emancipation south send the people north? People of any color seldom run unless there be something to run from. Heretofore colored people, to some extent, have fled north from bondage; and now, perhaps, from both bondage and destitution. But if gradual emancipation and deportation be adopted, they will have neither to flee from. Their old masters will give them wages at least until new laborers can be procured; and the freedmen, in turn, will gladly give their labor for the wages till new homes can be found for them in congenial climes and with people of their own blood and race. This proposition can be trusted on the mutual interests involved. And, in any event, cannot the North decide for itself whether to receive them?

Again, as practice proves more than theory, in any case, has there been any irruption of colored people northward because of the abolishment of slavery in this District last spring?

What I have said of the proportion of free colored persons to the whites in the District is from the census of 1860, having no reference to persons called contrabands, nor to those made free by the act of Congress abolishing slavery here.

The plan consisting of these articles is recommended, not but that a restoration of the national authority would be accepted without its adoption.

Nor will the war, nor proceedings under the proclamation of September 22, 1862, be stayed because of the recommendation of this plan. Its timely adoption, I doubt not, would bring restoration, and thereby stay both.

And, notwithstanding this plan, the recommendation that Congress provide by law for compensating any State which may adopt emancipation before this plan shall have been acted upon, is hereby earnestly renewed. Such would be only an advance part of the plan, and the same arguments apply to both.

This plan is recommended as a means, not in exclusion of, but additional to, all others for restoring and preserving the national authority throughout the Union. The subject is presented exclusively in its economical aspect. The plan would, I am confident, secure peace more speedily, and maintain it more permanently, than can be done by force alone; while all it would cost, considering amounts, and manner of payment, and times of payment, would be easier paid than will be the additional cost of the war if we rely solely upon force. It is much—very much—that it would cost no blood at all.

The plan is proposed as permanent constitutional law. It cannot become such without the concurrence of, first two-thirds of Congress and, afterwards, three-fourths of the States. The requisite three-fourths of the States will necessarily include seven of the slave States. Their concurrence, if obtained, will give assurance of their severally adopting emancipation at no very distant day upon the new constitutional terms. This assurance would end the struggle now, and save the Union forever.

I do not forget the gravity which should characterize a paper addressed to the Congress of the nation by the Chief Magistrate of the nation. Nor do I forget that some of you are my seniors, nor that many of you have more experience than I in the conduct of public affairs. Yet I trust that in view of the great responsibility resting upon me, you will perceive no want of respect to yourselves in any undue earnestness I may seem to display.

Is it doubted, then, that the plan I propose, if adopted, would shorten the war, and thus lessen its expenditure of money and of blood? Is it doubted that it would restore the national authority and national prosperity, and perpetuate both indefinitely? Is it doubted that we here—Congress and Executive—can secure its adoption? Will not the good people respond to a united and earnest appeal from us? Can we, can they, by any other means so certainly or so speedily assure these vital objects? We can succeed only by concert. It is not "Can any of us imagine better?" but, "Can we all do better?" Object whatsoever is possible, still the question occurs, "Can we do better?" The dogmas of the quiet past are inadequate to the stormy present. The occasion is piled high with difficulty, and we must rise with the occasion. As our case is new, so we must think anew and act anew. We must disenthrall ourselves, and then we shall save our country.

Fellow-citizens, we cannot escape history. We of this Congress and this administration will be remembered in spite of ourselves. No personal significance or insignificance can spare one or another of us. The fiery trial through which we pass will light us down, in honor or in dishonor, to the latest generation. We say we are for the Union. The world will not forget that we say this. We know how to save the Union. The world knows we do know how to save it. We—even we here—hold the power and bear the responsibility. In giving freedom to the slave, we assure freedom to the free—honorable alike in what we give and what we preserve. We shall nobly save or meanly lose the last, best hope of earth. Other means may succeed; this could not fail. The way is plain, peaceful, generous, just—a way which, if followed, the world will forever applaud, and God must forever bless.

ABRAHAM LINCOLN.

December 1, 1862.

FINAL EMANCIPATION PROCLAMATION, JANUARY 1, 1863 [1]

> On the first day of 1863 Lincoln issued his promised proclamation freeing the slaves in the seceded states. He based his right to emancipate on the war powers of the President and he stated that the proclamation was a measure of military necessity. It was significant that he excepted from the proclamation the only areas in the South occupied by Union armies and hence the only area where the proclamation could have had any immediate practical effect.

BY THE PRESIDENT OF THE UNITED STATES OF AMERICA:

A Proclamation

WHEREAS, on the twenty-second day of September, in the year of our Lord one thousand eight hundred and sixty-two, a proclamation was issued by the President of the United States, containing, among other things, the following, to wit:

"That on the first day of January, in the year of our Lord one thousand eight hundred and sixty-three, all persons held as slaves within any State, or designated part of a State, the people whereof shall then be in rebellion against the United States, shall be then, thenceforward, and forever free; and the Executive Government of the United States, including the military and naval authority thereof, will recognize and maintain the freedom of such persons, and will do no act or acts to repress such persons, or any of them, in any efforts they

---

[1] Lincoln, *Complete Works*, VIII, 161-164.

may make for their actual freedom.

"That the Executive will, on the first day of January aforesaid, by proclamation, designate the States and parts of States, if any, in which the people thereof respectively shall then be in rebellion against the United States; and the fact that any State, or the people thereof, shall on that day be in good faith represented in the Congress of the United States by members chosen thereto at elections wherein a majority of the qualified voters of such State shall have participated, shall in the absence of strong countervailing testimony be deemed conclusive evidence that such State and the people thereof are not then in rebellion against the United States."

Now, therefore, I, Abraham Lincoln, President of the United States, by virtue of the power in me vested as commander-in-chief of the army and navy of the United States, in time of actual armed rebellion against the authority and government of the United States, and as a fit and necessary war measure for suppressing said rebellion, do, on this first day of January, in the year of our Lord one thousand eight hundred and sixty-three, and in accordance with my purpose so to do, publicly proclaimed for the full period of 100 days from the day first above mentioned, order and designate as the States and parts of States wherein the people thereof, respectively, are this day in rebellion against the United States, the following, to wit:

Arkansas, Texas, Louisiana (except the parishes of St. Bernard, Plaquemines, Jefferson, St. John, St. Charles, St. James, Ascension, Assumption, Terre Bonne, Lafourche, St. Mary, St. Martin, and Orleans, including the city of New Orleans), Mississippi, Alabama, Florida, Georgia, South Carolina, North Carolina, and Virginia (except the forty-eight counties designated as West Virginia, and also the counties of Berkeley, Accomac, Northampton, Elizabeth City, York, Princess Anne, and Norfolk, including the cities of Norfolk and Portsmouth), and which excepted parts are for the present left precisely as if this proclamation were not issued.

And by virtue of the power and for the purpose aforesaid, I do order and declare that all persons held as slaves within said designated States and parts of States are, and henceforward shall be, free; and that the Executive Government of the United States, including the military and naval authorities thereof, will recognize and maintain the freedom of said persons.

And I hereby enjoin upon the people so declared to be free to abstain from all violence, unless in necessary self-defense; and I recommend to them that, in all cases where allowed, they labor faithfully for reasonable wages.

And I further declare and make known that such persons of suitable condition will be received into the armed service of the United States to garrison forts, positions, stations, and other places, and to man vessels of all sorts in said service.

And upon this act, sincerely believed to be an act of justice, warranted by the Constitution upon military necessity, I invoke the considerate judgment of mankind and the gracious favor of Almighty God.

In witness whereof, I have hereunto set my hand and caused the seal of the United States to be affixed.

Done at the city of Washington, this first day of January, in the year of our Lord one thousand eight hundred and sixty-three, and of the independence of the United States of America the eighty-seventh.

\ABRAHAM LINCOLN.

LETTER TO GENERAL JOHN A. McCLERNAND [1]

In this letter to McClernand, an old Illinois friend, Lincoln explained why he had issued the emancipation proclamation.

Executive Mansion, January· 8, 1863.

MY dear Sir: Your interesting communication by the hand of Major Scates is received. I never did ask more, nor

[1] Lincoln, *Complete Works*, VIII, 181-183.

ever was willing to accept less, than for all the States, and the people thereof, to take and hold their places and their rights in the Union, under the Constitution of the United States. For this alone have I felt authorized to struggle and I seek neither more nor less now. Still, to use a coarse but an expressive figure, "Broken eggs cannot be mended." I have issued the Emancipation Proclamation, and I cannot retract it. After the commencement of hostilities, I struggled nearly a year and a half to get along without touching the "institution"; and when finally I conditionally determined to touch it, I gave a hundred days' fair notice of my purpose to all the States and people, within which time they could have turned it wholly aside by simply again becoming good citizens of the United States.

They chose to disregard it, and I made the peremptory proclamation on what appeared to me to be a military necessity. And being made, it must stand. As to the States not included in it, of course they can have their rights in the Union as of old. Even the people of the States included, if they choose, need not be hurt by it. Let them adopt systems of apprenticeship for the colored people, conforming substantially to the most approved plans of gradual emancipation; and with the aid they can have from the General Government they may be nearly as well off, in this respect, as if the present trouble had not occurred, and much better off than they can possibly be if the contest continues persistently.

As to any dread of my having a "purpose to enslave or exterminate the whites of the South," I can scarcely believe that such dread exists. It is too absurd. I believe you can be my personal witness that no man is less to be dreaded for undue severity in any case.

If the friends you mention really wish to have peace upon the old terms, they should act at once. Every day makes the case more difficult. They can so act with entire safety, so far as I am concerned.

I think you had better not make this letter public; but you may rely confidently on my standing by whatever I have said in it. Please write me if anything more comes to light.

Yours very truly,   A. LINCOLN.

———

LETTER TO GENERAL JOSEPH HOOKER [1]

Lincoln had appointed Ambrose Burnside to succeed Mc-Clellan as Commander of the Army of the Potomac. Burnside suffered a disastrous defeat at Fredericksburg in December. Soon afterward he resigned. Lincoln then decided to give the command to Hooker, a favorite with the radicals. Hooker had ability but he had intrigued to undermine Burnside in order to get the command himself. He had also done a lot of loose talking about the necessity of having a dictator at the head of the government.

Executive Mansion,

Washington, D. C., January 26, 1862.

GENERAL: I have placed you at the head of the Army of the Potomac. Of course I have done this upon what appear to me to be sufficient reasons, and yet I think it best for you to know that there are some things in regard to which I am not quite satisfied with you. I believe you to be a brave and skilful soldier, which of course I like. I also believe you do not mix politics with your profession, in which you are right. You have confidence in yourself, which is a valuable if not an indispensable quality. You are ambitious, which, within reasonable bounds, does good rather than harm; but I think that during General Burnside's command of the army you have taken counsel of your ambition and thwarted him as much as you could, in which you did a great wrong to the country and to a most meritorious and honorable brother officer. I have heard, in such a way as to believe it, of your recently saying that both the army and the government needed

---

[1] Lincoln, *Complete Works*, VIII, 206-207.

a dictator. Of course it was not for this, but in spite of it, that I have given you the command. Only those generals who gain successes can set up dictators. What I now ask of you is military success, and I will risk the dictatorship. The government will support you to the utmost of its ability, which is neither more nor less than it has done and will do for all its commanders. I much fear that the spirit which you have aided to infuse into the army, of criticising their commander and withholding confidence from him, will now turn upon you. I shall assist you as far as I can to put it down. Neither you nor Napoleon, if he were alive again, could get any good out of an army while such a spirit prevails in it; and now beware of rashness. Beware of rashness, but with energy and sleepless vigilance go forward and give us victories.

Yours very truly,   A. LINCOLN.

LETTER TO GOVERNOR HORATIO SEYMOUR [1]

Seymour was the Democratic governor of New York. His support of the war effort had not been enthusiastic. Lincoln's appeal to Seymour was typical of the President's efforts to persuade men of all shades of opinion to sustain the prosecution of the war.

(Private and Confidential)
Executive Mansion,
Washington, March 23, 1863.

DEAR Sir: You and I are substantially strangers, and I write this chiefly that we may become better acquainted. I, for the time being, am at the head of a nation which is in great peril, and you are at the head of the greatest State of that nation. As to maintaining the nation's life and integrity, I assume and believe that there cannot be a difference of purpose between you and me. If we should differ as to the means, it is important that such difference should be as small as pos-

---

[1] Lincoln, *Complete Works*, VIII, 230-231.

sible; that it should not be enhanced by unjust suspicions on one side or the other. In the performance of my duty the cooperation of your State, as that of others, is needed—in fact, is indispensable. This alone is a sufficient reason why I should wish to be at a good understanding with you. Please write me at least as long a letter as this, of course saying in it just what you think fit.

Yours very truly,

A. LINCOLN.

———

PROCLAMATION APPOINTING A NATIONAL FAST-DAY, MARCH 30, 1863 [1]

> This proclamation illustrates the rich development of Lincoln's prose style during the war years and the mystic, religious qualities of his nature.

BY THE PRESIDENT OF THE UNITED STATES OF AMERICA:

A Proclamation.

WHEREAS, the Senate of the United States, devoutly recognizing the supreme authority and just government of Almighty God in all the affairs of men and of nations, has by a resolution requested the President to designate and set apart a day for national prayer and humiliation:

And whereas, it is the duty of nations as well as of men to own their dependence upon the overruling power of God; to confess their sins and transgressions in humble sorrow, yet with assured hope that genuine repentance will lead to mercy and pardon; and to recognize the sublime truth, announced in the Holy Scriptures and proven by all history, that those nations only are blessed whose God is the Lord:

And insomuch as we know that by his divine law nations,

---

[1] Lincoln, *Complete Works*, VIII, 235-237.

like individuals, are subjected to punishments and chastisements in this world, may we not justly fear that the awful calamity of civil war which now desolates the land may be but a punishment inflicted upon us for our presumptuous sins, to the needful end of our national reformation as a whole people? We have been the recipients of the choicest bounties of Heaven. We have been preserved, these many years, in peace and prosperity. We have grown in numbers, wealth, and power as no other nation has ever grown; but we have forgotten God. We have forgotten the gracious hand which preserved us in peace, and multiplied and enriched and strengthened us; and we have vainly imagined, in the deceitfulness of our hearts, that all these blessings were produced by some superior wisdom and virtue of our own. Intoxicated with unbroken success, we have become too self-sufficient to feel the necessity of redeeming and preserving grace, too proud to pray to the God that made us:

It behooves us, then, to humble ourselves before the offended Power, to confess our national sins, and to pray for clemency and forgiveness.

Now, therefore, in compliance with the request, and fully concurring in the views, of the Senate, I do by this my proclamation designate and set apart Thursday the 30th day of April, 1863, as a day of national humiliation, fasting, and prayer. And I do hereby request all the people to abstain on that day from their ordinary secular pursuits, and to unite at their several places of public worship and their respective homes in keeping the day holy to the Lord, and devoted to the humble discharge of the religious duties proper to that solemn occasion. All this being done in sincerity and truth, let us then rest humbly in the hope authorized by the divine teachings, that the united cry of the nation will be heard on high, and answered with blessings no less than the pardon of our national sins, and the restoration of our now divided and suffering country to its former happy condition of unity and peace.

In witness whereof, I have hereunto set my hand, and caused the seal of the United States to be affixed.

Done at the city of Washington, this thirtieth day of March, in the year of our Lord one thousand eight hundred and sixty-three, and of the independence of the United States the eighty-seventh.

ABRAHAM LINCOLN.

TELEGRAM TO GENERAL JOSEPH HOOKER [1]

> When Lincoln wrote this telegram, Lee was moving his army northward for an invasion of Pennsylvania. In homely, vivid language, Lincoln advised Hooker how to meet the threat.

Washington, June 5, 1863, 4 p. m.

MAJOR-GENERAL Hooker: Yours of to-day was received an hour ago. So much of professional military skill is requisite to answer it, that I have turned the task over to General Halleck.[2] He promises to perform it with his utmost care. I have but one idea which I think worth suggesting to you, and that is, in case you find Lee coming to the north of the Rappahannock, I would by no means cross to the south of it. If he should leave a rear force at Fredericksburg, tempting you to fall upon it, it would fight in intrenchments and have you at disadvantage, and so, man for man, worst you at that point, while his main force would in some way be getting an advantage of you northward. In one word, I would not take any risk of being entangled upon the river, like an ox jumped half over a fence and liable to be torn by dogs front and rear without a fair chance to gore one way or kick the other. If Lee would come to my side of the river, I would

---

[1] Lincoln, *Complete Works,* VIII, 291-292.
[2] Henry W. Halleck was Lincoln's military adviser.

keep on the same side, and fight him or act on the defense, according as might be my estimate of his strength relatively to my own. But these are mere suggestions which I desire to be controlled by the judgment of yourself and General Halleck.

A. LINCOLN.

————

LETTER TO ERASTUS CORNING AND OTHERS [1]

> During the war Lincoln used his war powers vigorously to suspend civil liberties wherever he thought such action necessary to prevent obstruction of the war effort. Many people were placed under military arrest and denied the right to a trial. The most important figure to be incarcerated was Clement L. Vallandigham of Ohio, leader of the Peace Democrats. Protests against the government's policy were numerous and came in some cases from people who supported the war.
>
> Corning and a committee representing the New York Democrats transmitted to Lincoln a protest against arbitrary arrests. In this public letter in reply Lincoln presented a complete defence of the government's right to suspend civil liberties in a crisis that threatened the existence of the government.

Executive Mansion, June 12, 1863.

GENTLEMEN: Your letter of May 19, inclosing the resolutions of a public meeting held at Albany, New York, on the 16th of the same month, was received several days ago.

The resolutions, as I understand them, are resolvable into two propositions—first, the expression of a purpose to sustain the cause of the Union, to secure peace through victory, and to support the administration in every constitutional and lawful measure to suppress the rebellion; and, secondly, a declaration of censure upon the administration for supposed unconstitutional action, such as the making of military arrests. And from the two propositions a third is deduced, which is that

---

[1] Lincoln, *Complete Works*, VIII, 298-314.

the gentlemen composing the meeting are resolved on doing their part to maintain our common government and country, despite the folly or wickedness, as they may conceive, of any administration. This position is eminently patriotic and as such I thank the meeting, and congratulate the nation for it. My own purpose is the same; so that the meeting and myself have a common object, and can have no difference, except in the choice of means or measures for effecting that object.

And here I ought to close this paper, and would close it, if there were no apprehension that more injurious consequences than any merely personal to myself might follow the censures systematically cast upon me for doing what, in my view of duty, I could not forbear. The resolutions promise to support me in every constitutional and lawful measure to suppress the rebellion; and I have not knowingly employed, nor shall knowingly employ, any other. But the meeting, by their resolutions, assert and argue that certain military arrests and proceedings following them, for which I am ultimately responsible are unconstitutional. I think they are not. The resolutions quote from the Constitution the definition of treason, and also the limiting safeguards and guarantees therein provided for the citizen on trials for treason, and on his being held to answer for capital or otherwise infamous crimes, and in criminal prosecutions his right to a speedy and public trial by an impartial jury. They proceed to resolve "that these safeguards of the rights of the citizen against the pretensions of arbitrary power were intended more especially for his protection in times of civil commotion." And, apparently to demonstrate the proposition, the resolutions proceed: "They were secured substantially to the English people after years of protracted civil war, and were adopted into our Constitution at the close of the revolution." Would not the demonstration have been better if it could have been truly said that these safeguards had been adopted and applied during the civil wars and during our revolution, instead of after the one and at the close of the other? I, too, am devotedly for them after civil war and before civil war, and at all times, "except when in cases of rebellion or invasion, the public safety may require" their suspension. The resolutions proceed to tell us that these safeguards "have stood the test of seventy-six years of trial under our republican system under circumstances which show that while they constitute the foundation of all free government, they are the elements of the enduring stability of the republic." No one denies that they have so stood the test up to the beginning of the present rebellion . . . nor does any one question that they will stand the same test much longer after the rebellion closes. But these provisions of the Constitution have no application to the case we have in hand, because the arrests complained of were not made for treason—that is, not for the treason defined in the Constitution, and upon the conviction of which the punishment is death—nor were the proceedings following, in any constitutional or legal sense, "criminal prosecutions." The arrests were made on totally different grounds, and the proceedings following accorded with the grounds of the arrests. Let us consider the real case with which we are dealing, and apply to it the parts of the Constitution plainly made for such cases.

Prior to my installation here it had been inculcated that any State had a lawful right to secede from the national Union, and that it would be expedient to exercise the right whenever the devotees of the doctrine should fail to elect a president to their own liking. I was elected contrary to their liking; and, accordingly, so far as it was legally possible, they had taken seven States out of the Union, had seized many of the United States forts, and had fired upon the United States flag, all before I was inaugurated, and, of course, before I had done any official act whatever. The rebellion thus began soon ran into the present civil war; and, in certain respects, it began on very unequal terms between the parties. The insurgents had been preparing for it more than thirty years, while the government had taken no steps to resist them. The former had carefully considered all the means which could be turned to their account. It undoubtedly was a well-pondered reliance with them that in their own unrestricted effort to destroy Union, Constitution and law, all together, the government would, in great degree, be restrained by the same Constitution and law from arresting their progress. Their sympathizers pervaded all departments of the government and nearly all communities of the people. From this material, under cover of "liberty of speech," "liberty of the press" and *"habeas corpus,"* they hoped to keep on foot amongst us a most efficient corps of spies, informers, suppliers and aiders and abettors of their cause in a thousand ways. They know that in times such as they were inaugurating, by the Constitution itself the *"habeas corpus"* might be suspended; but they also know they had friends who would make a question as to who was to suspend it; meanwhile their spies and others might remain at large to help on their cause. Or if, as has happened, the Executive should suspend the writ without ruinous waste of time, instances of arresting innocent persons might occur, as are always likely to occur in such cases; and then a clamor could be raised in regard to this, which might be at least of some service to the insurgent cause. It needed no very keen perception to discover this part of the enemy's program, so soon as by open hostilities their machinery was fairly put in motion. Yet, thoroughly imbued with a reverence for the guaranteed rights of individuals, I was slow to adopt the strong measures which by degrees I have been forced to regard as within the exceptions of the Constitution, and as indispensable to the public safety. Nothing is better known to history than that courts of justice are utterly incompetent to such cases. Civil courts are organized chiefly for trials of individuals, or, at most, a few individuals acting in concert—and this in quiet times, and on charges of crimes well defined in law. Even in times of peace bands of horse-thieves and robbers frequently grow too numerous and powerful for the ordinary courts of justice. But what comparison, in numbers, have such bands ever borne to the insurgent sympathizers even in many of the loyal States? Again, a jury too frequently has at least one member more ready to hang the panel than to hang the traitor. And yet again, he who dissuades one man from volunteering, or induces one soldier to desert, weakens the Union cause as much as he who kills a Union soldier in battle. Yet this dissuasion or inducement may be so conducted as to be no defined crime of which any civil court would take cognizance.

Ours is a case of rebellion—so called by the resolutions before me—in fact, a clear, flagrant, and gigantic case of rebellion; and the provision of the Constitution that "the privilege of the writ of *habeas corpus* shall not be suspended unless when, in cases of rebellion or invasion, the public safety may require it," is the provision which specially applies to our present case. This provision plainly attests the understanding of those who made the Constitution that ordinary courts of justice are inadequate to "cases of rebellion"—attests their purpose that, in such cases, men may be held in custody whom the courts, acting on ordinary rules, would discharge. *Habeas corpus* does not discharge men who are proved to be guilty of defined crime; and its suspension is allowed by the Constitution on purpose that men may be arrested and held who cannot be proved to be guilty of defined crime, "when, in cases of rebellion or invasion, the public safety may require it."

This is precisely our present case—a case of rebellion wherein the public safety does require the suspension. Indeed, arrests by process of courts and arrests in cases of rebellion do not proceed altogether upon the same basis. The former is directed at the small percentage of ordinary and continuous perpetration of crime, while the latter is directed at sudden and extensive uprisings against the government, which, at most, will succeed or fail in no great length of time. In the latter case arrests are made not so much for what has been done, as for what probably would be done. The latter is more for the preventive and less for the vindictive than the former. In such cases the purposes of men are much more easily understood than in cases of ordinary crime. The man who stands by and says nothing when the peril of his government is discussed, cannot be misunderstood. If not hindered, he is sure to help the enemy; much more if he talks ambiguously—talks for his country with "buts," and "ifs" and "ands." Of how little value the constitutional provision I have quoted will be rendered if arrests shall never be made until defined crimes shall have been committed, may be illustrated by a few notable examples: General John C. Breckenridge, General Robert E. Lee, General Joseph E. Johnston, General John B. Magruder, General William B. Preston, General Simon B. Buckner, and Commodore Franklin Buchanan, now occupying the very highest places in the rebel war service, were all within the power of the government since the rebellion began, and were nearly as well known to be traitors then as now. Unquestionably if we had seized and held them, the insurgent cause would be much weaker. But no one of them had then committed any crime defined in the law. Every one of them, if arrested, would have been discharged on *habeas corpus* were the writ allowed to operate. In view of these and similar cases, I think the time not unlikely to come when I shall be blamed for having made too few arrests rather than too many.

By the third resolution the meeting indicate their opinion that military arrests may be constitutional in localities where rebellion actually exists, but that such arrests are unconstitutional in localities where rebellion or insurrection does not actually exist. They insist that such arrests shall not be made "outside of the lines of necessary military occupation and the scenes of insurrection." Inasmuch, however, as the Constitution itself makes no such distinction, I am unable to believe that there is any such constitutional distinction. I concede that the class of arrests complained of can be constitutional only when, in cases of rebellion or invasion, the public safety may require them; and I insist that in such cases they are constitutional wherever the public safety does require them, as well as in places to which they may prevent the rebellion extending, as in those where it may be already prevailing; as well where they may restrain mischievous interference with the raising and supplying of armies to suppress the rebellion, as where the rebellion may actually be; as well where they may restrain the enticing men out of the army, as where they would prevent mutiny in the army; equally constitutional at all places where they will conduce to the public safety, as against the dangers of rebellion or invasion. Take the particular case mentioned by the meeting. It is asserted in substance, that Mr. Vallandigham was, by a military commander, seized and tried "for no other reason than words addressed to a public meeting in criticism of the course of the administration, and in condemnation of the military orders of the general." Now, if there be no mistake about this, if this assertion is the truth and the whole truth, if there was no other reason for the arrest, then I concede that the arrest was wrong. But the arrest, as I understand, was made for a very different reason. Mr. Vallandigham avows his hostility to the war on the part of the Union; and his arrest was made because he was laboring, with some effect, to prevent the raising of troops, to encourage desertions from the army, and to leave the rebellion without an adequate military force to suppress it. He was not arrested because he was damaging the political prospects of the administration or the personal interests of the commanding general but because he was damaging the army, upon the existence and vigor of which the life of the nation depends. He was warring upon the military, and this gave the military constitutional jurisdiction to lay hands upon him. If Mr. Vallandigham was not damaging the military power of the country, then his arrest was made on mistake of fact, which I would be glad to correct on reasonably satisfactory evidence.

I understand the meeting whose resolutions I am considering to be in favor of suppressing the rebellion by military force—by armies. Long experience has shown that armies cannot be maintained unless desertion shall be punished by the severe penalty of death. The case requires, and the law and the Constitution sanction, this punishment. Must I shoot a simple-minded soldier boy who deserts, while I must not touch a hair of a wily agitator who induces him to desert? This is none the less injurious when effected by getting a father, or brother, or friend into a public meeting, and there working upon his feelings till he is persuaded to write the soldier boy that he is fighting in a bad cause, for a wicked administration of a contemptible government, too weak to arrest and punish him if he shall desert. I think that, in such a case, to silence the agitator and save the boy is not only constitutional, but withal a great mercy.

If I be wrong on this question of constitutional power, my error lies in believing that certain proceedings are constitutional when, in cases of rebellion or invasion, the public safety requires them, which would not be constitutional when, in absence of rebellion or invasion, the public safety does not require them: in other words, that the Constitution is not in its application in all respects the same in cases of rebellion or invasion involving the public safety, as it is in times of profound peace and public security. The Constitution itself makes the distinction, and I can no more be persuaded that the government can constitutionally take no strong measures in time of rebellion, because it can be shown that the same could not be lawfully taken in time of peace, than I can be persuaded that a particular drug is not good medicine for a sick man because it can be shown to not be good food for a well one. Nor am I able to appreciate the danger apprehended by the meeting, that the American people will by means of military arrests during the rebellion lose the right of public discussion, the liberty of speech and the press, the law of evidence, trial by jury, and *habeas corpus* throughout the indefinite peaceful future which I trust lies before them, any more than I am able to believe that a man could contract so strong an appetite for emetics during temporary illness as to persist in feeding upon them during the remainder of his healthful life.

In giving the resolutions that earnest consideration which

you request of me, I cannot overlook the fact that the meeting speak as "Democrats." Nor can I, with full respect for their known intelligence, and the fairly presumed deliberation with which they prepared their resolutions, be permitted to suppose that this occurred by accident, or in any way other than that they preferred to designate themselves "Democrats" rather than "American citizens." In this time of national peril I would have preferred to meet you upon a level one step higher than any party platform, because I am sure that from such more elevated position we could do better battle for the country we all love than we possibly can from those lower ones where, from the force of habit, the prejudices of the past, and selfish hopes of the future, we are sure to expend much of our ingenuity and strength in finding fault with and aiming blows at each other.

* * * *

One of the resolutions expresses the opinion of the meeting that arbitrary arrests will have the effect to divide and distract those who should be untied in suppressing the rebellion and I am specifically called on to discharge Mr. Vallandigham. I regard this as, at least, a fair appeal to me on the expediency of exercising a constitutional power which I think exists. In response to such appeal I have to say, it gave me pain when I learned that Mr. Vallandigham had been arrested (that is, I was pained that there should have seemed to be a necessity for arresting him), and that it will afford me great pleasure to discharge him so soon as I can by any means believe the public safety will not suffer by it.

I further say that, as the war progresses, it appears to me, opinion and action, which were in great confusion at first, take shape and fall into more regular channels, so that the necessity for strong dealing with them gradually decreases. I have every reason to desire that it should cease altogether, and far from the least is my regard for the opinions and wishes of those who, like the meeting at Albany, declare their purpose to sustain the government in every constitutional and lawful measure to suppress the rebellion. Still, I must continue to do so much as may seem to be required by the public safety.

A. LINCOLN.

––––

LETTER TO GENERAL ULYSSES S. GRANT [1]

After a hard campaign Grant had taken Vicksburg, the last great Confederate stronghold on the Mississippi river. He had been forced to run his fleet past Vicksburg's guns, march his army down the west bank of the river and then cross it to the east bank, and come at Vicksburg from the rear. Lincoln had watched the campaign with misgivings as to its success. Then, after Grant's capture of the city, Lincoln wrote this graceful note of thanks to the general.

Executive Mansion, July 13, 1863.

MY dear General: I do not remember that you and I ever met personally. I write this now as a grateful acknowledgement for the almost inestimable service you have done the country. I wish to say a word further. When you first reached the vicinity of Vicksburg, I thought you should do what you finally did—march the troops across the neck, run the batteries with the transports, and thus go below; and I never had any faith, except a general hope that you knew better than I, that the Yazoo Pass expedition and the like could succeed. When you got below and took Port Gibson, Grand Gulf, and vicinity, I thought you should go down the river and join General Banks, and when you turned northward, east of the Big Black, I feared it was a mistake. I now wish to make the personal acknowledgment that you were right and I was wrong.

Yours very truly,

A. LINCOLN.

––––

<hr />

[1] Lincoln, *Complete Works*, IX, 26.

DRAFT OF LETTER TO GENERAL GEORGE G. MEADE [1]

> Meade had succeeded Hooker as commander of the Army of the Potomac. In July he had met Lee's invading army at Gettysburg, Pennsylvania, and forced it to retreat to Virginia. Lincoln thought that Meade could have crushed the Confederates if he had pursued them vigorously, that an opportunity to end the war had been lost. Lincoln wrote this letter to Meade but never sent it.

Executive Mansion,

Washington, D. C., July 14, 1863.

MAJOR-GENERAL Meade: I have seen your despatch to General Halleck, asking to be relieved of your command because of a supposed censure of mine. I am very, very grateful to you for the magnificent success you gave the cause of the country at Gettysburg; and I am sorry now to be the author of the slightest pain to you. But I was in such deep distress myself that I could not restrain some expression of it. I have been oppressed nearly ever since the battles of Gettysburg by what appeared to be evidences that yourself and General Couch and General Smith [2] were not seeking a collision with the enemy, but were trying to get him across the river without another battle. What these evidences were, if you please, I hope to tell you at some time when we shall both feel better. The case, summarily stated, is this: You fought and beat the enemy at Gettysburg and, of course, to say the least, his loss was as great as yours. He retreated, and you did not, as it seemed to me, pressingly pursue him; but a flood in the river detained him till, by slow degrees, you were again upon him. You had at least twenty thousand veteran troops directly with you, and as many more raw ones within supporting distance, all in addition to those who fought with you at Gettysburg, while it was not possible that he had received a single recruit, and yet you stood and let the flood run down, bridges be built, and the enemy move away at his leisure without attacking him.

---

[1] Lincoln, *Complete Works*, IX, 28-30.
[2] Couch and Smith were generals in Meade's army.

And Couch and Smith! The latter left Carlisle in time, upon all ordinary calculation, to have aided you in the last battle at Gettysburg, but he did not arrive. At the end of more than ten days, I believe twelve, under constant urging, he reached Hagerstown from Carlisle, which is not an inch over fifty-five miles, if so much, and Couch's movement was very little different.

Again, my dear general, I do not believe you appreciate the magnitude of the misfortune involved in Lee's escape. He was within your easy grasp, and to have closed upon him would, in connection with our other late successes, have ended the war. As it is, the war will be prolonged indefinitely. If you could not safely attack Lee last Monday, how can you possibly do so south of the river, when you can take with you very few more than two thirds of the force you then had in hand?

It would be unreasonable to expect, and I do not expect [that], you can now effect much. Your golden opportunity is gone, and I am distressed immeasurably because of it.

I beg you will not consider this a prosecution or persecution of yourself. As you had learned that I was dissatisfied, I have thought it best to kindly tell you why.

(Indorsement on the Envelope.)

To General Meade, never sent or signed.

LETTER TO GENERAL NATHANIEL P. BANKS [1]

> Banks was in command in Louisiana; he had advanced some suggestions about the establishment of a loyal state government under military supervision. Lincoln was anxious to get the process of reconstruction started, and he thought Louisiana offered a convenient laboratory. He encouraged

[1] Lincoln, *Complete Works*, IX, 56-58.

Banks to go ahead and outlined a tentative reconstruction plan.

Executive Mansion, August 5, 1863.

MY dear General Banks: Being a poor correspondent is the only apology I offer for not having sooner tendered my thanks for your very successful and very valuable military operations this year. The final stroke in opening the Mississippi never should, and I think never will, be forgotten.

* * * *

While I very well know what I would be glad for Louisiana to do, it is quite a different thing for me to assume direction of the matter. I would be glad for her to make a new constitution recognizing the emancipation in those parts of the State to which the proclamation does not apply. And while she is at it, I think it would not be objectionable for her to adopt some practical system by which the two races could gradually live themselves out of the old relation to each other, and both come out better prepared for the new. Education for young blacks should be included in the plan. After all, the power or element of "contract" may be sufficient for this probationary period; and, by its simplicity and flexibility, may be the better.

As an anti-slavery man, I have a motive to desire emancipation which pro-slavery men do not have; but even they have strong enough reason to thus place themselves again under the shield of the Union; and to thus perpetually hedge against the recurrence of the scenes through which we are now passing.

Governor Shepley has informed me that Mr. Durant is now taking a registry, with a view to the election of a constitutional convention in Louisiana. This to me appears proper. If such convention were to ask my views, I could present little else than what I now say to you. I think the thing should be pushed forward, so that, if possible, its mature work may reach here by the meeting of Congress.

For my own part, I think I shall not, in any event, retract the emancipation proclamation; nor, as executive, ever return to slavery any person who is freed by the terms of that proclamation, or by any of the acts of Congress.

If Louisiana shall send members to Congress, their admission to seats will depend, as you know, upon the respective Houses, and not upon the President.

If these views can be of any advantage in giving shape and impetus to action there, I shall be glad for you to use them prudently for that object. Of course you will confer with intelligent and trusty citizens of the State, among whom I would suggest Messrs. Flanders, Hahn, and Durant; and to each of whom I now think I may send copies of this letter.

Still, it is perhaps better to not make the letter generally public.

Yours very truly,

A. LINCOLN.

LETTER TO JAMES C. CONKLING [1]

A committee in Lincoln's home town of Springfield planned to hold a mass-meeting of supporters of the war. They invited Lincoln to attend and speak. He was unable to go but he sent this letter to be read at the meeting. The letter was a defence of his policy of using any means to save the Union and particularly of the emancipation proclamation.

Executive Mansion, August 26, 1863.

MY dear Sir: Your letter inviting me to attend a mass-meeting of unconditional Union men, to be held at the capital of Illinois on the 3d day of September has been received. It would be very agreeable to me to thus meet

----

[1] Lincoln, *Complete Works*, IX, 95-102.

my old friends at my own home, but I cannot just now be absent from here so long as a visit there would require.

The meeting is to be of all those who maintain unconditional devotion to the Union; and I am sure my old political friends will thank me for tendering, as I do, the nation's gratitude to those and other noble men whom no partizan malice or partizan hope can make false to the nation's life.

There are those who are dissatisfied with me. To such I would say: You desire peace, and you blame me that we do not have it. But how can we attain it? There are but three conceivable ways: First, to suppress the rebellion by force of arms. This I am trying to do. Are you for it? If you are, so far we are agreed. If you are not for it, a second way is to give up the Union. I am against this. Are you for it? If you are, you should say so plainly. If you are not for force, nor yet for dissolution, there only remains some imaginable compromise. I do not believe any compromise embracing the maintenance of the Union is now possible. All I learn leads to a directly opposite belief. The strength of the rebellion is its military, its army. That army dominates all the country and all the people within its range. Any offer of terms made by any man or men within that range, in opposition to that army, is simply nothing for the present, because such man or men have no power whatever to enforce their side of a compromise, if one were made with them.

To illustrate: Suppose refugees from the South and peace men of the North get together in convention, and frame and proclaim a compromise embracing a restoration of the Union. In what way can that compromise be used to keep Lee's army out of Pennsylvania? Meade's army can keep Lee's army out of Pennsylvania, and, I think, can ultimately drive it out of existence. But no paper compromise to which the controllers of Lee's army are not agreed can at all affect that army. In an effort at such compromise we should waste time which the enemy would improve to our disadvantage; and that would be all. A compromise, to be effective, must be made either with those who control the rebel army, or with the people first liberated from the domination of that army by the success of our own army. Now, allow me to assure you that no word or intimation from that rebel army, or from any of the men controlling it, in relation to any peace compromise, has ever come to my knowledge or belief. All charges and insinuations to the contrary are deceptive and groundless. And I promise you that if any such proposition shall hereafter come, it shall not be rejected and kept a secret from you. I freely acknowledge myself the servant of the people, according to the bond of service—the United States Constitution—and that, as such, I am responsible to them.

But to be plain. You are dissatisfied with me about the negro. Quite likely there is a difference of opinion between you and myself upon that subject. I certainly wish that all men could be free, while I suppose you do not. Yet, I have neither adopted nor proposed any measure which is not consistent with even your view, provided you are for the Union. I suggested compensated emancipation, to which you replied you wished not to be taxed to buy negroes. But I had not asked you to be taxed to buy negroes, except in such way as to save you from greater taxation to save the Union exclusively by other means.

You dislike the emancipation proclamation, and perhaps would have it retracted. You say it is unconstitutional. I think differently. I think the Constitution invests its commander-in-chief with the law of war in time of war. The most that can be said—if so much—is that slaves are property. Is there—has there ever been—any question that by the law of war, property, both of enemies and friends, may be taken when needed? And is it not needed whenever taking it helps us, or hurts the enemy? Armies, the world over, destroy enemies' property when they cannot use it;

and even destroy their own to keep it from the enemy. Civilized belligerents do all in their power to help themselves or hurt the enemy, except a few things regarded as barbarous or cruel. Among the exceptions are the massacre of vanquished foes and non-combatants, male and female.

But the proclamation, as law, either is valid or is not valid. If it is not valid, it needs no retraction. If it is valid, it cannot be retracted any more than the dead can be brought to life. Some of you profess to think its retraction would operate favorably for the Union. Why better after the retraction than before the issue? There was more than a year and a half of trial to suppress the rebellion before the proclamation [was] issued; the last one hundred days of which passed under an explicit notice that it was coming, unless averted by those in revolt returning to their allegiance. The war has certainly progressed as favorably for us since the issue of the proclamation as before. I know, as fully as one can know the opinions of others, that some of the commanders of our armies in the field, who have given us our most important successes, believe the emancipation policy and the use of the colored troops constitute the heaviest blow yet dealt to the rebellion, and that at least one of these important successes could not have been achieved when it was but for the aid of black soldiers. Among the commanders holding these views are some who have never had any affinity with what is called Abolitionism, or with Republican party politics, but who hold them purely as military opinions. I submit these opinions as being entitled to some weight against the objections often urged that emancipation and arming the blacks are unwise as military measures, and were not adopted as such in good faith.

You say you will not fight to free negroes. Some of them seem willing to fight for you; but no matter. Fight you, then, exclusively, to save the Union. I issued the proclamation on purpose to aid you in saving the Union. Whenever you shall have conquered all resistance to the Union, if I shall urge you to continue fighting, it will be an apt time then for you to declare you will not fight to free negroes.

I thought that in your struggle for the Union, to whatever extent the negroes should cease helping the enemy, to that extent it weakened the enemy in his resistance to you. Do you think differently? I thought that whatever negroes can be got to do as soldiers, leaves just so much less for white soldiers to do in saving the Union. Does it appear otherwise to you? But negroes, like other people, act upon motives. Why should they do anything for us if we will do nothing for them? If they stake their lives for us they must be prompted by the strongest motive, even the promise of freedom. And the promise, being made, must be kept.

The signs look better. The Father of Waters again goes unvexed to the sea. Thanks to the great Northwest for it. Nor yet wholly to them. Three hundred miles up they met New England, Empire, Keystone, and Jersey, hewing their way right and left. The sunny South, too, in more colors than one, also lent a hand. On the spot, their part of the history was jotted down in black and white. The job was a great national one, and let none be banned who bore an honorable part in it. And while those who have cleared the great river may well be proud, even that is not all. It is hard to say that anything has been more bravely and well done than at Antietam, Murfreesboro', Gettysburg, and on many fields of lesser note. Nor must Uncle Sam's web-feet be forgotten. At all the watery margins they have been present. Not only on the deep sea, the broad bay, and the rapid river, but also up the narrow, muddy bayou, and wherever the ground was a little damp, they have been and made their tracks. Thanks to all: for the great republic— for the principle it lives by and keeps alive—for man's vast future—thanks to all.

Peace does not appear so distant as it did. I hope it will come soon, and come to stay; and so come as to be worth

the keeping in all future time. It will then have been proved
that among free men there can be no successful appeal from
the ballot to the bullet, and that they who take such appeal
are sure to lose their case and pay the cost. And then there
will be some black men who can remember that with silent
tongue, and clenched teeth, and steady eye, and well-poised
bayonet, they have helped mankind on to this great consummation, while I fear there will be some white ones unable
to forget that with malignant heart and deceitful speech
they strove to hinder it.

Still, let us not be over-sanguine of a speedy final triumph.
Let us be quite sober. Let us diligently apply the means,
never doubting that a just God, in his own good time, will
give us the rightful result.

Yours very truly,

A. LINCOLN.

———

LETTER TO GENERAL HENRY H. HALLECK [1]

Halleck was Lincoln's military adviser in Washington. When
Lincoln wrote this letter, a Union army was fighting the
Confederates in Tennessee. The issue had been raised as to
whether Meade should try to relieve the Union forces in the
West by advancing against Lee or by sending reenforce-
ments to Tennessee. Lincoln favored the latter plan. This
letter is evidence of Lincoln's steadily improving military
judgment.

Executive Mansion,

Washington, September 19, 1863.

MAJOR-GENERAL Halleck: By General Meade's despatch to you of yesterday it appears that he desires
your views and those of the government as to whether he
shall advance upon the enemy. I am not prepared to order,

---

[1] Lincoln, *Complete Works,* IX, 128-130.

or even advise, an advance in this case, wherein I know so little of particulars, and wherein he, in the field, thinks the risk is so great, and the promise of advantage so small.

And yet the case presents matters for very serious consideration in another aspect. These two armies confront each other across a small river, substantially midway between the two capitals, each defending its own capital, and menacing the other. General Meade estimates the enemy's infantry in front of him at not less than 40,000. Suppose we add fifty per cent. to this for cavalry, artillery, and extra-duty men stretching as far as Richmond, making the whole force of the enemy 60,000.

General Meade, as shown by the returns, has with him, and between him and Washington, of the same classes of well men, over 90,000. Neither can bring the whole of his men into a battle; but each can bring as large a percentage in as the other. For a battle, then, General Meade has three men to General Lee's two. Yet, it having been determined that choosing ground and standing on the defensive gives so great advantage that the three cannot safely attack the two, the three are left simply standing on the defensive also.

If the enemy's 60,000 are sufficient to keep our 90,000 away from Richmond, why, by the same rule, may not 40,-000 of ours keep their 60,000 away from Washington, leaving us 50,000 to put to some other use? Having practically come to the mere defensive, it seems to be no economy at all to employ twice as many men for that object as are needed. With no object, certainly, to mislead myself, I can perceive no fault in this statement, unless we admit we are not the equal of the enemy, man for man. I hope you will consider it.

To avoid misunderstanding, let me say that to attempt to fight the enemy slowly back into his intrenchments at Richmond, and then to capture him, is an idea I have been trying to repudiate for quite a year.

My judgment is so clear against it that I would scarcely

allow the attempt to be made if the general in command should desire to make it. My last attempt upon Richmond was to get McClellan, when he was nearer there than the enemy was, to run in ahead of him. Since then I have constantly desired the Army of the Potomac to make Lee's army, and not Richmond, its objective point. If our army cannot fall upon the enemy and hurt him where he is, it is plain to me it can gain nothing by attempting to follow him over a succession of intrenched lines into a fortified city.

Yours truly,

A. LINCOLN.

PROCLAMATION FOR THANKSGIVING, OCTOBER 3, 1863 [1]

Lincoln asked the American people to observe the last Thursday in November as a day of thanksgiving for the victories and blessings of the year.

BY THE PRESIDENT OF THE UNITED STATES OF AMERICA:

A Proclamation.

THE year that is drawing toward its close has been filled with the blessings of fruitful fields and healthful skies. To these bounties, which are so constantly enjoyed that we are prone to forget the source from which they come, others have been added, which are of so extraordinary a nature that they cannot fail to penetrate and soften the heart which is habitually insensible to the ever-watchful providence of almighty God. In the midst of a civil war of unequal magnitude and severity, which has sometimes seemed to foreign states to invite and provoke their aggressions, peace has been preserved with all nations, order has been maintained, the laws have been respected and obeyed, and harmony has

---

[1] Lincoln, *Complete Works,* IX, 151-153.

prevailed everywhere, except in the theater of military conflict; while that theater has been greatly contracted by the advancing armies and navies of the Union.

Needful diversions of wealth and of strength from the fields of peaceful industry to the national defense have not arrested the plow, the shuttle, or the ship; the ax has enlarged the borders of our settlements, and the mines, as well of iron and coal as of the precious metals, have yielded even more abundantly than heretofore. Population has steadily increased, notwithstanding the waste that has been made in the camp, the siege, and the battle-field, and the country, rejoicing in the consciousness of augmented strength and vigor, is permitted to expect continuance of years with large increase of freedom.

No human counsel hath devised, nor hath any mortal hand worked out these great things. They are the gracious gifts of the most high God, who, while dealing with us in anger for our sins, hath nevertheless remembered mercy.

It has seemed to me fit and proper that they should be solemnly, reverently, and gratefully acknowledged as with one heart and one voice by the whole American people. I do, therefore, invite my fellow-citizens in every part of the United States, and also those who are at sea and those who are sojourning in foreign lands, to set apart and observe the last Thursday of November next as a day of thanksgiving and praise to our beneficent Father who dwelleth in the heavens. And I recommend to them that, while offering up the ascriptions justly due to him for such singular deliverances and blessings, they do also, with humble penitence for our national perverseness and disobedience, commend to his tender care all those who have become widows, orphans, mourners, or sufferers in the lamentable civil strife in which we are unavoidably engaged, and fervently implore the interposition of the almighty hand to heal the wounds of the nation, and to restore it, as soon as may be consistent with the Divine purposes, to the full enjoyment of peace, harmony, tranquillity, and union.

In testimony whereof, I have hereunto set my hand, and caused the seal of the United States to be affixed.

> Done at the city of Washington, this third day of October, in the year of our Lord one thousand eight hundred and sixty-three, and of the independence of the United States the eighty-eighth.

A. LINCOLN.

ADDRESS AT THE DEDICATION OF THE GETTYS-BURG NATIONAL CEMETERY, NOVEMBER 19, 1863 [1]

> Soon after the battle of Gettysburg certain state governors and other individuals discussed plans to convert the battlefield into a national cemetery to honor the dead who had fallen there. The sponsors of the movement decided to have the dedication ceremony in November. They asked Edward Everett, the most noted orator of the day, to make the principal address. Printed invitations to attend the dedication were sent to members of the government and to well-known public figures. One went to Lincoln, and he accepted. The sponsors realized that the President could not well be present without taking some part in the ceremonies. So they invited him to deliver a few remarks after Everett had finished speaking. It is doubtful if many people in the crowd heard or appreciated Lincoln's brief address. Nor did the general public at first understand the immortal quality of what Lincoln had said, even after the address was printed. Literary men like James Russell Lowell were the first to call attention to its greatness. And it is as literature that the Gettysburg address should be studied, not as oratory. It is a beautiful and supreme statement of the democratic faith. There are five copies of the address in Lincoln's handwriting: the first, partially written in Washington before his trip to Gettysburg and finished on his arrival there; the second, written in Gettysburg; and three revised copies made by Lincoln at different and later times. In addition there is a

---

[1] Lincoln, *Complete Works*, IX, 209-210.

printed version of the Address, taken down by the short-hand reporter on the speaker's stand. All the versions differ in unessential details. The one reproduced here is Lincoln's first revision. For a complete treatment of the Address the reader is referred to William E. Barton's excellent book, *Lincoln at Gettysburg.*

FOURSCORE and seven years ago our fathers brought forth on this continent a new nation, conceived in liberty, and dedicated to the proposition that all men are created equal.

Now we are engaged in a great civil war, testing whether that nation, or any nation so conceived and so dedicated, can long endure. We are met on a great battle-field of that war. We have come to dedicate a portion of that field as a final resting-place for those who here gave their lives that that nation might live. It is altogether fitting and proper that we should do this.

But, in a larger sense, we cannot dedicate—we cannot consecrate—we cannot hallow—this ground. The brave men, living and dead, who struggled here, have consecrated it far above our poor power to add or detract. The world will little note nor long remember what we say here, but it can never forget what they did here. It is for us, the living, rather, to be dedicated here to the unfinished work which they who fought here have thus far so nobly advanced. It is rather for us to be here dedicated to the great task remaining before us—that from these honored dead we take increased devotion to that cause for which they gave the last full measure of devotion; that we here highly resolve that these dead shall not have died in vain; that this nation, under God, shall have a new birth of freedom; and that government of the people, by the people, for the people, shall not perish from the earth.

PROCLAMATION OF AMNESTY AND RECON-
STRUCTION, DECEMBER 8, 1863 [1]

> This proclamation was Lincoln's first public announcement
> of his reconstruction plan. His purpose was to get the
> Southern states back into the Union as speedily as possible.
> He wished to make it easy for them to return by imposing
> only a minimum of conditions as the price of restoration.
> This mild and merciful program was defeated by the radical
> Republicans.

BY THE PRESIDENT OF THE UNITED STATES OF AMERICA:

A Proclamation.

WHEREAS, in and by the Constitution of the United
States, it is provided that the President "shall have
power to grant reprieves and pardons for offenses against
the United States, except in cases of impeachment"; and

Whereas a rebellion now exists whereby the loyal State
governments of several States have for a long time been
subverted, and many persons have committed, and are now
guilty of, treason against the United States; and

Whereas, with reference to said rebellion and treason,
laws have been enacted by Congress, declaring forfeitures
and confiscation of property and liberation of slaves, all
upon terms and conditions therein stated, and also declaring that the President was thereby authorized at any time
thereafter, by proclamation, to extend to persons who may
have participated in the existing rebellion, in any State or
part thereof, pardon and amnesty, with such exceptions and
at such times and on such conditions as he may deem expedient for the public welfare; and

Whereas the congressional declaration for limited and
conditional pardon accords with well-established judicial
exposition of the pardoning power; and

Whereas, with reference to said rebellion, the President
of the United States has issued several proclamations, with

---

[1] Lincoln, *Complete Works*, IX, 218-223.

provisions in regard to the liberation of slaves; and

Whereas it is now desired by some persons heretofore engaged in said rebellion to resume their allegiance to the United States, and to reinaugurate loyal State governments within and for their respective States; therefore

I, Abraham Lincoln, President of the United States, do proclaim, declare, and make known to all persons who have, directly or by implication, participated in the existing rebellion, except as hereinafter excepted, that a full pardon is hereby granted to them and each of them, with restoration of all rights of property, except as to slaves, and in property cases where rights of third parties shall have intervened, and upon the condition that every such person shall take and subscribe an oath, and thenceforward keep and maintain said oath inviolate; and which oath shall be registered for permanent preservation, and shall be of the tenor and effect following, to-wit:

I, _____, do solemnly swear, in presence of almighty God, that I will henceforth faithfully support, protect, and defend the Constitution of the United States, and the union of the States thereunder; and that I will, in like manner, abide by and faithfully support all acts of Congress passed during the existing rebellion with reference to slaves, so long and so far as not repealed, modified, or held void by Congress, or by decision of the Supreme Court; and that I will, in like manner, abide by and faithfully support all proclamations of the President made during the existing rebellion having reference to slaves, so long and so far as not modified or declared void by decision of the Supreme Court. So help me God.

The persons exempted from the benefits of the foregoing provisions are all who are, or shall have been, civil or diplomatic officers or agents of the so-called Confederate Government; all who have left judicial stations under the United States to aid the rebellion; all who are or shall have been military or naval officers of said so-called Confederate Government above the rank of colonel in the army or of lieutenant in the navy; all who left seats in the United States Congress to aid the rebellion; all who resigned commissions in the army or navy of the United States and afterward aided the rebellion; and all who have engaged in any way in treating colored persons, or white persons in charge of such, otherwise than lawfully as prisoners of war, and which persons may have been found in the United States service as soldiers, seamen, or in any other capacity.

And I do further proclaim, declare, and make known that whenever, in any of the States of Arkansas, Texas, Louisiana, Mississippi, Tennessee, Alabama, Georgia, Florida, South Carolina, and North Carolina, a number of persons, not less than one tenth in number of the votes cast in such State at the presidential election of the year of our Lord one thousand eight hundred and sixty, each having taken the oath aforesaid and not having since violated it, and being a qualified voter by the election law of the State existing immediately before the so-called act of secession, and excluding all others, shall reestablish a State government which shall be republican, and in no wise contravening said oath, such shall be recognized as the true government of the State, and the State shall receive thereunder the benefits of the constitutional provision which declares that "the United States shall guaranty to every State in this Union a republican form of government, and shall protect each of them against invasion; and, on application of the legislature, or the executive (when the legislature cannot be convened), against domestic violence."

And I do further proclaim, declare, and make known, that any provision which may be adopted by such State government in relation to the freed people of such State, which shall recognize and declare their permanent freedom, provide for their education, and which may yet be consistent as a temporary arrangement with their present condition as a laboring, landless, and homeless class, will not be objected to by the national executive.

And it is suggested as not improper that, in constructing a loyal State Government in any State, the name of the State, the boundary, the subdivisions, the constitution, and the general code of laws, as before the rebellion, be maintained, subject only to the modifications made necessary by the conditions hereinbefore stated, and such others, if any, not contravening said conditions, and which may be deemed expedient by those framing the new State government.

To avoid misunderstanding, it may be proper to say that this proclamation, so far as it relates to State governments, has no reference to States wherein loyal State governments have all the while been maintained.

And, for the same reason, it may be proper to further say, that whether members sent to Congress from any State shall be admitted to seats, constitutionally rests exclusively with the respective houses, and not to any extent with the executive. And still further, that this proclamation is intended to present the people of the States wherein the national authority has been suspended, and loyal State governments have been subverted, a mode in and by which the national authority and loyal State governments may be reestablished within said States, or in any of them; and while the mode presented is the best the executive can suggest, with his present impressions, it must not be understood that no other possible mode would be acceptable.

> Given under my hand at the city of Washington, the eighth day of December, in the year of our Lord one thousand eight hundred and sixty-three, and of the independence of the United States of America the eighty-eighth.

> ABRAHAM LINCOLN.

ANNUAL MESSAGE TO CONGRESS,
DECEMBER 8, 1863 [1]

This message reviewed events of the past year, civil and
military. Lincoln sensed that the end of the war was near at
hand and that the Union would triumph. He was now becoming concerned about the problems of reconstruction. In
the message he explained why he had issued his proclamation of amnesty and reconstruction. He stated that his plan
had been advanced to get the process of reconstruction
started, that the plan was not complete, and that he was not
inflexibly committed to it. Obviously he hoped to avoid a
conflict with the radicals.

FELLOW-CITIZENS of the Senate and House of Representatives: Another year of health, and of sufficiently
abundant harvests, has passed. For these, and especially for
the improved condition of our national affairs, our renewed
and profoundest gratitude to God is due.

* * * *

When Congress assembled a year ago the war had already
lasted nearly twenty months, and there had been many con-
flicts on both land and sea with varying results. The rebellion had been pressed back into reduced limits; yet the tone
of public feeling and opinion, at home and abroad, was not
satisfactory. With other signs, the popular elections, then
just past, indicated uneasiness among ourselves while, amid
much that was cold and menacing, the kindest words coming
from Europe were uttered in accents of pity that we were
too blind to surrender a hopeless cause. Our commerce was
suffering greatly by a few armed vessels built upon, and furnished from, foreign shores, and we were threatened with
such additions from the same quarter as would sweep our
trade from the sea and raise our blockade. We had failed to
elicit from European governments anything hopeful upon
this subject. The preliminary emancipation proclamation,

---

[1] Lincoln, *Complete Works*, IX, 224-252.

issued in September, was running its assigned period to the beginning of the new year. A month later the final proclamation came, including the announcement that colored men of suitable condition would be received into the war service. The policy of emancipation, and of employing black soldiers, gave to the future a new aspect, about which hope, and fear, and doubt contended in uncertain conflict. According to our political system, as a matter of civil administration, the General Government had no lawful power to effect emancipation in any State, and for a long time it had been hoped that the rebellion could be suppressed without resorting to it as a military measure. It was all the while deemed possible that the necessity for it might come, and that if it should, the crisis of the contest would then be presented. It came, and, as was anticipated, it was followed by dark and doubtful ways. Eleven months having now passed, we are permitted to take another review. The rebel borders are pressed still further back, and, by the complete opening of the Mississippi, the country dominated by the rebellion is divided into distinct parts, with no practical communication between them. Tennessee and Arkansas have been substantially cleared of insurgent control, and influential citizens in each, owners of slaves and advocates of slavery at the beginning of the rebellion, now declare openly for emancipation in their respective States. Of those States not included in the Emancipation Proclamation, Maryland and Missouri, neither of which three years ago would tolerate any restraint upon the extension of slavery into new Territories, only dispute now as to the best mode of removing it within their own limits.

Of those who were slaves at the beginning of the rebellion, full one hundred thousand are now in the United States military service, about one half of which number actually bear arms in the ranks; thus giving the double advantage of taking so much labor from the insurgent cause, and supplying the places which otherwise must be filled with so many white men. So far as tested, it is difficult to say they are not as good soldiers as any. No servile insurrection, or tendency to violence or cruelty, has marked the measures of emancipation and arming the blacks. These measures have been much discussed in foreign countries, and contemporary with such discussion the tone of public sentiment there is much improved. At home the same measures have been fully discussed, supported, criticized, and denounced and the annual elections following are highly encouraging to those whose official duty it is to bear the country through this great trial. Thus we have the new reckoning. The crisis which threatened to divide the friends of the Union is past.

Looking now to the present and future, and with reference to a resumption of the national authority within the States wherein that authority has been suspended, I have thought fit to issue a proclamation, a copy of which is herewith transmitted. On examination of this proclamation it will appear, as is believed, that nothing is attempted beyond what is amply justified by the Constitution. True, the form of an oath is given, but no man is coerced to take it. The man is only promised a pardon in case he voluntarily takes the oath. The Constitution authorizes the executive to grant or withhold the pardon at his own absolute discretion; and this includes the power to grant on terms, as is fully established by judicial and other authorities.

It is also proffered that if, in any of the States named, a State government shall be, in the mode prescribed, set up, such government shall be recognized and guaranteed by the United States, and that under it the State shall, on the constitutional conditions, be protected against invasion and domestic violence. The constitutional obligation of the United States to guarantee to every State in the Union a republican form of government, and to protect the State in the cases stated, is explicit and full. But why tender the benefits of this provision only to a State government set up in this particular way? This section of the Constitution contemplates a case wherein the element within a State favorable to republican government in the Union may be too feeble for an opposite and hostile element external to, or even within, the State; and such are precisely the cases with which we are now dealing.

An attempt to guarantee and protect a revised State government, constructed in whole, or in preponderating part, from the very element against whose hostility and violence it is to be protected, is simply absurd. There must be a test by which to separate the opposing elements, so as to build only from the sound; and that test is a sufficiently liberal one which accepts as sound whoever will make a sworn recantation of his former unsoundness.

But if it be proper to require, as a test of admission to the political body, an oath of allegiance to the Constitution of the United States, and to the Union under it, why also to the laws and proclamations in regard to slavery? Those laws and proclamations were enacted and put forth for the purpose of aiding in the suppression of the rebellion. To give them their fullest effect, there had to be a pledge for their maintenance. In my judgment they have aided, and will further aid, the cause for which they were intended. To now abandon them would be not only to relinquish a lever of power, but would also be a cruel and an astounding breach of faith. I may add, at this point, that while I remain in my present position I shall not attempt to retract or modify the Emancipation Proclamation; nor shall I return to slavery any person who is free by the terms of that proclamation, or by any of the acts of Congress. For these and other reasons it is thought best that support of these measures shall be included in the oath; and it is believed the executive may lawfully claim it in return for pardon and restoration of forfeited rights, which he has clear constitutional power to withhold altogether, or grant upon the terms which he shall deem wisest for the public interest. It should be observed, also, that this part of the oath is subject to the modifying and abrogating power of legislation and supreme judicial decision.

The proposed acquiescence of the national executive in any

reasonable temporary State arrangement for the freed people is made with the view of possibly modifying the confusion and destitution which must at best attend all classes by a total revolution of labor throughout whole States. It is hoped that the already deeply afflicted people in those States may be somewhat more ready to give up the cause of their affliction, if, to this extent, this vital matter be left to themselves; while no power of the national executive to prevent an abuse is abridged by the proposition.

The suggestion in the proclamation as to maintaining the political framework of the States on what is called reconstruction is made in the hope that it may do good without danger of harm. It will save labor, and avoid great confusion.

But why any proclamation now upon this subject? This question is beset with the conflicting views that the step might be delayed too long or be taken too soon. In some States the elements for resumption seem ready for action, but remain inactive apparently for want of a rallying-point—a plan of action. Why shall A adopt the plan of B, rather than B that of A? And if A and B should agree, how can they know but that the General Government here will reject their plan? By the proclamation a plan is presented which may be accepted by them as a rallying-point, and which they are assured in advance will not be rejected here. This may bring them to act sooner than they otherwise would.

The objection to a premature presentation of a plan by the national executive consists in the danger of committals on points which could be more safely left to further developments. Care has been taken to so shape the document as to avoid embarrassments from this source. Saying that, on certain terms, certain classes will be pardoned, with rights restored, it is not said that other classes, or other terms will never be included. Saying that reconstruction will be accepted if presented in a specified way, it is not said it will never be accepted in any other way.

The movements, by State action, for emancipation in several

of the States not included in the Emancipation Proclamation, are matters of profound gratulation. And while I do not repeat in detail what I have heretofore so earnestly urged upon this subject, my general views and feelings remain unchanged; and I trust that Congress will omit no fair opportunity of aiding these important steps to a great consummation.

In the midst of other cares, however important, we must not lose sight of the fact that the war power is still our main reliance. To that power alone can we look, yet for a time, to give confidence to the people in the contested regions that the insurgent power will not again overrun them. Until that confidence shall be established, little can be done anywhere for what is called reconstruction. Hence our chiefest care must still be directed to the army and navy, who have thus far borne their harder part so nobly and well. And it may be esteemed fortunate that in giving the greatest efficiency to these indispensable arms, we do also honorably recognize the gallant men, from commander to sentinel, who compose them, and to whom, more than to others, the world must stand indebted for the home of freedom disenthralled, regenerated, enlarged and perpetuated.

ABRAHAM LINCOLN.

LETTER TO GOVERNOR MICHAEL HAHN [1]

With Lincoln's encouragement, a reconstructed state government was established in Louisiana. Hahn, a Louisiana politician who had taken an important part in the movement for reconstruction, was elected governor. Lincoln advised Hahn to permit some of the Negroes to vote in Louisiana. The President's purpose was to guard the reconstructed government against the criticism of the radical Republicans. This counsel was not followed. The radicals defeated Congressional recognition of Louisiana.

[1] Lincoln, *Complete Works*, X, 38-39.

(Private)

Executive Mansion, March 13, 1864.

MY dear Sir: I congratulate you on having fixed your name
in history as the first free-State governor of Louisiana.
Now you are about to have a convention, which, among other
things, will probably define the elective franchise. I barely
suggest for your private consideration, whether some of the
colored people may not be let in—as, for instance, the very
intelligent, and especially those who have fought gallantly in
our ranks. They would probably help, in some trying time to
come, to keep the jewel of liberty within the family of freedom.
But this is only a suggestion, not to the public, but to you alone.

Yours truly,   A. LINCOLN.

LETTER TO A. G. HODGES [1]

Hodges was a member of a delegation from Kentucky which
came to Washington to protest the employment of slaves
freed by the emancipation proclamation in the Union armies.
In this letter Lincoln defended the proclamation and the
practice of using Negroes in a military capacity. He knew
that the border slave states resented this policy, but he hoped
to convince them that it was an imperative necessity.

Executive Mansion, April 4, 1864.

MY dear Sir: You ask me to put in writing the substance
of what I verbally said the other day in your presence,
to Governor Bramlette and Senator Dixon. It was about as
follows:

"I am naturally antislavery. If slavery is not wrong, nothing
is wrong. I cannot remember when I did not so think and feel,
and yet I have never understood that the presidency conferred
upon me an unrestricted right to act officially upon this judg-

------
[1] Lincoln, *Complete Works*, X, 65-68.

ment and feeling. It was in the oath I took that I would, to the best of my ability, preserve, protect, and defend the Constitution of the United States. I could not take the office without taking the oath. Nor was it my view that I might take an oath to get power, and break the oath in using the power. I understood, too, that in ordinary civil administration this oath even forbade me to practically indulge my primary abstract judgment on the moral question of slavery. I had publicly declared this many times, and in many ways. And I aver that, to this day, I have done no official act in mere deference to my abstract judgment and feeling on slavery. I did understand, however, that my oath to preserve the Constitution to the best of my ability imposed upon me the duty of preserving, by every indispensable means, that government—that nation, of which that Constitution was the organic law. Was it possible to lose the nation and yet preserve the Constitution? By general law, life and limb must be protected, yet often a limb must be amputated to save a life; but a life is never wisely given to save a limb. I felt that measures otherwise unconstitutional might become lawful by becoming indispensable to the preservation of the Constitution through the preservation of the nation. Right or wrong, I assume this ground, and now avow it. I could not feel that, to the best of my ability, I had even tried to preserve the Constitution, if, to save slavery or any minor matter, I should permit the wreck of government, country, and Constitution all together. When, early in the war, General Frémont attempted military emancipation, I forbade it, because I did not then think it an indispensable necessity. When, a little later, General Cameron, then Secretary of War, suggested the arming of the blacks, I objected because I did not yet think it an indispensable necessity. When, still later, General Hunter attempted military emancipation, I again forbade it, because I did not yet think the indispensable necessity had come. When in March and May and July, 1862, I made earnest and successive appeals to the border States to favor compensated emancipation, I believed the indispensable necessity for military emancipation and arming the blacks would come unless averted by that measure. They declined the proposition, and I was, in my best judgment, driven to the alternative of either surrendering the Union, and with it the Constitution, or of laying strong hand upon the colored element. I chose the latter. In choosing it, I hoped for greater gain than loss; but of this, I was not entirely confident. More than a year of trial now shows no loss by it in our foreign relations, none in our home popular sentiment, none in our white military force—no loss by it anyhow or anywhere. On the contrary it shows a gain of quite a hundred and thirty thousand soldiers, seamen, and laborers. These are palpable facts, about which, as facts, there can be no caviling. We have the men; and we could not have had them without the measure.

"And now let any Union man who complains of the measure test himself by writing down in one line that he is for subduing the rebellion by force of arms; and in the next, that he is for taking these hundred and thirty thousand men from the Union side, and placing them where they would be but for the measure he condemns. If he cannot face his case so stated, it is only because he cannot face the truth."

I add a word which was not in the verbal conversation. In telling this tale I attempt no compliment to my own sagacity. I claim not to have controlled events, but confess plainly that events have controlled me. Now, at the end of three years' struggle, the nation's condition is not what either party, or any man, devised or expected. God alone can claim it. Whither it is tending seems plain. If God now wills the removal of a great wrong, and wills also that we of the North, as well as you of the South, shall pay fairly for our complicity in that wrong, impartial history will find therein new cause to attest and revere the justice and goodness of God.

Yours truly,
A. LINCOLN.

———

LETTER TO GENERAL ULYSSES S. GRANT [1]

In 1864 Grant became general-in-chief of the Union armies. When Lincoln wrote this letter, Grant was about to start his long, hard campaign to seize Richmond. Not until 1865 did he achieve his goal.

Executive Mansion, April 30, 1864.

L IEUTENANT-GENERAL Grant: Not expecting to see you again before the spring campaign opens, I wish to express in this way my entire satisfaction with what you have done up to this time, so far as I understand it. The particulars of your plans I neither know nor seek to know. You are vigilant and self-reliant; and, pleased with this, I wish not to obtrude any constraints or restraints upon you. While I am very anxious that any great disaster or capture of our men in great numbers shall be avoided, I know these points are less likely to escape your attention than they would be mine. If there is anything wanting which is within my power to give, do not fail to let me know it. And now, with a brave army and a just cause, may God sustain you.

Yours very truly,

A. LINCOLN.

REPLY TO THE COMMITTEE NOTIFYING PRESIDENT LINCOLN OF RENOMINATION, JUNE 9, 1864 [2]

In 1864 the radical Republicans made a determined attempt to prevent Lincoln's renomination for the Presidency. They failed because of his popularity with the masses. The Republican party, now calling itself the Union party, met in national convention on June 8 and named Lincoln as its candidate. In accepting the nomination, Lincoln indorsed the proposed Thirteenth Amendment abolishing slavery.

[1] Lincoln, *Complete Works*, X, 90-91.
[2] Lincoln, *Complete Works*, X, 116-117.

MR. Chairman and Gentlemen of the Committee: I will neither conceal my gratification nor restrain the expression of my gratitude that the Union people, through their convention, in their continued effort to save and advance the nation, have deemed me not unworthy to remain in my present position. I know no reason to doubt that I shall accept the nomination tendered; and yet perhaps I should not declare definitely before reading and considering what is called the platform. I will say now, however, I approve the declaration in favor of so amending the Constitution as to prohibit slavery throughout the nation. When the people in revolt, with a hundred days of explicit notice that they could within those days resume their allegiance without the overthrow of their institution, and that they could not so resume it afterward, elected to stand out, such amendment of the Constitution as now proposed became a fitting and necessary conclusion to the final success of the Union cause. Such alone can meet and cover all cavils. Now the unconditional Union men, North and South, perceive its importance and embrace it. In the joint names of Liberty and Union, let us labor to give it legal form and practical effect.

———

ANNOUNCEMENT CONCERNING TERMS OF PEACE [1]

> In the summer of 1864 rumors were prevalent that the South wanted peace and reunion. Many people came to Lincoln to urge him to negotiate a peace. Lincoln was skeptical that the Confederacy would give up the war, but he was ready to conclude peace provided the South would agree to two vital conditions.

Executive Mansion, July 18, 1864.

TO whom it may concern: Any proposition which embraces the restoration of peace, the integrity of the whole Union, and the abandonment of slavery, and which comes by and with

[1] Lincoln, *Complete Works*, X, 161.

an authority that can control the armies now at war against the United States, will be received and considered by the executive government of the United States, and will be met by liberal terms on other substantial and collateral points, and the bearer or bearers thereof shall have safe conduct both ways.

ABRAHAM LINCOLN.

———

ADDRESS TO THE 166th OHIO REGIMENT, AUGUST 22, 1864 [1]

> Lincoln often spoke to soldiers who were being mustered out of service in Washington when their term of enlistment had expired. It was significant that he usually talked to them about the democratic nature of the Union cause and the democratic objectives of the war.

SOLDIERS: I suppose you are going home to see your families and friends. For the service you have done in this great struggle in which we are all engaged, I present you sincere thanks for myself and the country.

I almost always feel inclined, when I happen to say anything to soldiers, to impress upon them, in a few brief remarks, the importance of success in this contest. It is not merely for to-day, but for all time to come, that we should perpetuate for our children's children that great and free government which we have enjoyed all our lives. I beg you to remember this, not merely for my sake, but for yours. I happen, temporarily, to occupy this White House. I am a living witness that any one of your children may look to come here as my father's child has. It is in order that each one of you may have, through this free government which we have enjoyed, an open field and a fair chance for your industry, enterprise, and intelligence; that you may all have equal privileges in the race of life, with all its desirable human aspirations. It is for this the struggle

———

[1] Lincoln, *Complete Works*, X, 202-203.

should be maintained, that we may not lose our birthright—not only for one, but for two or three years. The nation is worth fighting for, to secure such as inestimable jewel.

———

RESPONSE TO A SERENADE, NOVEMBER 10, 1864 [1]

> In the election of 1864 Lincoln was opposed by McClellan, the Democratic candidate. At one time it seemed that McClellan would certainly be the victor. Lincoln himself was ready to concede defeat. But triumphs by the Union armies turned the tide, and Lincoln was reelected. After the election a crowd came to the White House to serenade Lincoln. He spoke to them about the necessity of holding free elections even in the crisis of war.

IT has long been a grave question whether any government, not too strong for the liberties of its people, can be strong enough to maintain its existence in great emergencies. On this point the present rebellion brought our republic to a severe test, and a presidential election occurring in regular course during the rebellion, added not a little to the strain.

If the loyal people united were put to the utmost of their strength by the rebellion, must they not fail when divided and partially paralyzed by a political war among themselves? But the election was a necessity. We cannot have free government without elections; and if the rebellion could force us to forego or postpone a national election, it might fairly claim to have already conquered and ruined us. The strife of the election is but human nature practically applied to the facts of the case. What has occurred in this case must ever recur in similar cases. Human nature will not change. In any future great national trial, compared with the men of this, we shall have as weak and as strong, as silly and as wise, as bad and as good. Let us, therefore, study the incidents of this as philosophy to learn wisdom from, and none of them as wrongs to be revenged. But

---

[1] Lincoln, *Complete Works,* X, 263-265.

the election, along with its incidental and undesirable strife, has done good too. It has demonstrated that a people's government can sustain a national election in the midst of a great civil war. Until now, it has not been known to the world that this was a possibility. It shows, also, how sound and how strong we still are. It shows that, even among candidates of the same party, he who is most devoted to the Union and most opposed to treason can receive most of the people's votes. It shows, also, to the extent yet known, that we have more men now than we had when the war began. Gold is good in its place, but living, brave, patriotic men are better than gold.

But the rebellion continues, and now that the election is over, may not all having a common interest reunite in a common effort to save our common country? For my own part, I have striven and shall strive to avoid placing any obstacle in the way. So long as I have been here I have not willingly planted a thorn in any man's bosom. While I am deeply sensible to the high compliment of a reëlection, and duly grateful, as I trust, to Almighty God for having directed my countrymen to a right conclusion, as I think, for their own good, it adds nothing to my satisfaction that any other man may be disappointed or pained by the result.

May I ask those who have not differed from me to join with me in this same spirit toward those who have? And now let me close by asking three hearty cheers for our brave soldiers and seamen and their gallant and skilful commanders.

LETTER TO MRS. LYDIA A. BIXBY [1]

This letter has been called Lincoln's "beautiful blunder." It is probably his best known letter. Mrs. Bixby, a Boston widow needing financial assistance, told the governmental authorities of Massachusetts that her five sons had been killed in battle. Governor Andrew asked Lincoln to write a letter of consolation to Mrs. Bixby. Lincoln responded

[1] Lincoln, *Complete Works*, X, 274-275.

with this fine production. Later it became known that only two of the sons had been killed. One had been captured and exchanged before the mother told her story. Another had been captured and had enlisted in the Confederate army. The youngest deserted and went to sea. The entire episode is discussed in William E. Barton's book, *A Beautiful Blunder.*

Executive Mansion, November 21, 1864.

DEAR Madam: I have been shown in the files of the War Department a statement of the Adjutant-General of Massachusetts that you are the mother of five sons who have died gloriously on the field of battle. I feel how weak and fruitless must be any words of mine which should attempt to beguile you from the grief of a loss so overwhelming. But I cannot refrain from tendering to you the consolation that may be found in the thanks of the Republic they died to save. I pray that our heavenly Father may assuage the anguish of your bereavement, and leave you only the cherished memory of the loved and lost, and the solemn pride that must be yours to have laid so costly a sacrifice upon the altar of freedom.

Yours very sincerely and respectfully,

ABRAHAM LINCOLN.

ANNUAL MESSAGE TO CONGRESS, DECEMBER 6, 1864 [1]

This is an exultant message. The war was nearly over, and victory was assured. Lincoln could boast that despite the terrible losses of the war the Union's resources in men and materials were greater than ever.

*   *   *   *

THE war continues. Since the last annual message, all the important lines and positions then occupied by our forces

---

[1] Lincoln, *Complete Works,* X, 283-310.

have been maintained, and our arms have steadily advanced, thus liberating the regions left in rear; so that Missouri, Kentucky, Tennessee, and parts of other States have again produced reasonably fair crops.

The most remarkable feature in the military operations of the year is General Sherman's attempted march of three hundred miles, directly through the insurgent region. It tends to show a great increase of our relative strength, that our general-in-chief should feel able to confront and hold in check every active force of the enemy, and yet to detach a well-appointed large army to move on such an expedition. The result not yet being known, conjecture in regard to it is not here indulged.

Important movements have also occurred during the year to the effect of molding society for durability in the Union. Although short of complete success, it is much in the right direction that 12,000 citizens in each of the States of Arkansas and Louisiana have organized loyal State governments, with free constitutions, and are earnestly struggling to maintain and administer them. The movements in the same direction, more extensive though less definite, in Missouri, Kentucky, and Tennessee, should not be overlooked. But Maryland presents the example of complete success. Maryland is secure to liberty and Union for all the future. The genius of rebellion will no more claim Maryland. Like another foul spirit, being driven out, it may seek to tear her, but it will woo her no more.

At the last session of Congress a proposed amendment of the Constitution, abolishing slavery throughout the United States, passed the Senate, but failed for lack of the requisite two-thirds vote in the House of Representatives. Although the present is the same Congress, and nearly the same members, and without questioning the wisdom or patriotism of those who stood in opposition, I venture to recommend the reconsideration and passage of the measure at the present session. Of course the abstract question is not changed, but an intervening election shows, almost certainly, that the next Congress will pass the measure if this does not. Hence there is only a question of time as to when the proposed amendment will go to the States for their action. And as it is to so go, at all events, may we not agree that the sooner the better? It is not claimed that the election has imposed a duty on members to change their views or their votes any further than as an additional element to be considered, their judgment may be affected by it. It is the voice of the people now for the first time heard upon the question. In a great national crisis like ours, unanimity of action among those seeking a common end is very desirable—almost indispensable. And yet no approach to such unanimity is attainable unless some deference shall be paid to the will of the majority, simply because it is the will of the majority. In this case the common end is the maintenance of the Union, and among the means to secure that end, such will, through the election, is most clearly declared in favor of such constitutional amendment.[1]

The most reliable indication of public purpose in this country is derived through our popular elections. Judging by the recent canvass and its result, the purpose of the people within the loyal States to maintain the integrity of the Union, was never more firm nor more nearly unanimous than now. The extraordinary calmness and good order with which the millions of voters met and mingled at the polls give strong assurance of this. Not only all those who supported the Union ticket, so called, but a great majority of the opposing party also, may be fairly claimed to entertain, and to be actuated by, the same purpose. It is an unanswerable argument to this effect, that no candidate for any office whatever, high or low, has ventured to seek votes on the avowal that he was for giving up the Union. There has been much impugning of motives, and much heated controversy as to the proper means and best mode of advancing the Union cause; but on the distinct issue of Union or no Union the politicians have shown their instinctive knowledge that there is no diversity among the people. In affording the people the fair opportunity of showing one to another and

---

[1] The Thirteenth amendment was ratified in 1865.

to the world this firmness and unanimity of purpose, the election has been of vast value to the national cause.

The election has exhibited another fact, not less valuable to be known—the fact that we do not approach exhaustion in the most important branch of national resources—that of living men. While it is melancholy to reflect that the war has filled so many graves, and carried mourning to so many hearts, it is some relief to know that compared with the surviving, the fallen have been so few. While corps, and divisions, and brigades, and regiments have formed, and fought, and dwindled, and gone out of existence, a great majority of the men who composed them are still living. The same is true of the naval service. The election returns prove this. So many voters could not else be found. The States regularly holding elections, both now and four years ago—to wit: California, Connecticut, Delaware, Illinois, Indiana, Iowa, Kentucky, Maine, Maryland, Massachusetts, Michigan, Minnesota, Missouri, New Hampshire, New Jersey, New York, Ohio, Oregon, Pennsylvania, Rhode Island, Vermont, West Virginia, and Wisconsin—cast 3,982,011 votes now, against 3,870,222 cast then; showing an aggregate now of 3,982,011. To this is to be added 33,762 cast now in the new States of Kansas and Nevada, which States did not vote in 1860; thus swelling the aggregate to 4,015,773, and the net increase during the three years and a half of war, to 145,551. A table is appended, showing particulars. To this again should be added the number of all soldiers in the field from Massachusetts, Rhode Island, New Jersey, Delaware, Indiana, Illinois, and California, who by the laws of those States could not vote away from their homes, and which number cannot be less than 90,000. Nor yet is this all. The number in organized Territories is triple now what it was four years ago, while thousands, white and black, join us as the national arms press back the insurgent lines. So much is shown, affirmatively and negatively, by the election.

It is not material to inquire how the increase has been produced, or to show that it would have been greater but for the

war, which is probably true. The important fact remains
demonstrated that we have more men now than we had when
the war began; that we are not exhausted, nor in process of
exhaustion; that we are gaining strength, and may, if need be,
maintain the contest indefinitely. This as to men. Material
resources are now more complete and abundant than ever.

The national resources, then, are unexhausted, and, as we
believe, inexhaustible. The public purpose to restablish and
maintain the national authority is unchanged, and, as we believe, unchangeable. The manner of continuing the effort remains to choose. On careful consideration of all the evidence
accessible, it seems to me that no attempt at negotiation with
the insurgent leader could result in any good. He would accept
nothing short of severance of the Union—precisely what we
will not and cannot give. His declarations to this effect are
explicit and oft repeated. He does not attempt to deceive us.
He affords us no excuse to deceive ourselves. He cannot voluntarily re-accept the Union; we cannot voluntarily yield it.

Between him and us the issue is distinct, simple, and inflexible. It is an issue which can only be tried by war, and decided
by victory. If we yield, we are beaten; if the Southern people
fail him, he is beaten. Either way it would be the victory and
defeat following war. What is true, however, of him who
heads the insurgent cause, is not necessarily true of those who
follow. Although he cannot re-accept the Union, they can.
Some of them, we know, already desire peace and reunion. The
number of such may increase.

They can at any moment have peace simply by laying down
their arms and submitting to the national authority under the
Constitution. After so much the government could not, if it
would, maintain war against them. The loyal people would
not sustain or allow it. If questions should remain, we would
adjust them by the peaceful means of legislation, conference,
courts, and votes, operating only in constitutional and lawful
channels. Some certain, and other possible, questions are, and
would be, beyond the executive power to adjust; as, for in-

stance, the admission of members into Congress, and whatever might require the appropriation of money. The executive power itself would be greatly diminished by the cessation of actual war. Pardons and remissions of forfeitures, however, would still be within executive control. In what spirit and temper this control would be exercised, can be fairly judged of by the past.

A year ago general pardon and amnesty, upon specified terms, were offered to all except certain designated classes, and it was at the same time made known that the excepted classes were still within contemplation of special clemency. During the year many availed themselves of the general provision, and many more would only that the signs of bad faith in some led to such precautionary measures as rendered the practical process less easy and certain. During the same time, also, special pardons have been granted to individuals of the excepted classes, and no voluntary application has been denied.

Thus, practically, the door has been for a full year open to all, except such as were not in condition to make free choice— that is, such as were in custody or under constraint. It is still so open to all; but the time may come—probably will come— when public duty shall demand that it be closed; and that in lieu more rigorous measures than heretofore shall be adopted.

In presenting the abandonment of armed resistance to the national authority on the part of the insurgents as the only indispensable condition to ending the war on the part of the government, I retract nothing heretofore said as to slavery. I repeat the declaration made a year ago, that "while I remain in my present position I shall not attempt to retract or modify the Emancipation Proclamation, nor shall I return to slavery any person who is free by the terms of that proclamation, or by any of the acts of Congress."

If the people should, by whatever mode or means, make it an executive duty to reenslave such persons, another, and not I, must be their instrument to perform it.

In stating a single condition of peace, I mean simply to say, that the war will cease on the part of the government whenever it shall have ceased on the part of those who began it.

ABRAHAM LINCOLN.

———

LETTER TO GENERAL WILLIAM T. SHERMAN [1]

When Grant started his campaign against Richmond in the spring of 1864, Sherman moved against Atlanta. He captured the city in September and then drove toward Savannah which he seized in December. He announced the fall of Savannah as his Christmas present to the nation. The Confederates had tried to draw off Sherman from Savannah by sending an army under General Hood to invade Tennessee. Hood was smashed by a Union army in Tennessee commanded by General George Thomas.

Executive Mansion, December 26, 1864.

MY dear General Sherman: Many, many thanks for your Christmas gift, the capture of Savannah.

When you were about leaving Atlanta for the Atlantic coast, I was anxious, if not fearful; but feeling that you were the better judge, and remembering that "nothing risked, nothing gained," I did not interfere. Now, the undertaking being a success, the honor is all yours; for I believe none of us went further than to acquiesce.

And taking the work of General Thomas into the count, as it should be taken, it is indeed a great success. Not only does it afford the obvious and immediate military advantages; but in showing to the world that your army could be divided, putting the stronger part to an important new service, and yet leaving enough to vanquish the old opposing force of the whole,—Hood's army,—it brings those who sat in darkness to see a great light. But what next?

I suppose it will be safe if I leave General Grant and yourself to decide.

---

[1] Lincoln, *Complete Works*, X, 325-326.

Please make my grateful acknowledgments to your whole army—officers and men.

Yours very truly,

A. LINCOLN.

INSTRUCTIONS TO SECRETARY SEWARD [1]

Early in 1865 the Confederate government appointed three commissioners to negotiate an armistice with the Union. Lincoln thought the commissioners wanted to conclude peace and he authorized Secretary of State Seward to deal with them. At the last moment he decided to go with Seward to the conference. The commissioners had no authority to meet Lincoln's conditions, and the meeting accomplished nothing.

Executive Mansion, January 31, 1865.

HON. William H. Seward: You will proceed to Fortress Monroe, Virginia, there to meet and informally confer with Messrs. Stephens, Hunter, and Campbell, on the basis of my letter to F. P. Blair, Esq., on January 18, 1865, a copy of which you have.[2] You will make known to them that three things are indispensable—to wit:

1. The restoration of the national authority throughout all the States.

2. No receding by the executive of the United States on the slavery question from the position assumed thereon in the late annual message to Congress, and in preceding documents.

3. No cessation of hostilities short of an end of the war, and the disbanding of all forces hostile to the government.

You will inform them that all propositions of theirs, not inconsistent with the above, will be considered and passed upon

---

[1] Lincoln, *Complete Works*, X, 351-352.

[2] Blair had gone to Richmond hoping to arrange peace terms. He had heard that the Confederacy wanted to quit the war and he asked Lincoln for permission to negotiate with the Confederate government as a private citizen. Blair's mission failed.

in a spirit of sincere liberality. You will hear all they may choose to say and report it to me. You will not assume to definitely consummate anything.

Yours, etc.,

ABRAHAM LINCOLN.

DRAFT OF A MESSAGE TO CONGRESS, FEBRUARY 5, 1865 [1]

This was Lincoln's last attempt to secure compensated emancipation. The Cabinet told him his plan was hopeless, and he dropped the project.

(Not signed or sent)

FELLOW-CITIZENS of the Senate and House of Representatives: I respectfully recommend that a joint resolution, substantially as follows, be adopted so soon as practicable by your honorable bodies: "Resolved by the Senate and House of Representatives of the United States of America, in Congress assembled, That the President of the United States is hereby empowered, in his discretion to pay $400,000,000 to the States of Alabama, Arkansas, Delaware, Florida, Georgia, Kentucky, Louisiana, Maryland, Mississippi, Missouri, North Carolina, South Carolina, Tennessee, Texas, Virginia, and West Virginia, in the manner and on the conditions following, to wit: The payment to be made in six per cent. government bonds, and to be distributed among said States *pro rata* on their respective slave populations as shown by the census of 1860, and no part of said sum to be paid unless all resistance to the national authority shall be abandoned and cease, on or before the first day of April next; and upon such abandonment and ceasing of resistance one half of said sum to be paid in manner aforesaid, and the remaining half to be paid only upon the amendment of the National Constitution recently proposed by

---

[1] Lincoln, *Complete Works*, XI, 1-3.

Congress becoming valid law, on or before the first day of July next, by the action thereon of the requisite number of States." [1]

The adoption of such resolution is sought with a view to embody it, with other propositions, in a proclamation looking to peace and reunion.

Whereas, a joint resolution has been adopted by Congress, in the words following, to wit:

Now, therefore, I, Abraham Lincoln, President of the United States, do proclaim, declare, and make known, that on the conditions therein stated, the power conferred on the executive in and by said joint resolution will be fully exercised; and that war will cease and armies be reduced to a basis of peace; that all political offenses will be pardoned; that all property, except slaves, liable to confiscation or forfeiture, will be released therefrom, except in cases of intervening interests of third parties; and that liberality will be recommended to Congress upon all points not lying within executive control.

(Indorsement)

February 5, 1865. To-day these papers, which explain themselves, were drawn up and submitted to the cabinet and unanimously disapproved by them.

A. LINCOLN.

———

SECOND INAUGURAL ADDRESS, MARCH 4, 1865 [2]

The second inaugural is the finest example of Lincoln's prose style. In the hour of victory he was humbly thankful that the nation had weathered its greatest crisis. No malice toward the South was in his heart as he faced the future and reconstruction.

FELLOW-COUNTRYMEN: At this second appearing to take the oath of the presidential office, there is less occasion

---

[1] The Thirteenth amendment.
[2] Lincoln, *Complete Works*, XI, 44-47.

for an extended address than there was at the first. Then a statement, somewhat in detail, of a course to be pursued, seemed fitting and proper. Now, at the expiration of four years, during which public declarations have been constantly called forth on every point and phase of the great contest which still absorbs the attention and engrosses the energies of the nation, little that is new could be presented. The progress of our arms, upon which all else chiefly depends, is as well known to the public as to myself; and it is, I trust, reasonably satisfactory and encouraging to all. With high hope for the future, no prediction in regard to it is ventured.

On the occasion corresponding to this four years ago, all thoughts were anxiously directed to an impending civil war. All dreaded it—all sought to avert it. While the inaugural address was being delivered from this place, devoted altogether to saving the Union without war, insurgent agents were in the city seeking to destroy it without war—seeking to dissolve the Union, and divide effects, by negotiation. Both parties deprecated war; but one of them would make war rather than let the nation survive; and the other would accept war rather than let it perish. And the war came.

One-eighth of the whole population were colored slaves, not distributed generally over the Union, but localized in the Southern part of it. These slaves constituted a peculiar and powerful interest. All know that this interest was, somehow, the cause of the war. To strengthen, perpetuate, and extend this interest was the object for which the insurgents would rend the Union, even by war; while the government claimed no right to do more than to restrict the territorial enlargement of it.

Neither party expected for the war the magnitude or the duration which it has already attained. Neither anticipated that the cause of the conflict might cease with, or even before, the conflict itself should cease. Each looked for an easier triumph, and a result less fundamental and astounding. Both read the same Bible, and pray to the same God; and each invokes his aid against the other. It may seem strange that any men should dare to ask a just god's assistance in wringing their bread from the sweat of other men's faces; but let us judge not, that we be not judged. The prayers of both could not be answered—that of neither has been answered fully.

The Almighty has his own purposes. "Woe unto the world because of offenses! for it must needs be that offenses come; but woe to that man by whom the offense cometh." If we shall suppose that American slavery is one of those offenses which, in the providence of God, must needs come, but which, having continued through his appointed time, he now wills to remove, and that he gives to both North and South this terrible war, as the woe due to those by whom the offense came, shall we discern therein any departure from those divine attributes which the believers in a living God always ascribe to him? Fondly do we hope—fervently do we pray—that this mighty scourge of war may speedily pass away. Yet, if God wills that it continue until all the wealth piled by the bondsman's two hundred and fifty years of unrequited toil shall be sunk, and until every drop of blood drawn with the lash shall be paid by another drawn with the sword, as was said three thousand years ago, so still it must be said, "The judgments of the Lord are true and righteous altogether."

With malice toward none; with charity for all; with firmness in the right, as God gives us to see the right, let us strive on to finish the work we are in; to bind up the nation's wounds; to care for him who shall have borne the battle, and for his widow, and his orphan—to do all which may achieve and cherish a just and lasting peace among ourselves, and with all nations.

———

LETTER TO THURLOW WEED [1]

In this letter Lincoln advanced an interesting opinion about the second inaugural address and a reason why it might not be popular.

Executive Mansion, March 16, 1865.

DEAR Mr. Weed: Every one likes a compliment. Thank you for yours on my little notification speech and on the recent inaugural address. I expect the latter to wear as well as —perhaps better than—anything I have produced; but I believe it is not immediately popular. Men are not flattered by being shown that there has been a difference of purpose between the Almighty and them. To deny it, however, in this case, is to deny that there is a God governing the world. It is a truth which I thought needed to be told, and, as whatever of humiliation there is in it falls most directly on myself, I thought others might afford for me to tell it.

Truly yours,

A. LINCOLN.

———

UNSIGNED MEMORANDUM GIVEN TO JOHN A. CAMPBELL, APRIL 5, 1865 [2]

On April 3 Union troops occupied Richmond. Two days later Lincoln came to the fallen city. Campbell, a Virginia leader and Confederate official, went to Lincoln and asked upon what terms Virginia could have peace. Lincoln then wrote this memorandum. Campbell said he thought he could get the Virginia legislature to meet and take the state out of the war. Lincoln gave permission for the legislature to come together.

AS to peace, I have said before, and now repeat, that three things are indispensable:

---

[1] Lincoln, *Complete Works*, XI, 54.
[2] Lincoln, *Complete Works*, XI, 71-73.

1. The restoration of the national authority throughout the United States.

2. No receding by the executive of the United States on the slavery question from the position assumed thereon in the late annual message, and in preceding documents.

3. No cessation of hostilities short of an end of the war, and the disbanding of all forces hostile to the government. That all propositions coming from those now in hostility to the government, not inconsistent with the foregoing, will be respectfully considered and passed upon in a spirit of sincere liberality.

I now add that it seems useless for me to be more specific with those who will not say that they are ready for the indispensable terms, even on conditions to be named by themselves. If there be any who are ready for these indispensable terms, on any conditions whatever, let them say so, and state their conditions, so that the conditions can be known and considered. It is further added, that the remission of confiscation being within the executive power, if the war be now further persisted in by those opposing the government, the making of confiscated property at the least to bear the additional cost will be insisted on, but that confiscations (except in case of third party intervening interests) will be remitted to the people of any State which shall now promptly and in good faith withdraw its troops from further resistance to the government. What is now said as to the remission of confiscation has not reference to supposed property in slaves.

TELEGRAM TO GENERAL GODFREY WEITZEL[1]

After the conference with Campbell, Lincoln directed Weitzel, commander of the troops occupying Richmond, to let the Virginia legislature meet. Later Lincoln revoked this

[1] Lincoln, *Complete Works*, XI, 75.

permission, mainly because he realized his action opened
him to a dangerous attack by the radicals.

Headquarters Armies of the U.S.,
City Point, April 6, 1865.

MAJOR-GENERAL Weitzel, Richmond, Va.: It has been
intimated to me that the gentlemen who have acted as
the legislature of Virginia in support of the rebellion may now
desire to assemble at Richmond and take measures to withdraw
the Virginia troops and other support from resistance to the
General Government. If they attempt it, give them permission
and protection, until, if at all, they attempt some action hostile
to the United States, in which case you will notify them, give
them reasonable time to leave, and at the end of which time
arrest any who remain. Allow Judge Campbell to see this,
but do not make it public.

A. LINCOLN.

———

LAST PUBLIC ADDRESS, APRIL 11, 1865 [1]

> On April 11 a crowd came to the White House to serenade
> Lincoln, celebrate the end of the war, and hear Lincoln de-
> liver a previously announced address. This speech was Lin-
> coln's challenge to the radicals on the issue of reconstruction.
> It was a plea for his reconstructed government in Louisiana
> and his reconstruction policy in general. He was trying to
> rally public opinion behind his program and against the
> radicals.

WE meet this evening not in sorrow, but in gladness of
heart. The evacuation of Petersburg and Richmond, and
the surrender of the principal insurgent army, give hope of a
righteous and speedy peace, whose joyous expression cannot
be restrained. In the midst of this, however, He from whom
all blessings flow must not be forgotten. A call for a national

___
[1] Lincoln, *Complete Works*, XI, 84-92.

thanksgiving is being prepared, and will be duly promulgated. Nor must those whose harder part give us the cause of rejoicing be overlooked. Their honors must not be parceled out with others. I myself was near the front, and had the high pleasure of transmitting much of the good news to you; but no part of the honor for plan or execution is mine. To General Grant, his skilful officers and brave men, all belongs. The gallant navy stood ready, but was not in reach to take active part.

By these recent successes the reinauguration of the national authority—reconstruction—which has had a large share of thought from the first, is pressed much more closely upon our attention. It is fraught with great difficulty. Unlike a case of war between independent nations, there is no authorized organ for us to treat with—no one man has authority to give up the rebellion for any other man. We simply must begin with and mold from disorganized and discordant elements. Nor is it a small additional embarrassment that we, the loyal people, differ among ourselves as to the mode, manner, and measure of reconstruction. As a general rule, I abstain from reading the reports of attacks upon myself, wishing not to be provoked by that to which I cannot properly offer an answer. In spite of this precaution, however, it comes to my knowledge that I am much censured for some supposed agency in setting up and seeking to sustain the new State government of Louisiana.

In this I have done just so much, and no more than, the public knows. In the annual message of December, 1863, and in the accompanying proclamation, I presented a plan of reconstruction as the phrase goes, which I promised, if adopted by any State, should be acceptable to and sustained by the executive government of the nation. I distinctly stated that this was not the only plan which might possibly be acceptable, and I also distinctly protested that the executive claimed no right to say when or whether members should be admitted to seats in Congress from such States. This plan was in advance submitted to the then Cabinet, and distinctly approved by every member of it. One of them suggested that I should then and in that connection apply the Emancipation Proclamation to the theretofore excepted parts of Virginia and Louisiana; that I should drop the suggestion about apprenticeship for freed people, and that I should omit the protest against my own power in regard to the admission of members to Congress. But even he approved every part and parcel of the plan which has since been employed or touched by the action of Louisiana.

The new constitution of Louisiana, declaring emancipation for the whole State, practically applies the proclamation to the part previously excepted. It does not adopt apprenticeship for freed people, and it is silent, as it could not well be otherwise, about the admission of members to Congress. So that, as it applies to Louisiana, every member of the Cabinet fully approved the plan. The message went to Congress, and I received many commendations of the plan, written and verbal, and not a single objection to it from any professed emancipationist came to my knowledge until after the news reached Washington that the people of Louisiana had begun to move in accordance with it. From about July, 1862, I had corresponded with different persons supposed to be interested [in] seeking a reconstruction of a State government for Louisiana. When the message of 1863, with the plan before mentioned, reached New Orleans, General Banks wrote me that he was confident that the people, with his military cooperation, would reconstruct substantially on that plan. I wrote to him and some of them to try it. They tried it, and the result is known. Such has been my only agency in getting up the Louisiana government.

As to sustaining it, my promise is out, as before stated. But as bad promises are better broken than kept, I shall treat this as a bad promise, and break it whenever I shall be convinced that keeping it is adverse to the public interest; but I have not yet been so convinced. I have been shown a letter on this subject, supposed to be an able one, in which the writer expresses regret that my mind has not seemed to be definitely fixed on the question whether the seceded States, so called, are in the

Union or out of it. It would perhaps add astonishment to his regret were he to learn that since I have found professed Union men endeavoring to make that question, I have purposely forborne any public expression upon it. As appears to me, that question has not been, nor yet is, a practically material one, and that any discussion of it, while it thus remains practically immaterial, could have no effect other than the mischevious one of dividing our friends. As yet, whatever it may hereafter become, that question is bad as the basis of a controversy, and good for nothing at all— a merely pernicious abstraction.

We all agree that the seceded States, so called, are out of their proper practical relation with the Union, and that the sole object of the government, civil and military, in regard to those States is to again get them into that proper practical relation. I believe that it is not only possible, but in fact easier, to do this without deciding or even considering whether these States have ever been out of the Union, than with it. Finding themselves safely at home, it would be utterly immaterial whether they had ever been abroad. Let us all join in doing the acts necessary to restoring the proper practical relations between these States and the Union, and each forever after innocently indulge his own opinion whether in doing the acts he brought the States from without into the Union, or only gave them proper assistance, they never having been out of it. The amount of constituency, so to speak, on which the new Louisiana government rests, would be more satisfactory to all if it contained 50,000 or 30,000 or even 20,000, instead of only about 12,000, as it does. It is also unsatisfactory to some that the election franchise is not given to the colored man. I would myself prefer that it were now conferred on the very intelligent, and on those who serve our cause as soldiers.

Still, the question is not whether the Louisiana government, as it stands, is quite all that is desirable. The question is, will it be wiser to take it as it is and help to improve it, or to reject and disperse it? Can Louisiana be brought into proper practical relation with the Union sooner by sustaining or by disre-

garding her new State government? Some twelve thousand
voters in the heretofore slave State of Louisiana have sworn
allegiance to the Union, assumed to be the rightful political
power of the State, held elections, organized a State government, adopted a free-State constitution, giving the benefit of
public schools equally to black and white, and empowering the
legislature to confer the elective franchise upon the colored
man. Their legislature has already voted to ratify the constitutional amendment recently passed by Congress, abolishing
slavery throughout the nation. These 12,000 persons are thus
fully committed to the Union and to perpetual freedom in the
States—committed to the very things, and nearly all the things,
the nation wants—and they ask the nations' recognition and
its assistance to make good their committal.

Now, if we reject and spurn them, we do our utmost to dis-
organize and disperse them. We, in effect, say to the white
man: You are worthless or worse; we will neither help you,
nor be helped by you. To the blacks, we say: This cup of liberty which these, your old masters, hold to your lips we will
dash from you, and leave you to the chances of gathering the
spilled and scattered contents in some vague and undefined
when, where, and how. If this course, discouraging and para-
lyzing both white and black has any tendency to bring Louisiana into proper practical relations with the Union, I have so
far been unable to perceive it. If, on the contrary, we recognize
and sustain the new government of Louisiana, the converse of
all this is made true. We encourage the hearts and never the
arms of the 12,000 to adhere to their work, and argue for it,
and proselyte for it, and fight for it, and feed it, and grow it,
and ripen it to a complete success. The colored man, too, in
seeing all united for him, is inspired with vigilance, and energy,
and daring, to the same end. Grant that he desires the election
franchise, will he not attain it sooner by saving the already advanced steps toward it than by running backward over them?
Concede that the new government of Louisiana is only what it
should be as the egg is to the fowl, we shall sooner have the

fowl by hatching the egg than by smashing it.

Again, if we reject Louisiana we also reject one vote in favor of the proposed amendment to the national Constitution. To meet this proposition it has been argued that no more than three-fourths of those States which have not attempted secession are necessary to validly ratify the amendment. I do not commit myself against this further than to say that such a ratification would be questionable, and sure to be persistently questioned, while a ratification by three-fourths of all the States would be unquestioned and unquestionable. I repeat the question: Can Louisiana be brought into proper practical relation with the Union sooner by sustaining or by discarding her new State government? What has been said of Louisiana will apply generally to other States. And yet so great peculiarities pertain to each State, and such important and sudden changes occur in the same State, and withal so new and unprecedented is the whole case that no exclusive and inflexible plan can safely be prescribed as to details and collaterals. Such exclusive and inflexible plan would surely become a new entanglement. Important principles may and must be inflexible. In the present situation, as the phrase goes, it may be my duty to make some new announcement to the people of the South. I am considering, and shall not fail to act when satisfied that action will be proper.